Thanks Mosquito for the Great Ride

MEMOIRS OF A LIFE WITH PARABILITIES

Jan Cocks-Salvemini

JAN COCKS-SALVEMINI

"Don't underestimate yourself.
You are capable of more than you can ever imagine."

Les Brown

Thanks Mosquito for the Great Ride

MEMOIRS OF A LIFE WITH PARABILITIES

Jan Cocks-Salvemini

DoctorZed
Publishing
www.doctorzed.com

Copyright © 2022 by Jan Cocks-Salvemini

All rights reserved. No part of this book may be used or reproduced by any means, graphic, electronic, or mechanical, including photocopying, recording, taping or by any information storage retrieval system without the written permission of the publisher except in the case of brief quotations embodied in critical articles and reviews.

All the stories contained within are true, but some of the locations and people's names have been changed.

First published 2022 by DoctorZed Publishing.

DoctorZed Publishing books may be ordered through booksellers or by contacting:

DoctorZed Publishing
IDAHO
10 Vista Ave
Skye, South Australia 5072
www.doctorzed.com
info@doctorzed.com

ISBN: 978-0-6454665-1-5 (hc)
ISBN: 978-0-6454665-2-2 (sc)
ISBN: 978-0-6454665-3-9 (e)

A CIP number for this book is available at the National Library of Australia. This is a work of non-fiction. The views expressed in this work are solely those of the author and do not necessarily reflect the views of the publisher, and the publisher hereby disclaims any responsibility for them.

Wedding Photo pg. 154 © Owen E. D'A. Tomlins
Cover design © Hari Teah
Printed in Australia, Uk & USA

DoctorZed Publishing rev. date: 22/06/2022

This book is dedicated to four people I deeply love.

To the memory of, and the thanks to, my wonderful parents, Harry and Irene Gardner. Thank you for your unconditional love and belief in me. Also, for teaching me the proper way to dream the biggest and wildest dreams to keep me happy; a fantastic gift.

To the love of my life, my husband, Graham. Thank you for your unconditional love and believing in me. Always being there for me when I need you, and respecting my need to be my normal self.

To our loving son, Lee. I love those spontaneous hugs and you are always looking for ways to make life easier for me. Such as buying a portable keyboard so that I could comfortably write this book. Thank you. We are so very proud of you and we feel the love you show us. You keep us young at heart. You are our best friend. We love you heaps.

ACKNOWLEDGEMENTS

My husband, Graham Cocks
Our son, Lee Salvemini
My parents, the late Harry and Irene Gardner
Colleen Hammet
Joan Bateman, daughter of the late Mrs Guerin
Neville Bonney
Family of the late Keith Wadlow
Jill Stanton (nee O'Toole)
Rita Cole (nee Keane)
Reena Eden
Tricia and Len McQuade
Denis Healy
Di Harvey (nee Caldow)
Christine Sharkey (nee Hembrow)
Family of the late orthopaedic specialist, Mr Rodney White
Margaret Wells (nee Evens)
Dan Andersen
Merle Salvemini
Madeleine Holland (nee Andersen)
Marina Aston
Trena Van Roosmalen (nee Andersen)
Lisbeth and Karin, the daughters of the late Finn and Kirsten Deleuran
Allen Haines, brother of the late Elaine Haines
Robin Foster
Sir Paul McCartney
Ian Rigney
Barry Hill
Dr. James Brown
Patrea Smallacombe, niece of the late Betty Quin
Pam Western
Lewis O'Brien
Margaret O'Brien, wife of the late Douglas O'Brien
Grant Rollins, son of the late Des Rollins and Rosemary Rollins (nee O'Brien)
Natalie Hyde
Peter Hyde
Gary Pascoe
Pam Charles
Peter, Cathy, and James Crotti
Peter Smith
Peter Russ
Ron and Karina Van Dok
Libby Thompson
Elena Rorie
Marcia Walsh
Sylvia Holzapfel
Gem and Lina Somerville, granddaughters of the late Len Somerville
Blackwood Writers Group
Lincoln Brady
Ton Roosendaal
Chris Plush
Greg and Amanda Wood
Dr. Craig Jurisevic
Norrie and Liz Balacco
Peter Dempsey
Warren Entsch MP
Temara Srhoj
Dr. Scott Zarcinas
Hari Teah

CONTENTS

CHAPTER 1: Family, Heritage, and a Country Start
CHAPTER 2: Childhood Years
CHAPTER 3: My Innocence Meets Death
CHAPTER 4: Teenage Years
CHAPTER 5: Getting a Job
CHAPTER 6: Overseas Trip
CHAPTER 7: Meeting The Beatles, Minus Ringo
CHAPTER 8: Q Theatre
CHAPTER 9: Employment
CHAPTER 10: Marriage
CHAPTER 11: Being a Nanny
CHAPTER 12: 'Parking For The Disabled' Campaigns
CHAPTER 13: My Hand and The Pretty Blue Screw
CHAPTER 14: Lee
CHAPTER 15: Poetry Performances, Radio Presentation Course, and Making a CD
CHAPTER 16: Lee's Health Scares
CHAPTER 17: Pole Sitting
CHAPTER 18: Dad
CHAPTER 19: Mother
CHAPTER 20: The Partial Removal of My Lung
CHAPTER 21: Public Speaking
CHAPTER 22: Karate
CHAPTER 23: Australasian Masters Games - Darts
CHAPTER 24: Changing Driving Regulations
CHAPTER 25: Cairns
CHAPTER 26: Knee Replacement
CHAPTER 27: Para-abled and Parability

CHAPTER 1

Family, Heritage, and a Country Start

It was a cool October morning in 2006, and I hoped it was going to be a good day – the day that I would finally learn whether or not the operation had been a success.

My husband Graham and I were sitting in my orthopaedic specialist's office. It was a small room with a big desk occupying most of the space that wasn't taken up by my wheelchair. I gazed out of the window at the view of uneven buildings beyond, as Graham and I chatted quietly.

After several minutes my orthopaedic specialist walked into the room and placed several x-rays side-by-side on the wall-mounted light box, before sitting down behind the desk. He was classically tall, blond, and handsome, and had a presence about him that was impressive.

He greeted us warmly, then drew our attention to the x-rays. There was the inside of my right ankle in all its glory, the lower leg bones and the three bolts that held my ankle in place. The bolts were white and looked like a child's attempt to make a triangle. I tried to read my specialist's face before he spoke. After ten weeks in hospital—eight weeks longer than expected—I didn't want to wait another minute to find out what my future held.

He looked into my eyes and said, 'The bone hasn't healed. There is another operation we can do, but it will take longer. It is a bigger operation and may not work, because your bones are weak and starting to crumble.' He paused, before gently uttering the words, 'You may have to get used to never walking again.'

Ten little words, but as they left his lips my eyes filled with tears and a feeling of anguish moved through me from deep inside my stomach. He went on talking, but I could no longer hear. My thoughts were on fast-forward. I wiped the tears away and apologised for not hearing what he had been saying. He told me that Graham could fill me in and asked if I would like to think about the operation and get back to him. I said that I did want time to think about it, and that I would let him know.

On the way home, Graham tried to go over what the specialist had said. He told me that my leg bone was being held together by cartilage that could give way at any time. I didn't want to talk. I had already decided not to have another operation. My thoughts turned to amputation. I knew if I had my foot chopped off that I may not be a suitable candidate for an artificial leg, but I decided that it was the way to go. After all, if it didn't work I would be no worse off.

I had already been in the wheelchair for a long time. Although I can only use my left hand I had still been able to drive myself to the shopping centre and use my wheelchair successfully once I was there, even though my method for getting around was a little unconventional. I controlled the chair by putting my left leg on the ground while pushing the wheel along with my working hand. It sounds odd, but worked very well for the most part.

The occasions when it got interesting were when I encountered a slope. If I had to go up a slope then I would need to get enough momentum. At the shopping mall this meant starting on the far side of the car park crossing, waiting until there were no cars, and then getting up as much speed as I could. If I wasn't moving fast enough then I would get halfway up the ramp into the mall, before rolling back down and doing my best to stop before I was back on the crossing. The whole situation was so ridiculous that I would get the giggles. Sometimes someone would ask if I would like a push up the ramp. I always appreciated being asked, rather than having people assume that they could just take over and push me.

The other interesting situation was when I realised that the shopping mall walkway was on an incline. One day I was pushing myself along and suddenly discovered that I was on a downhill slope. I tried to slow myself down but couldn't get control. I looked down and screamed out to a group of teenagers who were mooching along in front of me, 'Get out of the way, I'm dangerous!' Well, they moved fast. When I got down to the bottom and managed to stop myself I said to them, 'When you woke up this morning you didn't know that you'd have to save yourself from an old duck in a wheelchair,' and we all had a good laugh.

In spite of the bad news from my orthopaedic specialist, I knew it was vital that I had a go at getting back to walking. I have a chronic lung disease, and walking helps keep my lungs working to the best of their ability. I only have three out of the five lobes of my lung left, and there is scarring on both my lungs. I made my mind up to speak to Graham and our son Lee about what I saw as the best way forward, and decided that sooner was better than later.

That night after dinner, I told them I didn't want the operation. I knew it would be useless as my bones were crumbling. I said that I'd decided my foot was passed its 'use-by' date, and I wanted it chopped off. Before I finished speaking they both got up and walked away. I understood their reaction and decided to leave it, so I put the kettle on for a cuppa.

The next day, I went to my doctor to talk it through with him. He stopped my little speech about my foot being passed its use-by date, and said, 'No, I don't want to talk about this!' I smiled and replied, 'You're my doctor, you have to listen.' When I pointed out that my lung disease meant that I needed to keep as healthy as possible, and so walking was extremely important, he agreed that I was right. We made an appointment for Graham and Lee to go in and talk everything through with him, but before the day arrived my doctor rang me and said he'd done some research and found a company that made boots which would allow me to keep my right foot and enable me to walk. The boot would be designed to fit me comfortably, just under the kneecap. At the back of my leg it would curve in comfortably to hold my knee firmly in place, allowing me to walk. I immediately agreed that it was a good idea. I felt so excited to have a solution that would keep everyone happy. It was worth a try, at least.

Graham drove me to my appointments with the boot manufacturers. First came the plaster cast to create the mould, and then all the fittings. I chose to have the boot made in black, because I could wear a black shoe on my left foot and not many people would notice the difference. There were a lot of frustrating teething problems before we got it absolutely right for my needs, and at times I felt that perhaps it was just a waste of everyone's time. Finally, the boot was complete and I got to walk unaided, very shakily at first, but gradually the boot became second nature. It was such an amazing feeling of freedom.

When I was out of the house I decided that a walking stick was an intelligent way to go, as I didn't want to take the chance of a fall. After seeing an elderly gentleman on television using his walking stick to protect a woman from being attacked, I figured I had a legal lethal weapon with me whenever I left the house. There is always a positive if you think hard enough.

About two months after I regained my freedom with my boot, I had a follow-up appointment with my orthopaedic specialist. Graham and I were sitting in the waiting room when my specialist called my name. I stood up and made my way into his room, with Graham following.

My specialist's jaw dropped open and the words tumbled out of his mouth, 'What are you doing?'

With a huge smile on my face I said, 'I am walking.'

'Yes, but how?' he asked, incredulously.

I unstrapped the boot and he examined it for some time. I told him I was very happy with the boot and would be pleased to pass on the details of the company to him. I believe that he now has other patients walking with the aid of these boots, who may otherwise have had to spend the rest of their lives in wheelchairs.

Even though my orthopaedic specialist had believed we'd come to the end of the road, my general practitioner looked outside the box to find a solution that was less dramatic than amputation. No matter how much knowledge you have, it's so important to continue searching for new ways of seeing things.

***

As a small child, I became very aware that I could manipulate everyone. Well, everyone except my dad. But as I grew older I realised I needed to work out who I really was. I decided that I was different, but so was everyone else. It is as simple as that. Somewhere along the way people will find labels for us all, one way or another, because they look at us from their perspective of life.

People say I am disabled, and that's okay. The reality is that everyone has some sort of disability, just as each of us has certain abilities. For example, after an operation on my right hand, I learned to do my shoelaces up with one hand. You may think that is clever. However, if you were offered your dream job, but the catch was that the dream job was in Denmark, wouldn't you learn Danish? Doing my shoelaces up with one hand is the same thing – it is an ability I acquired to meet my needs.

I prefer to be called 'para-abled', rather than 'disabled.' This word is smooth sounding and partners well with 'paramedics' and 'Paralympics.' The words 'disabled' and 'disability' are negative and sharp sounding. Not one single person in this world has immunity against acquiring a parability. If you or a loved one gained a parability what would you rather be called—para-abled or disabled? Para means 'alongside of' in Ancient Greek, and I believe that this is an accurate description of people with physical and cognitive differences— our differences place us alongside others, not behind. We are equal human beings.

For this reason, from this point on I will use only the words 'para-abled' and 'parability', rather than 'disabled' and 'disability.'

People can't imagine being me, but I am fine with that. I wouldn't want to be anyone else. I am so happy being me. Having my parability comes with certain challenges—the hardest of which is putting up with 'do-gooders.' It is important to point out the difference between people who do good and 'do-gooders.'

People who do good respect everyone as an equal. They ask people with parabilities if they can help, and if the answer is, 'No thanks, I am fine' then they say, 'Okay, I am just over here if you want anything.' They don't ask if they can help and then disrespect the answer by taking the para-abled person's independence away. My independence is as important to me as yours is to you.

Do-gooders, on the other hand, get their self-worth from 'helping' people, and think that those around them will be impressed with their efforts. Do-gooders can so easily underestimate what other people are capable of. They make assumptions that if someone has a parability that they couldn't possibly achieve a task, because they are sure that if it were them, they wouldn't be able to manage.

For example, I had to stop going to a particular club because the people drove me nuts with continual comments such as, 'Watch that step', 'I'll get your drink for you', 'The seat closest to the door will be good for you', and, 'Let me know when you need to go to the toilet and I'll come with you and help.' This is caring taken to the extreme. Seriously, treating someone with a parability as though they are a helpless child instead of treating them as an equal is likely to make them feel so distressed on the inside, even if they must politely say 'Thank you, I am fine.'

I have been para-abled for more than 69 years as I write this. I am an expert in lived experience. Do-gooders are amateurs. I am far from perfect, mind you. I loved my power as a child, as I realised I could play the game of using my parability to get out of things I didn't want to do. I was, in those days, the only para-abled child in my school, as far as I was aware. The teachers and other students had no experience with para-abled children.

One girl, Judith—a lovely girl with bright red hair and chronic asthma—used to worry about me a lot. I was probably guilty of bringing on some of her asthma attacks, now that I think about it, but as a child I was not the least bit interested in why Judith had her attacks, I just got upset when she did. I was more interested in playing the game of using my parability to get out of things I didn't like doing. I had everyone wrapped around my little finger. I saw it as fun.

I realised that I had a hold over adults, and I felt powerful. I loved every minute of it and revelled in the attention. Because I was constantly distracted by playing my power games, I didn't concentrate on learning. This meant that my future wasn't as easy as it could have been. Even so, I did enjoy discovering how to do things to suit my lifestyle. Despite the gaps in my education I didn't have to copy what others did. I found my own way.

I was born Janice Mary Gardner on 22nd January 1950, in the small town of Millicent, in the South-East of South Australia. I am very proud of my heritage, and am grateful to the long line of people who came before me, and made it possible for me to arrive in the world. They came to Australia from different parts of the world, and lived through hardship, wars, and the depression—but they also found love and happiness within the complexity of life. My family history has been passed down by word of mouth. None of my ancestors wrote anything down, and so a lot of their experiences have fallen through the cracks of time, never to be heard of again. However, the decisions of my ancestors, all the way from the distant past, right through to my parents, have brought me to the point of documenting the fantastic highs and dreadful lows of my life, so that there will be a more permanent record for future generations, and particularly for our son, Lee.

***

I was born a happy and very healthy baby, and was the only daughter of Harry William and Irene Laura Nellie Gardner (nee Andersen). Our family home at that time was in the small country town of Mount Burr, in the South-East of South Australia.

My dad was born in Bishop Stortford, England, on the 1st of February 1919. His father, William, was an Australian stretcher-bearer soldier during the First World War, and his mother, Daisy, was an English nurse, working in a London hospital. William received a stomach wound due to an explosion, and was transported to the hospital where Daisy worked. She was his nurse, and over the course of his recovery they fell in love, and then married. Their first child, Harry, my dad, was three months old when they headed for Australia on the ship RMS *Lucie Woermann*. During the voyage, my dad won first prize in the ship's 'Under Six-Months Baby Competition.' After arriving in Adelaide, South Australia, they settled in Cheltenham, a western suburb of Adelaide.

Dad always joked that he crawled out from England as soon as he could. But I know he was proud of his heritage, and always called himself a 'Pommy bastard', a moniker that his mates also used. This was back in the days when it was given and taken as a jovial expression.

My mother was born on the 1st March 1919, one month to the day after my dad's birth. My mother was born at Alberton, a western suburb of Adelaide. Alberton was the suburb next to Cheltenham, where Dad was to grow up.

My maternal grandmother was born in Broken Hill, New South Wales, and my maternal grandfather, Niels Emil Andersen, was born in Denmark. Niels Emil, who was a seaman, jumped ship in Port Adelaide as an illegal immigrant and met my grandma. He heard that if he signed up with the Australian Army he would automatically become an Australian citizen, and so that is what he did. He fought in France in the First World War, and served in the American Merchant Navy in the Second World War. One of my cousins, Paul Andersen, told me that they were responsible for shipments of weapons. Grandpa always sent money home to his family.

Grandma and Grandpa met at Port Adelaide. Grandma was the second youngest in a family of six sisters and one brother. Grandma's sisters never approved of Grandpa being Danish. In their eyes he was a foreigner, and they never fully accepted him.

Over the years Grandma became angry and unforgiving of Grandpa. I could never understand her anger. I have a memory of sitting at her kitchen table and asking if she had loved Grandpa when they got married. She told me that she had, and that was the end of the conversation. I had hoped for more of an explanation that would make sense of the complexity of their marriage, how their love had got lost, and why. I was being shielded from all the facts, of course. I never saw him drunk, I didn't experience his anger or violence, and had no knowledge of his womanising. I later found out that he was always in trouble on the ships, as there are records showing he spent time in the brig, due to being drunk and involved in fights, but this is all I know of his past. I wish I knew the back-story of his life, so that I might understand why he carried such huge anger. Apparently his brother, George, had the opposite personality and was a loving, and much loved, man. Grandma said she had married the wrong brother.

Dad signed up for the army in 1940, at the beginning of World War II. He was one of the first Australians to do so. He was posted to the Middle East and then to New Guinea, serving in the Army Engineers Corp.

Mother and Dad first met at school. Mother told me she thought he was the biggest show off in the school. Dad was expelled after standing up to a teacher who continually singled him out and victimised him. Dad's revenge was to push a wardrobe on top of the teacher, and to then sit on top of the wardrobe. All hopes of a fresh start were dashed when he discovered that his teacher at the new school was a friend of the very teacher he had pushed the wardrobe on to. He continued having trouble at the new school.

Dad had an outgoing, fun-loving personality, a combination that was not acceptable at school, and so he was always in trouble. His mother was very strict, and determined that her children would grow up to be model citizens, so his naturally exuberant personality meant that he didn't get the love from his mother that he needed. At the age of twelve he had a breakdown after the death of his grandmother, who had been the primary source of love and affection for him. Dad recovered, and I believe the experience helped to shape the wonderful man he became.

Mother and Dad met again when they were seventeen. Dad was working as an usher at the Ozone picture theatre in Alberton, and Mother was working in the lolly shop next to the theatre. She had not long been out of hospital, after suffering from tuberculosis. Dad was too shy to ask her out, so he asked her brother, Keith, who he knew from school, to ask her if she would go out with him. Mother's reply was, 'If Harry Gardner wants to take me out he can ask me himself!'

So he did.

They dated from 1936 until Dad went to war in 1940. They then wrote to each other all through the war. Mother kept the letters until the last years of her life, when she offered those special letters to me. I felt that they should stay with her, but she misunderstood and told Dad that the letters no longer needed to be kept, and so they were thrown away, lost forever.

Dad got five days' leave from the army, and on the 3rd June 1942 he married my mother. After the wedding Mother stayed living with her parents until the war was over. When Dad returned to Australia in 1945 the government offered him a job at a sawmill at Mount Burr.

Mother and Dad made a fine picture as a young, good-looking couple, ready to embrace country life. He was a handsome, solid-built man of about six feet tall, with blue eyes and blond hair that went darker over the years. He was a very sociable man, with a lovely sense of humour, and could get away with saying just about anything. He had a very strong, deep voice. He loved his sports and won trophies for cricket in the late 1940s. In his senior years he won trophies for lawn bowls, while proudly playing for the Lockley's Bowling Club. I treasure those trophies.

Mother was a very pretty young lady. She was slim, with blue eyes and light brown hair, which she curled with rags and then rollers. She always reminded me of Queen Elizabeth II. Mother was a very sensitive, gentle, and caring person.

Mother found it hard to be accepted in Mount Burr. She loved cooking and would ask the country ladies for a recipe of something that they had made, be it a special tart or a wonderful meat dish she had tasted. They obliged by giving her the recipe, but one or two deliberately left an ingredient out so that mother had no success with it. When mother realised what the ladies were doing it affected her confidence, as she was a very sensitive person. However, with encouragement from friends, she eventually became a confident cook. She was also good at sewing, and kept the housework under control far better than I have ever succeeded in doing.

When I was very young, Mother had a luncheon at the home of a woman whose son called her 'Mother.' This made an impression on my mother, and so when she came home she asked if I would call her 'Mother' and, of course, that was fine with me. Over the years it has been suggested that it sounds too formal and cold, but I always said it with love and warmth.

So there we were, a happy, healthy and stable country family. I was content, and although I now live in the city I still have a great love for country life.

I fitted into the swing of things for the first ten months of my life. However, in November of 1950 I became ill with the flu, which turned into bronchial pneumonia. During my illness, without anyone noticing, I was bitten by a pesky little mosquito, which was carrying a disease called Murray Valley Encephalitis. The mosquito had got the disease from an infected bird, and then passed it on to me. It didn't take long before Mother realised that there was something seriously wrong, as I became limp and started grunting. Mother went to seek help from the next-door neighbour, Mrs Guerin, who was also a wonderful friend. It was decided that I should be taken to the hospital.

I was admitted to Thyne Memorial Hospital at Millicent, where I remained for three weeks. After an assessment was made on my health, the latest drugs were flown in from Adelaide. Mr Court, from the chemist shop at Millicent, met the plane and took the drugs to the hospital. It was thought that I had polio. I also had bronchial pneumonia, but my condition was not improving. As my condition became critical, doctors at the Adelaide Children's Hospital recommended that I should be airlifted to Adelaide. Mother accompanied me on the aeroplane, which was met by an ambulance to rush me to the hospital. The dreadful shock and fear of losing her beloved baby was a feeling I was to experience myself later in life. It was only then that I realised how horrendous my illness would have been for Mother.

Once I was settled in the hospital in Adelaide I was found to be paralysed all the way down my right side. Gradually, movement returned to the top of my leg and the top of my arm, but this movement stopped at my knee and my elbow. It was still believed by the doctors in Adelaide that I had contracted polio. It wasn't until many years later that I discovered it was not polio but encephalitis.

Encephalitis is swelling of the brain. It was this swelling that caused the paralysing of the right side of my body. The most affected areas being from my right elbow—down to and including my fingers, and from my right knee—down to and including my foot. The bronchial pneumonia that I experienced at the same time permanently affected my lung, and left me with a disease called chronic bronchiectasis. As a result, my lung produces an excessive amount of phlegm as soon as the temperature drops below about twenty-three degrees Celcius. In my late twenties I wanted it confirmed that the encephalitis had definitely not affected me mentally, and so I had a full evaluation carried out by a psychologist. The results proved that my mind was okay. The swelling in my brain had only stopped the oxygen getting to my leg and arm. I was in the Adelaide Children's Hospital for eight months. Through that time Mother stayed with Grandma Andersen at her home at Ozone Street, Alberton, and worked part-time in Adelaide while I was in hospital.

Dad gave one month's notice at the sawmill, which meant the surrender of a permanent government job. At the time, Wadlow Timber Merchants at Port Adelaide was advertising for a head saw doctor, which was the position my dad held at Mount Burr. Mother rang Keith Wadlow, the managing director, and explained that her husband was interested in the job but would not be available for four weeks, as he insisted on giving one month's notice to his current employers. Keith Wadlow was impressed, and said they would wait for Dad to finish up at Mount Burr. So Dad packed up the Mount Burr home, sold it, and relocated to Adelaide. My sickness completely changed the direction of all our lives.

Dad was in charge of the saw shop at Wadlow's. He told me that he would be constantly on the phone to the hospital while I was undergoing my many operations. On one occasion he was called into the managing director's office about all the time he was wasting. Dad was furious and said, 'My daughter is having major surgery. I will continue to "waste time", as you put it.'

This was accepted, and his phone calls to the hospital were not questioned again. Dad worked at Wadlow's until he retired at the age of sixty. He didn't get a great retirement payout, as a result of changing jobs. After moving to Adelaide, he'd had the opportunity to become the part-owner of a business, but turned it down because of my needs. He didn't want to take the chance when he already had security, even though the job he turned down would have paid substantially more money. Dad's uncle, George Gardner, passed away some years later and left some money to my dad, which enabled my family to have a bit more financial comfort.

After spending eight months in hospital, I was sent home strapped to a frame, which I continued to use for the rest of 1950 all the way through to 1953. I had to lie flat on my back, which was not good for my lung disease, but they didn't realise that back then, with my legs straight and apart. My mother was good at dressmaking, so I was a patient making a fashion statement among the 'frame gang', with pretty covers made of the latest fabrics, stiched to perfection.

Once home, the frame rested on a converted pram so that I could be wheeled around. Dad converted the pram by removing the front, hood and back, while leaving the sides and wooden base in place. The metal frame was then laid out on blankets over the base, and Mother made removable fabric covers which fitted over the metal frame. I was strapped in with bandages, which were secured to the frame, with my arms bandaged to the metal and then covered with the fabric covers. My head rested on a pretty pillow, which was on an extension of the metal frame. I spent about two and a half years on the frame, and could only see people from the knees up.

Mother and Dad bought land at Thanet Street, Brooklyn Park, a western suburb of Adelaide, and had a house built. We lived with Grandma and Grandpa until the house was built. I should imagine that Mother was glad of the help that Grandma gave her, as the routine was that I would have to be taken out of my frame three times a day for exercises. That meant undoing all the bandages, holding my legs, arms and body in position, and then rolling the bandages up one by one, ready to be used again. I must have loved the freedom, as I was told in later years that when it was time to put me back in the frame and bandage me in, I would scream continually until I realised I was stuck there. It must have been so hard for everyone. I have no memory of it at all.

In 1952, the day came for us to move into our new home at Brooklyn Park. There was a smallish bathroom at the centre of the house, and a toilet out the back through the laundry attached to our home. The kitchen was large, to make it easy for my parents to manoeuvre my frame. My room was next to my parent's room, and both rooms had windows facing the street. We had a big backyard. After it was well-established, Mother called it the back garden, and was very rightly proud of it. Dad loved gardening too, and in later years, when I became a brat, that was their escape from me. Consequently, I never learnt to become a 'green thumb.'

I was now two years old, and they had no idea if I would ever be free from my frame. I have a lovely memory of Mr March, a neighbour from up the street. He arranged for 'Father Christmas' to visit me in our kitchen. I was by the back door, with the head of the frame up against the wall so I could see the kitchen hallway door. I remember lying there and suddenly Father Christmas came in, with a lovely smile on his face. He leaned over the frame and wished me a merry Christmas. A truly lovely memory.

I feel sad when I think of everyone back in the 1950's worrying about me, and having no idea of my future possibilities. They have now passed on. I wish I could go back in time to thank them and let them know that my life is great, so they don't need to worry. I would love to sit down with my parents and thank them for teaching me about how to dream, and how to let go of the dreams that don't work out so that I can chase after the next ones.

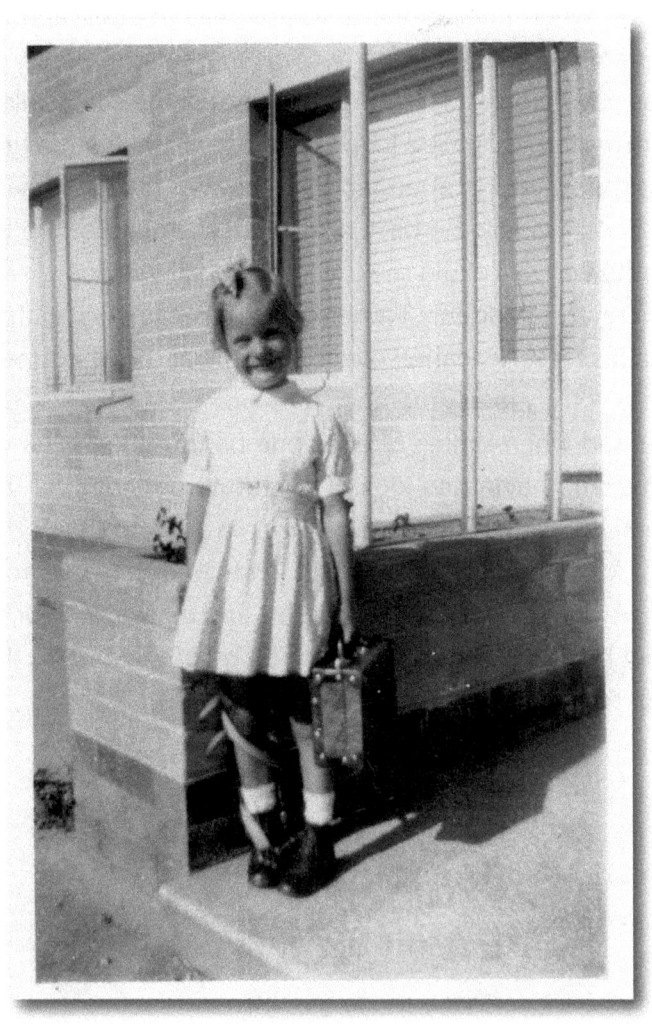

CHAPTER 2
Childhood Years

In 1952, our shift from Grandma and Grandpa's home to Thanet Street, Brooklyn Park, meant a new house—a house that my parents made into a lovely home to grow up in. It was a three-bedroom red double-brick home with red tiles on the roof, which extended to cover the small front porch.

The 'Kangaroo Ambulance' that had collected me from Grandma's home now collected me from our new home. The ambulance used to take me for treatments at the Children's Hospital, because I could not fit into a car on the frame. The Kangaroo Ambulances were wonderful. The ambulance I particularly remember had cartoon characters on the inside walls and a little kangaroo frieze around the top of the outer sides.

In 1950s Adelaide, the ambulances were made possible by the radio station 5AD, which raised money on air through their Kangaroo Club shows and birthday calls. The ambulances were presented to the Adelaide Children's Hospital on the 31 May 1951. I believe there were seven ambulances in Adelaide, with specialist drivers. I only remember one, by the name of David. He was older than my dad, and had a 'grandpa' way about him. He was of medium height and had a stomach that liked food. I recall his amazing kindness. He always smiled and made me feel special.

Those ambulances were our special ambulances. I am sure the times the Kangaroo Ambulance took me to the hospital for physio would have helped Mother to catch up on the housework, which was just plain hard work in those early years.

Our kitchen floor was covered in linoleum, with a pattern of large black squares with different light-coloured plain squares which seemed to cross under and off centre to the black squares. The floor showed any marks—even water marks. Our ice-chest cooler was old. There were more modern styles of ice-chests on the market but they were too expensive for us. The ice-man would come with a solid oblong ice brick, held by metal tongs. The ice bricks were big and heavy, and were for well-built men to carry. When the ice-man arrived at the back door he would put the ice brick down and slide it across the floor with his thick gloved hands, to where the ice-chest stood against the opposite wall. He arrived at no specific time, always unannounced, and just yell, 'Ice!' There was an ice compartment at the top of our ice-chest. He would lift the lid, place the ice in, and close the lid. That was his job done and he would leave. Our ice-chest had metal pipes that ran down the sides. As the ice melted the water would run down the pipes to the tray on the floor under the legs of the ice-chest. It was Mother's job to empty the tray full of water before it overflowed. When it did, Mother would get upset, as the clean up was time consuming.

Mother worked very hard to keep the kitchen lino sparkling clean in our large kitchen. In those early days, as Mother had to regularly clean and polish the lino by hand, she would put me out on the front porch while she worked. I would lie there on my frame, which was quite safe, as many wives and mothers in the neighbourhood stayed at home in those days, so there were plenty of people around to keep an eye on me. The floor was first swept, then washed and left to dry, then Mother would get down on her hands and knees and rub the polish on every area of that floor with an old rag. After waiting for it to dry she would again get down on her hands and knees and rub it with a clean dry rag, her elbow and arm in rapid movement, until it shone beautifully. She was very proud of her finished work. I remember, when I was a little older, Mother had only just finished her sparkling clean floor when the ice-man yelled 'Ice!' and immediately whizzed the ice across the floor. She just stood there in shock and started crying.

In those early years, another big job was the washing. This was always done on Mondays, using our large copper basin. Mother would fill the basin with cold water and light the gas copper from the bottom. It used to make a bang, which always frightened me. When the water was hot she would wash the clothes, empty the water, then re-fill with water to rinse. When finished, Mother would hand-wring the clothes and hang them on the line in the backyard.

She had added stress, because in those days we all had home incinerators to burn anything that would burn. Everyone could burn anytime they wished, and someone close by used to burn often when Mother had the white sheets on the line. Mother would rush out to grab the washing in before the incinerator smoke meant rewashing the lot.

With me in the frame Mother only had time to go to the shops when I was taken by ambulance for physio. The shops were around the corner from our street, on Airport Road and Henley Beach Road.

The evening meal was no easy chore, as the peas had to be hand-shelled and the string beans had to be topped and tailed—it all took time. Dad was a 'blue collar' worker and would expect his dinner on the table at 6pm sharp. That was the way it was, and I can never remember Mother letting him down.

One day, while I was out on the front veranda on my frame, I was crying. An older gentleman dressed in a uniform came and rang the doorbell, collecting money door-to-door for the Salvation Army. Mother and the gentleman, who was called Mr Simpson, got talking. He asked if he could pray for me. Mother agreed because of the wonderful work the Salvation Army had done through World War Two. Dad had relayed his experience of his five years in the Australian Army—heading for a hill, rifle in hand, expecting to find the enemy on the other side of the hill but instead finding a 'Salvo' with a billy hanging over a fire. The Salvo called them over to have a cuppa and a biscuit. Dad said the Salvos weren't armed, so when they left they weren't sure if the man would survive.

After that meeting on the front veranda, Mr Simpson visited regularly, and would give me birthday and Christmas presents, some of which I still have and treasure. He prayed regularly for me, and his visits to have a cuppa and a chat with Mother were a great comfort to her. Much later in our lives the Salvation Army were there again when we needed them.

Dad planted the lawn in the front and back yards, and Mother planted flowers. In those early years our kitchen window, with the sink under it, looked out onto the wooden paling fence that divided us from our side neighbour. Mother planted a camellia bush with beautiful deep rose-pink petals in view from the kitchen. I remember standing at the sink looking out of the window at the beautiful flowers. The neighbourhood dogs aimlessly roamed the streets. There were no laws to restrict them from visiting other neighbours or even other neighbourhoods, but around our way I never heard of anyone getting bitten.

While the husbands worked, the children played ball games in the street or played in friends' homes, and the mums got to know each other through their children. People tended to their gardens and watered their lawns with the hose. The greengrocer's van would drive up the streets, and the 'milky' in his van delivered milk to your door in the early morning.

There weren't as many distractions then as there are these days. Getting to know the neighbours was easy for my parents, with their chatty and friendly natures. Everyone walked to the local shops, and would say hello to others, sometimes stopping for a chat. Our immediate neighbours were great, and became an important part of our lives. Once we got to know the back neighbours, Dad took enough palings off the back fence to enable us to walk through. Mr and Mrs Wallis became good friends with our family. I called them 'Uncle Darcy' and 'Auntie Gail', and I loved them both.

I am not an organised person, and over my adult years with my family responsibilities and health problems I only managed to pop in to visit Uncle Darcy and Auntie Gail unannounced, or to make the occasional phone call, but not as often as I should have. I do wish I still had time, but I can't change the past. I have sadness within me that I disappointed them. They didn't know how special they were to me. I have the present and the future to try to do better with family and friends.

Uncle Darcy and Auntie Gail were Church of England, as it was known then (it is now the Anglican Church), and our local church, St Richards, was 'High Church', as Mother used to remind me. Uncle Darcy and Auntie Gail were wonderful. We didn't have a telephone all through my childhood, and they invited my parents to make calls from their phone at any time. Auntie Gail always made time for a chat whenever I wandered down through the gap in the fence in later years. I loved her homemade ice cream. Uncle Darcy and Dad enjoyed a chat and a beer together, and Auntie Gail and Mother often caught up for a cuppa and a chat.

Mr & Mrs O'Toole were the neighbours on the northern side of our house. Their daughter, Jill—their only child—was twelve years old when we moved in. Jill used to help Mother roll up the bandages when I was taken off my frame at exercise time and bath time. I remember Mr O'Toole being a tall thin man, and in later years I would hear him playing his piano. He was a gentle and kind man who always had a smile and a 'hello' for me. Mrs O'Toole was a very quiet person.

When Jill left school she gained employment at the Adelaide Airport, gradually working her way up to be secretary to the airport manager. Jill helped me to get quite close to famous people that I liked when they arrived at Adelaide Airport. I remember being at the airport in 1959, so excited to see Danny Kaye, the American comedian and actor. Jill always gave me her time just to chat. She also took me to the Adelaide 'Carols by Candlelight' as well as other outings. I have lovely memories of Jill coming into our home to share the news of trips she was planning to Japan and other great destinations. I got such a thrill sitting by the open fire in our lounge room and examining the tickets and maps. I think that inspired me to travel in later years. Jill was and, and still is, like a big sister to me.

The neighbours directly across the road were Mr & Mrs Keane, and their daughter, Rita, who was six years old when we moved in. Rita recently explained to me that she and her friends were instructed by their mums and dads to always include me. The sad thing is I have very little memory of spending time with them. I got Rita's hand-me-down clothes, which was lovely, as they were all hand-made by Mrs Keane. These gifts would have been a great help to my parents.

At the age of three, the Kangaroo Ambulance collected me for the usual physio visit to the hospital, taking me out of the house on my frame. However, I arrived home with a caliper on my leg, a hand splint, and standing – I was out of the frame and standing on my own two feet! I was only three years old, but I clearly remember that wonderful feeling of freedom.

My first thought after showing my very excited mother was to show Auntie Gail. Mother said I insisted on walking down to her place through the hole in the fence, stepping over the piece of wooden rail, to show her. I must have had some practice walking at the hospital before that day. I can clearly remember saying, 'I want to do this myself.' Mother was not far behind, in case I needed help, and was always there if I needed her—until in later years she needed me.

***

I loved being the centre of attention, as I had been when I was in hospital, but Dad wouldn't let me get away with anything. Mother's only sister, Auntie Dawn, who has now passed away, told me a story of a family gathering. I was trying to get attention when they were all sitting around chatting, by presenting myself among them and then falling over. Auntie Dawn got up to help me, but Dad ordered her to sit down, saying in an angry voice, 'Janice put herself down there and she can bloody well pick herself up.'

Dad was the only person who could call me Janice and get away with it, other than a lovely French couple who lived up the top end of Thanet Street who said 'Janice' in the most wonderful way - it came out as 'Jeneece.'

Dad was always very strict with me. He was a strong person in body and mind, and realised I was strong willed too. He would not give me an inch, knowing I would take ten miles if I could get away with it. I can remember not liking him but also loving him all at once. Dad was the only person I could not wrap around my finger in my childhood years.

Mother was so loving and giving of her time, offering me help if I needed it. When I was naughty she would just put me in my bedroom to be dealt with by Dad when he got home. I can still hear those words, 'Just wait 'til your father gets home.' The door handles in those days were high up, so I couldn't reach them. I was stuck in my room waiting to be dealt with by Dad. When dad did get home he would come in and back mother up by giving me a stern talking too, which I would get upset by, then he would leave me to think about what I had done.

At the age of four, the top right lobe of my right lung was presenting itself as a huge problem to my health. I was coughing a lot, day and night. The lung specialist decided to operate to remove the diseased lobe, hoping to stop the bronchiectasis disease from going to the two remaining lobes on my right side. I asked Mother what was going to happen to me, and she suggested that I ask the doctor who was going to do the operation, so I did. Doctors never scared me. I was constantly visiting them, and they were all kind and gentle. I can remember asking the doctor. He gently took my hand and walked me to a little office with glass windows. He sat me on his knee, got a pencil and paper, and drew a picture of lungs in a simple way, so I could understand without feeling overwhelmed. He told me about the sick part of my lung, explaining to me that he had to stop it making me cough by taking it away. He also told me that I would be asleep when he took the sick part of my lung away, and not to worry. The operation went well. I don't remember having any pain, just feeling safe and happy.

Another memory I have from that stay in hospital was triggered by a photo that was taken in 1954—I was standing on the Adelaide Children's Hospital balcony with other children, and a cake was brought out. In the photo the cake has '10 Years' written on it in icing. In a book by Margaret Barbalet, The Adelaide Children's Hospital 1876-1976, Margaret talks of two major developments in 1944, which the cake may have been celebrating. Both were important to my health. The first was the introduction at the hospital of penicillin - the wonder injection to stop infections, such as my lung infections. The second was a new wing of the building, which was built for the surgical care of babies and for physiotherapy rooms, which I used. The Premier (the Hon. T. Playford) laid the foundation stone on 14 April 1944 - ten years before the cake was made.

I remember being so overwhelmed and delighted with the amazing cake. I had never seen anything like it before or since. It was made in the shape of a beautiful house. It was perfect. But then I remember suddenly feeling very, very angry with a doctor who snatched the chimney off the cake and ate it, just before the photo was taken. I have that photo, but it is not possible to see the hole where the chimney was, as it was on my side away from the camera. I didn't give my usual smile because I was still angry with the doctor.

My parents had friends who lived on a farm at Kongorong, in the South-East of South Australia. The doctor said that I should get some country air and it was decided I should go with my parents to stay on the farm after my operation. 'Auntie' Marie and 'Uncle' Maurie Healy welcomed us into their home. They were warm hearted and caring people. At that time, they only had one child—their son, Denis. They were later to have two daughters. The first, Tricia, was born a few months after our visit.

Many years before, Uncle Maurie used to take my mother to the movies when they were both about 15 years old, but Uncle Maurie was Catholic and my mother wasn't, so their families split up the friendship. Mother met Dad at 17 years of age, and Maurie met Marie. The two couples became good friends, and stayed in touch through the years.

It was a long drive to the Kongorong farm. My parents entertained me by telling me to look for fox eyes shining from the bushes—we must have been travelling in the early hours before dawn. I can remember sitting on my mother's lap, as there were no seat belts in cars in those days.

The memory of that holiday has stayed with me all my life. It was around shearing time. Auntie Marie and Uncle Maurie were wonderful. I remember how kind they were. They had a thirteen-year old boy, named Tony, staying with them. Tony was given the job of baby-sitting me, in order to give my parents a break after their stress about my operation. Tony later worked on the farm again, when he was sixteen, and I have wonderful memories of walks around the farm with him, and of sitting with him in the long narrow lounge room, playing checkers with Denis. Denis got angry that Tony was helping me, and started throwing the checkers disks at me, but Tony protected me by holding up a lounge cushion. I remember sitting at the dinner table and Tony coming in late one night and apologising as he sat next to me. I felt so happy. I loved walking around the farm. Tony would let me pat the lambs, and I'd chat away while he listened. We stood watching the shearing of the sheep; so much wool came off each sheep! I asked him where he lived and he showed me his sleep-out room through the wire door.

I have a memory of standing on the lawn chatting to Uncle Maurie, when a wild magpie started talking like a parrot. I was sure that magpies should not have been talking.

I remember, too, the day we left to come home. In that one week Tony had totally won my heart. He had befriended me, protected me, given me his time, and cared for me. He was able to give me the time that my dad couldn't—in those days, with my strong personality, my dad had to be strict and not be my friend. As I sit here I can visualise that holiday and the last day, as we were leaving. Tony bent down on one knee in the hallway of the farmhouse, he gave me a kiss on my cheek and we hugged. I was crying—I did not want to leave him. Tony said, 'You have to go now, next time I see you, you won't have that caliper on.'

As amazing as it may seem, I never stopped loving Tony. He was like a perfect brother in my mind. I thought of him constantly during the following days, weeks, months, and years. Tony became my invisible friend and protector, but no one knew except my girlfriend Di.

When things got really hard, from that single week on the farm, I formulated a way of coping with the lonely times, the sad times, and the pain of operations. I imagined I had Tony protecting me. I could be strong because I imagined he was there with me. Adults would say, 'Be brave, little one.' and I would think, 'Yes, I can, Tony is helping me and protecting me.'

My wonderful parents never made going to hospital into a drama. They would talk about what fun I would have meeting new people, and I would start remembering the fun I had the last time I was there. I would be reminded of what a joy it would be for me after the treatment or operation. They never said it would or wouldn't hurt—that part of the process was never discussed, which was great, as it would not have been helpful. It just hurt when it hurt, and I would be comforted by my parents or the nurses. I don't know how Dad did it, with work obligations, but he was always there when I came out of recovery. I would wake up and he would have a big smile for me. I knew he hated hospitals, so that was a true gift from him.

On one of my hospital stays I met two sisters. They were both having operations on their legs. We had a lot of fun together, playing and having pillow fights. They both had wonderful singing voices and taught me a song called Summertime. I had no idea of timing or tone, but that didn't matter.

When I was making progress with my recovery, but still not strong enough to go home, I had to go to a place called Estcourt House in the Adelaide suburb of Grange. It was a huge home, with 17 rooms, built in 1894, which had been converted into a convalescent home. I would be collected from the hospital and transferred to Estcourt House. I enjoyed hospital and getting pampered, but the convalescent home meant less pampering, and I was probably busy being naughty. I remember little of my days there, but in my autograph book I have signatures of nurses and a teacher from the Estcourt House school. I hated going to convalesce, and David, the Kangaroo Ambulance driver, knew that. To make it easier for me, he would drive along the road overlooking the beach and stop at a shop and buy me some lollies. He was a perfect gentleman—we would just sit and watch the sea and he would talk to me and make me feel better, just like a caring grandpa would do.

Estcourt House was on the top of a hill, and had a big veranda. Many of the nurses there were young trainees. On one occasion after an operation, my leg was encased in plaster up to my knee. I had no control over the spasms, and my leg would jump when I got nervous or if my toes were touched. This jumping was very painful after operations. Two nurses entertained themselves by touching my toes, which made my leg jump. The pain was dreadful for me, but they were laughing and having fun.

In hospital and at Estcourt House there were always lights on, but at home in my room it was pitch black. When I was alone and very scared of the dark in my room at night I would tell myself that my invisible friend, Tony, was there with me, protecting me. It was my secret, because I thought there was something wrong with me. I felt ashamed that I had an invisible friend. As far as I knew, no one else had one.

Straight after my lung operation my parents were taught to give me postural draining. My lung disease meant that my lungs constantly created too much phlegm, which needed clearing.

My lungs still over-produce to this day, and need to be constantly drained or they will become infected. If my lungs are not drained it can cause pneumonia, and that part of my lung would become scarred and not work properly.

As a child, draining the lung meant one of my parents taking a kitchen chair, turning it upside down on the floor and then placing pillows over the chair for me to lie across. Then they would carry out percussion, by cupping their hands and banging on my back to shake the phlegm off the walls of the lobes of my lungs. I would then huff and cough the phlegm out into a cotton hanky. I now use tissues and do my own percussion for around one to two hours each night. There are five lobes in most people's lungs, two on the left side and three on the right side, but I had one missing on the right side.

Winter months have always been worse for my lungs. In those early years we couldn't have the heater on all night because of the expense, and my cough would become worse in the early hours. My mother went to the chemist shop and the chemist recommend cough mixture for me to have when needed; I remembered it tasted good and was dark red in colour. Mother was told to give me a sip whenever I was coughing. Regular sips were needed. No one knew in those days to question what substances were in medicines. It was blind trust for everyone.

My room had brightly coloured curtains, with many different colours all patched in different shapes. I remember when I had day naps, lying there staring at the curtains, and a little boy would emerge from the colours, swing around the curtains and wave to me. I would smile and wave back. He never worried me, as he seemed very friendly, and then he would disappear back into the colours.

Once when I went to the toilet, which meant walking through our laundry, I saw the most beautiful fairy standing on top of the cupboard; she was white and glowing with her wings fluttering. On another occasion, when I was lying in my bed, awake but with my eyes closed, I felt my inner body moving, and I was conscious that

I was moving down my body. At one point I found I could think of moving up and then moving down again, and it happened. I got to the point of having my head at my feet. I seemed to know that I had a choice of getting out of my body or moving back. I became scared that if I chose to get out of my body I may not be able to get back in, so I chose to go back up. I was fascinated that I had control.

Later we learned that the medicine had alcohol in it, and the curtain boy was a part of a tiddly elusion, and also possibly the fairy. But to this day I believe I had control over my movement within my body. I guess these days it would be known as an out-of-body experience.

I also remember dad getting out of bed and bringing me a teaspoon of butter that had been dipped into the sugar bowl. This seemed to help me to stop coughing.

Once I was well enough I went to kindy, which was a first step before starting school the next year. I met Christine Hembrow there, and we are still friends today. I remember us sitting on the floor and being handed a plate with wedges of orange, apple, and a handful of grapes. That is the sum total of my memories of kindy. I am sure those dear ladies worked very hard to make us happy. Christine's parents, whom I called Auntie Jean and Uncle John, were good friends with my parents. On Christmas Day mornings we would go to their home for Christmas drinks, and exchange gifts. Uncle John was CEO at McNiven Bros Ltd, who produced ice creams. I would sometimes go to Christine's after school, as she lived in the same street as the school, which was Lockley's Primary School. In the early years we would spend birthdays together, along with other friends. I can remember one year when Uncle John brought the most beautiful fairy house ice-cream cake for my birthday. We spent a lot more time together in our late teens and early twenties, as our homes were in adjacent suburbs.

Christine and I started school together, where we met Dianne Caldow, who was also in Grade One. Dianne and I have remained friends too. I remember standing in a line on the very first day and being so excited, and also feeling confused because some of the other kids were crying. I couldn't understand why they were not happy too. I quickly worked out that I was being treated differently to the other kids, and enjoyed the attention. My first year of school was wonderful. I remember sitting on the floor listening to the teacher reading us a story—that felt so special to me. I also have vague memories of a picture of a cartoon drawing of a town, with the shops and roads and buildings. I have no other memories of that school year.

In Grade Two things got a bit more serious, but I had lung infections during winter and had time off school, which meant I missed important information. I was starting to not like school. All of the sitting at desks and needing to be quiet and learn was a bore, and to make things worse I couldn't understand some of it. To add insult to injury, the school—in their wisdom—decided that I should repeat Grade Two, which meant that Christine and Dianne went up a grade higher than me. I found it hard to fit in with my new classmates, as their friendships had already been formed.

I remember Christine staying for a sleepover. At school my caliper was just a part of who I was. The following morning, I bounced out of bed and grabbed my caliper to put on as normal. I looked up to see Christine staring at me with a curious awareness, before we both raced out for breakfast. I have a strong memory of that moment.

The kids at school never worried about my caliper. Well, I wasn't aware of it if they did. It never entered my mind to think about how anyone else might view my caliper. I was comfortable and felt secure wearing it. The teachers were also aware that I had a portion of my lung removed. I think that, coupled with my caliper, worried them immensely. They weren't educated in how to deal with sick or para-abled children. Being used to getting so much attention at home, and then finding myself having to share attention with so many other children at school, was hard for me. I was spoilt, to an extent. Being treated differently by the teachers led me to realising that I could play on their caring. I discovered the art of manipulation, without knowing what it was. My manipulation worked well, because they all underestimated my naughty behaviour.

My Grade Three teacher, Mrs Grenville, gave me a wake up call. She stopped me from getting the other kids to help me write my name on the front of my books. I knew she was on to me, but this was my game—I had power, and she wasn't going to get power over me. I remember being shocked that she was as clever as my dad.

While I was in Grade Three I saw a girl faint. I remember being so interested in all the attention she got. Weeks later I was getting fed up with what we were doing in class. I remembered the girl fainting, so I decided to have a go at it myself. I wanted to see if I could get that attention and get out of the work, so I just went floppy. Everybody reacted, the teacher called for help, and I was rushed to the sick bay. My Auntie Gail got the phonecall and went through the fence to tell Mother. Mother then called Christine's mum, as she was close to the school. Auntie Jean collected me and took me to her place until Dad could drive to collect me, as Mother couldn't drive.

As I look back, I am sure Dad knew I was putting on an act. However, my dad saw schoolteachers as being high up on a pedestal, and so he felt powerless. My parents also felt that way about doctors or anyone else who had been to university.

I knew that the fainting act couldn't be done too many times. About a year later I knew I would be in trouble at school for refusing to do my homework, so the morning it was due in I told Mother that I had a sore throat. She peered down into my open mouth and said, 'Oh, it looks like you have an ulcerated throat.' I was surprised, because my throat wasn't hurting at all, but I didn't say anything. I got to stay home from school and off we went to the doctor. I started to worry. The doctor looked down my throat and, to my surprise, he agreed with my mother. I was confused but happy, because I didn't have to go to school. I didn't tell anyone, not even Christine or Di.

Making out I wasn't well was naughty, but I kept up the sore throat act as I was getting away with it.

Whenever I got bored I did the act. After a day or two I said I felt better, then back to school I went. The funny thing was that no one looked down my throat after I said I felt better. When I was an adult I asked my doctor about the white dots on my tonsils. I learnt that they could have appeared after my sickness as a baby. The doctor told me that I could have them removed, but the sound of my voice would change. They weren't bothering me and I got compliments about the tone of my voice, so I declined.

From my early childhood onwards, anytime I wanted I would put on a faint or have a sore throat. I had power over poor Mrs Grenville and the teachers in the following years, as well as my parents. I look back as an adult and realise that because of this game I was playing, coupled with all the appointments with doctors and specialists, as well as the operations, I missed out on a large chunk of important information that was vital to my future.

In Grade Five we were told during our art lesson to go home and draw one of our parents. I decided that I would draw my dad because he sat still the longest. He would sit in his favourite chair after dinner each evening and watch TV, hardly moving. So I sat in front of him out of his view of the TV with paper, a pencil, and a rubber. After a long period of drawing, rubbing bits out, and redrawing, I was very excited as it was finally finished. It was my dad on paper in pencil. Both my parents were amazed with the result, and I felt so proud. I presented it to my teacher the next day feeling so pleased with myself. The teacher looked at the drawing then looked at me. She ripped the paper in half and told me my parents should stop doing my homework for me. Obviously because I was para-abled, in her mind I was not capable: I was totally underestimated. I felt completely shattered by her response, tears welled in my eyes and I just stood, stunned, looking at her face. Yes, I was a hyperactive kid and was scatty in my behaviour. It was my work though, and she made an assumption, totally dismissing my effort. I told Mother and Dad, but I think they felt powerless to follow up. After that experience I lost interest in art. I felt it wasn't worth the effort.

Having the family together for Christmas Day was a special time for me. As a little girl, Father Christmas came during the night to bring us gifts. We would spend Christmas Day at my mother's parents' home in Alberton. My uncles, aunties, and cousins all came together for the day. Dad and the uncles would set up the trestle tables and chairs in the lounge room, and festive tablecloths covered the tables. Porcelain Father Christmases with a bag to put the Christmas mix lollies in were placed on the table as the finishing touch once the tables had been set. It was a wonderful sight, and I felt so very excited to catch up with all my relatives.

It didn't enter my head back then that we never caught up with Dad's parents or siblings on such a special day. Later I learnt, to my great sadness, that my mother and my dad's mum had never really got along. This went way back, to when Mother and Dad were courting. They were holding hands in the lounge room when Grandma caught them. She was so disgusted with their behaviour that she became very angry with them both. Mother was devastated that she hadn't been trusted, and then learnt that Dad's mum knew a young woman who owned a florist shop, and she thought Dad should date the florist. I can understand that Grandma only wanted the best for Dad's future, but it wasn't for her to decide. It's wonderful that she loved and cared about my dad, but thank goodness he made his own decision, or I may never have been born. I loved Grandma and Grandpa Gardner, and although we didn't see them at Christmas they always came to our home for New Year's Day.

Throughout my childhood, Grandma Andersen would cook a hot roast dinner on Christmas Day, the English tradition of the mid-winter feast, which had been brought to Australia by our ancestors. As the Australian Christmas falls in the summer, when temperatures are often so hot, even without the oven being on, the heat of the kitchen was extreme. We followed the main meal with a Christmas pudding, made by Grandma and later by mother, served with custard. Tradition was to put the Christmas pudding upside down on a big dinner plate, pour about a tablespoon of warmed-up rum over the pudding, and set it alight in the centre of the table. The fun with the pudding was to find the coins that had been cooked within it—a threepence or two. When one of us children found a coin in the pudding we would win a prize. When we changed from pounds, shillings, and pence to dollars and cents in 1966 the new coins could not be cooked, so we kept the old money for that special Christmas tradition.

There were two other yearly traditions from my childhood which I treasure the memories of to this day. Both were with my mother. One was on ANZAC Day, the 25th of April. The Australian and New Zealand Army Corps held an annual march through the city of Adelaide in memory of the fallen soldiers of the two world wars, as well as other conflicts our countries have been involved in. We would attend each year, to watch my dear dad march with his army mates. His army number was SX4028, and he served as a Sapper in the 2/23 Corps Field Park Company, which was a unit of the Royal Australian Engineers. On the 25th of April every year Dad would go to the dawn service at 6 am with his mates. Mother and I would catch the bus to the city a bit later in the morning, to stand watching the march and madly wave with pride when Dad marched by.

The other event was the Adelaide Christmas Pageant, when Father Christmas arrived at the big Adelaide department store, John Martins, run by the Hayward family. According to an article written by Anne Burrows, Mr Edward Hayward brought back the idea of the pageant from Toronto, Canada. On the 18th of November 1933 he started the Adelaide Christmas Pageant. I understand that John Martins already had the Magic Cave set up and going in the years before the pageant began. I loved the magical feeling of watching the parade of wonderfully decorated floats as each one passed by.

The music, colour, costumes, themes and so much sparkle gave me an amazing inner happiness. After the pageant, Mother and I would visit the amazing Magic Cave where Father Christmas would talk to the children. The Adelaide Christmas Pageant still takes place each year. It is now longer, but still filled with all the wonderment that children and their parents enjoy.

For Christmas, when I was ten years old, I got a two-wheeler bike, which dad patiently and calmly helped me gain the confidence to ride. All of a sudden, I had an amazing feeling of freedom, and I enjoyed every minute of it. We lived seven houses from the end of our street and my girlfriend Di lived just around the corner, so I could ride down to Di's on my own. I then progressed to being allowed to ride around the block. Later I was allowed to ride the back streets to school, which was in our neighbouring suburb.

The older I got the harder school became. I had corrective operations on my hand and leg. I loved going to hospital. I slept through the operation and the painkillers worked most of the time, so hospital meant getting to know the other kids on the ward and having a wonderful time. I had totally lost interest in school.

I remember seriously disliking a girl who had the same first name as mine, but I have no memory as to why. One night I had decided to get some paper and write as many times as I could, 'I hate Janice.' I wrote it and folded it up as small as I could get that paper to fold. I decided to give the piece of paper to the other Janice when I arrived at school the following day. The next morning, Mother was helping me to get my school bag ready and found the note. She confiscated it, never to be seen again.

At school my ability to 'faint' and have 'sore throats' had become an Academy Award standard performance. I no longer understood what to do in class or what the teacher was talking about, so I became disruptive. The school suggested to my parents that I should be transferred to Thebarton Primary School, as they had a special learning class. I was then in Grade Six, and the transfer was arranged.

Arriving at a new school was daunting. I met Elaine Haynes and we became friends. My new Grade Six teacher, Mrs Winston, was a lovely, calming and caring lady. I can remember her sitting with me and asking me how to spell 'mother.' I had no idea at all how to spell 'mother.' Mrs Winston was obviously shocked, but I wasn't a bit upset that I couldn't spell 'mother.' Mrs Winston was patient and kind. I went to the special classes. I did try, and I improved slightly.

During the whole of my schooling I have no memory of anyone bullying me or giving me a bad time about me being a person with a parability, probably because I never saw myself as being different, other than thinking I was clever to be able to get out of work whenever I wanted to. One day I was sitting waiting for my friend Elaine at the school. A Grade Seven student came up to me and said, 'I envy you', before going into the classroom. I sat there wondering what she meant, as I had no idea about the concept of envy. I thought it must mean something bad. I remember asking her later what she meant. Her answer surprised me. She said, 'I wish I were you.' That made me feel great. I had no idea why anyone would want to be plain and boring like me.

I know I had confidence in myself, because around that time my orthopaedic specialist, Mr Rodney White, asked my parents if I would agree to go to his lectures, so that his students could learn about my parability. He gave me a one pound note ($2) and a bar of chocolate for attending, which I thought was fantastic.

On one occasion Mr White told his students I had no feeling in my right hand. However, that statement wasn't true. I stood up in front of everyone and announced, 'I have feeling, Mr White.' He quickly went on to explain that if he stuck a pin in my hand I would have sensation, but not feeling. I replied that I had the same feeling in my right hand as I did in my left hand. Such a sweet man, he turned to me, smiling, and said, 'Okay Jan, let us test this.'

He stood me up, facing the wall, with a medical student on each side, so that I couldn't look. With my hands behind my back he placed something in my right hand, which spasmed into a fist. I declared the object felt sticky and had sharp bits, but not like a knife. It was actually a wide piece of masking tape with the sticky side folded out, and the sharp bits were where it was folded.

Mr White took the masking tape away, and put something else in my hand. I said, 'It is plastic, and is wide at one end and thin at the other.' There was a short silence and Mr White asked me what colour it was. I was holding a golf tee that he'd had in his pocket. As I turned to look at him he started laughing and we all joined in. I have complete feeling down my right side, and could feel the spasm in my foot as well.

***

From the age of three I wore brown shoes. Once I started school, after seeing the other girls had different coloured shoes, I wore black shoes. They needed to have alterations made in order to connect to my caliper. All the girls at school wore pretty shoes of all sorts of colours. I mentioned at home that I would like white shoes, and for Christmas 1962 they appeared. I was so very excited. The hospital 'boot man' made white straps for me, to blend in with my pretty white shoes.

At school, I would get bored with the dance classes. We danced in a group and I had trouble remembering the steps. I told the teacher that I couldn't do it because of my leg. In her caring way, she asked if I would like to put the records on for the other children to dance to. I had a great time, in charge of the record player, watching the rest of the kids prancing around like trained poodles. I think if I'd been able to remember the steps I would have enjoyed the classes, as I do have a wonderful memory of being in my kitchen with Mother watching on smiling as I stood on Dad's feet while he waltzed me around the room.

***

As my mother never learnt to drive, my dad always took me to my many appointments with doctors and physiotherapists. Miss Evens was my physio from when I was seven years old. Her dad and my dad met when they were in the army. Miss Evens was wonderful, and Dad loved chatting to her. Over 60 years since we first met, we are still in touch. Miss Evens became Mrs Wells, and is still as lovely and caring as ever.

As a result of all my appointments, Dad and I spent a lot of time together in the car, but unfortunately I only have a few memories of conversations we shared. There was of a bridge on the way to and from the Adelaide Children's Hospital, and it was possible to drive over or under the bridge. If Dad took me over the bridge I would comment that I wished we had gone under, and vice versa. One day my dad said with restrained frustration, 'When I take you under, you want to go over. When I take you over, you want to go under.' I remember looking at him, shocked, as I hadn't realised I had be doing that. He was such a lovely dad. Another time we were driving along and I asked if he would show me how to reverse the car. He looked at me and told me that was a very good question to ask. I remember feeling so very proud of myself. Later, he showed me how to reverse the car down our driveway.

Once when we were driving along, Dad pulled over to the side of the road next to a two-storey home with an ivy vine climbing up the front and the sides of the house, all the way around the windows. It was a beautiful home. Dad said quietly, 'That is my dream home, isn't it beautiful?' I smiled and agreed with him. Dad's dream home never materialised for him, but he was very proud of our own home. He put so much work into it. He built the shed with the help of some of his mates. They built it from asbestos, as no one knew of the danger back then. He also painted the inside of our home, and if anything broke he would do his best to try and fix it.

One day when I was leaving school for the day an elderly man yelled out. 'Just know these are the happiest days of your life.'

I thought he was mad! All I wanted to do was grow up. I was sure that then I would be happy. I didn't realise he was right. I had amazing parents caring for me and giving me unconditional love. I lived in a lovely middle-class home, and had a security that I later learned not all children were fortunate enough to have.

CHAPTER 3

My Innocence Meets Death

At eight years of age my life was bubbling along like a carefree brook. I felt secure. I was a brat, and my strong will got me into trouble. However, my behaviour was recognised as innocent and naive, and although I was disciplined, I was given unconditional love. My lung was reasonably healthy. My caliper remained just an extension of me. I didn't care that my right hand didn't work; I just used my left hand.

My loving Auntie and Uncle lived in the next street, and other close family and friends were also nearby. My Godfather, one of my favourite uncles, was Uncle Ross, my mother's youngest brother. Mother had cared for him a lot when they were young. Uncle Ross started dating a young woman named Betty Honey. I was six years old when I was first introduced to her, on a Sunday afternoon at my grandma Andersen's home, at a 'scones and cuppas' get together, where we all enjoyed Grandma's delicious homemade scones. Betty greeted me with a lovely smile and a smooth comforting voice; I instantly liked her.

Uncle Ross and Betty got married and had their honeymoon at Seacliff, a beachside suburb south of Adelaide. Two years later, Betty, now Auntie Bet, gave birth to a baby boy, whom they named Paul. We were so delighted for them. On one occasion I can remember visiting them at their home. Paul was in his pram, and as we came around the back Auntie Bet was hanging clothes on the line. Paul was sound asleep and Uncle Ross came out to greet us. We went into their home and saw Uncle Ross's work. He was a carpenter, and had made all the kitchen cabinets, the kitchen table set, and so much more. I have lovely memories of Uncle Ross. He always had a smile for me and would be happy to spend time with me, whether it was to chat or play 'catchy' with a balloon. I loved him.

When Paul was just four months old Uncle Ross went to work one day and didn't return. He was working as a carpenter on the roof of a building in Port Adelaide. His hammer was about to fall, and as he reached for it he overbalanced and slipped from the roof. He hadn't been issued with any safety equipment. He fell 50 feet, first onto an iron fence without capping, and then onto the concrete below. He was rushed to hospital with multiple internal and external injuries. Grandma Andersen was at home and heard the ambulance go by, not knowing that it was for her son.

Mother was home in Thanet Street doing the ironing. While ironing Mother was listening to the radio, and in the midday extended news there was an announcement about the accident, and that the person was Ross Andersen. In 1958 there were few media restrictions about announcing people's names before the family had been informed. Mother stopped ironing and questioned if she'd heard right. She immediately went down to our back neighbour's home and asked Auntie Gail if she could use their phone. Mother rang the radio station's newsroom to learn that it was her brother Ross. Then she called Dad at work. I was at school, and came home to find Auntie Gail waiting for me as I rounded the corner to our backyard. I was shocked to see her, but I was also excited because I had earned a gold star from school for being so good—which was rare. I have little memory of what followed. Uncle Ross was in intensive care for a day or two, and then passed away. Mother told me later that Auntie Bet was told of a man that had a problem with his leg and was in urgent need of a leg muscle, and asked Auntie Bet if they could take Uncle Ross's leg muscle. Auntie Bet gave her consent and signed the form. Mother explained later that a small part of Uncle Ross lived on.

Mother, in shock and devastated, lay on her bed crying. I felt completely lost. I couldn't quite comprehend the magnitude of death. I felt confused and so very upset. I was in my room listening to mother sobbing in the next room, and I was crying too. Dad was comforting Mother. She was different from that day. She carried the grief of her brother's death from then on. She hid it most of the time, but her love and distress were deep. My love for Uncle Ross and my feelings about his passing caused me extreme sadness and puzzlement.

I gradually started to realise that death meant never coming back, and never seeing my favourite uncle and Godfather again. I then became scared, realising that it could happen to anyone, even me—and at any time. Being scared of the dark I assumed that death was like being plunged into blackness and nothingness, while still being aware of being there. I wasn't allowed to go to the funeral. I think it would have helped me to be at the funeral and experience the farewell. At night, in the darkness and being scared that I could die, I trusted my invisible friend Tony to protect me while I slept.

Because Uncle Ross hadn't made a will, it was the law at that time that both Auntie Bet's and Uncle Ross' joint bank accounts were closed and all monies automatically passed to their four month of age Paul's trust account, held by the pubic trustee. This also meant that the new home they had built had to be sold, including all Uncle Ross' self-made built-in kitchen cupboards and all the other built-in items that he had made. The things that were free-standing, such as the bookshelf and a few other things that Uncle Ross had made, were moved out before the home was sold. All the money received from the sale of the house was kept for Paul.

I can only imagine the depth of despair and sadness that Auntie Bet must have felt. She had not only lost her wonderful husband but now her home was being sold from under her feet. She and Paul moved back in with her mum and dad, Mr and Mrs Honey. As a child, I had no understanding of the gravity of the situation. I know all the relatives helped where they could. Auntie Bet had to go back to full-time work, all while coping with her grief and caring for Paul each night, as well as at weekends. There was rarely time for her. Her mum and dad were a wonderful help with Paul. To care for Paul, such as for the purchase of clothes and school items, Auntie Bet had to apply for financial support from Paul's account held by the public trustee. There were forms to fill out and post, and then she needed to wait for a response—that process had to be repeated every time she needed something for her son.

Mother and Dad built a sunroom on to the back of our home so that Auntie Bet and Paul could stay over on weekends to give Mr and Mrs Honey a break. I became very close to them. She became like a second mum, and Paul became like a brother.

Every Friday afternoon at school we would have a movie in the hall. I loved Fridays, as it meant watching the afternoon movie at school, before going home and waiting for Auntie Bet and Paul arrived to share our evening meal and stay for the weekend. Many times at school I would start crying for no apparent reason and I couldn't understand why, but I realise now it was grief. Something must have triggered my emotions.

Time went by and Paul grew from a baby into the cutest, happiest little boy with a mop of white-blond curly hair. Auntie Bet loved the weekends with us, and we loved them being part of our family. Uncle Ross was rarely talked about. Later, when I was about eleven years old, and when Mother and Dad were working weekends, I went to stay for weekends with Auntie Bet. By this time her mum had passed away, so I was there with Auntie Bet, Paul and Mr Honey.

On Saturday nights, when Paul was in bed and Mr Honey was reading the paper in the kitchen, Auntie Bet and I would settle down in the lounge room to watch our favourite show, *The Andy William's Show*. Andy reminded us both of Uncle Ross. We were spellbound by his singing and laughed at the comedy. We were both like teenagers watching the show together. There was one song we both adored, called 'Moon River'. That song never stopped being our favourite. The show was special, because it allowed us to openly talk about our feelings for Uncle Ross, and we shared many chats and a deep connection. Thinking back, I wish I could have had those types of chats with Mother too. It would have helped her, as it helped Auntie Bet and me.

The black hole of death within me stayed with me for many, many years. My naivety and innocence had gone. It took the death of another very dear loved one, 40 years after the loss of Uncle Ross, to help me to finally be at peace with death.

10 years after Uncle Ross's passing. Auntie Betty and Uncle Keith, Mother's older brother, fell in love. They enjoyed a long and happy marriage. Paul's cousin, Trena, became his sister.

CHAPTER 4
Teenage Years

At the age of twelve, I was transferred from the Adelaide Children's Hospital to The Queen Elizabeth Hospital. From that point on, when having an operation, I was put on the teenagers' ward. My childhood orthopaedic specialist, Mr Rodney White, continued looking after my case.

Mr White had previously been called Dr. White, and my thoughts were that doctors were very special people in my life, who worked to help make my health and my life better. One day Mother told me that Dr. White had been given the special title of 'Mr' White. In my mind that wasn't fair, to make him just a 'mister', which was the title I used to address every man who wasn't related to me. To me, Doctor White was special, and as an adult I still feel that way. 'Senior Doctor' would be my choice of title, rather than reverting to 'Mr.'

Mr Rodney White had consistently worked towards helping me feel my best as I headed towards my teenage years. He was a wonderful, caring, compassionate man, and always had time to talk to me if he saw me in the hospital outpatients department for my lung appointments. Once he saw me and suggested I go to the outpatients' desk with him to make an appointment, so that he could talk about an operation he thought would help me. His goal had always been to have my hand and leg behaving the best they could, and to have me walking without my caliper by the time I was thirteen. It was decided that a corrective operation could achieve that goal. In addition, there was another operation that could have my hand under control. After the operations, both my leg and my hand would have the minimal spasm reaction possible.

Mother and I had that appointment, and Mr White decided to do the foot operation first. I was delighted. I would get out of school again! This would be the biggest foot operation I'd had. It meant that I would be in a plaster cast for three months, with the cast going all the way from my foot up to the top of my right leg, I had the operation, and was in hospital for quite a while. Even though my leg was encased in plaster straight after the operation, it would still constantly spasm and jump in the air.

My leg would react to all the usual day-to-day noises from the hospital open ward, which had six beds. Thinking about it now it is funny. A door would bang and my leg would fling itself into the air as though it was magically connected to the noise. This happened every time there was any loud noise, and I had absolutely no control over it whatsoever. Every time my leg jumped my foot would spasm too. As a result of the operation this caused horrific pain, and so the ward doctor put me on pain reduction tablets and Valium, which worked to calm my nerves. Valium was thought of differently in those days. The belief was that if it was needed, it should be used. They started me off with a minimal dosage of Valium. It didn't work—there would be a bang and my leg would spasm. So they kept upping the dosage, until I was only awake when the nurses woke me at mealtimes and to give me more medication. When I woke up all I wanted to know was which meal I was eating and what medication I was taking. The initial horrific pain gradually subsided as the weeks went by. The spasms grew less intense and less frequent, and so the Valium was stopped. I had no after effects.

After coming off the Valium the right side of my foot started hurting a bit, then gradually the pain became intense, until it was constantly painful each time I moved or a spasm occurred. I told a nurse and she told me that it couldn't possibly be hurting there, because that wasn't the operation site. The intense pain continued to the point that I just couldn't stop crying. The senior ward sister told me to stop being a naughty child and to stop seeking attention. I wasn't! It was really intense pain.

Mr White was doing his ward rounds and called in to see me. I was crying and he became quite concerned. I told him about the pain, and he asked why I hadn't told the nurses. When I told him what their reaction had been, the compassionate and caring look on his face turned to furious anger. He yelled for the nearest nurse to get the senior nurse. With that my leg performed a huge spasm. His anger quickly turned back to compassion for me, and he apologised for yelling. The senior nurse entered and again he yelled—my foot spasmed again, but he was too angry to notice. He told the senior nurse that he had known me for many years and that if I cried I was really in pain and needed help. A plaster saw was brought in immediately and a square was cut where I pointed to the area of the pain. The plaster square was removed and there it was—the biggest and meanest blister, for all to see.

***

I had a wonderful time with the teenagers on the ward. Although there were six of us to a room we socialised with all the kids from the other rooms on our ward. I enjoyed having people around all the time to talk to, as I was a real chatterbox. I also loved being made a fuss of with chocolates, balloons, and visitors. As an adult I rarely get that spontaneous reaction, and the little girl in me misses it.

Each floor had two sections, and each section had a TV room, which doubled during the day as a meeting room for doctors or whoever needed it. We kids arranged between ourselves who would push the kids who were unable to get out of bed, and those in wheelchairs, down to the TV room. It wasn't a very big room and would only take a limited number of beds. I wanted to get there early so I wouldn't miss out. I couldn't get out of bed after my operation, so I would always arrange my bed pushers early in the day.

Each evening it was visiting time, until 7.30 pm. It was wonderful when I had visitors, but if they didn't leave by 7.30 pm it became difficult, because my pushers would be waiting for them to go. As soon as my visitors made a move my pushers would race in, and I would be pushed out of the room, waving goodbye to my visitors as we passed them. They thought it was funny, and I think it pleased them that we were having a good time. Sometimes a nurse would help us organise the beds, but the kids would shift the beds into the best position, then the pushers would jump on the beds and we would all watch TV on a very small screen until the nurses would come and get us and take us back to our rooms to settle down and sleep.

When three of us were due to leave the hospital, a junior doctor told us he would come and visit us to have a quiet party. Later that day he crept in, making out it was a big surprise. He brought the three of us soft drinks, potato chips, and lollies. It was a nice farewell to leaving the hospital.

I was never aware of any of the kids hurting themselves in the wards. It was a wonderful, innocent time. I was always very sad leaving all the fun of the teenage ward, and all the friends I had to talk to.

At home it was quiet, because Mother and Dad had their own things to do. I remember on one occasion when Dad was driving me home and I couldn't stop myself from crying. Dad said quietly, 'See that transistor radio up on the dashboard. That is yours, you can have it.' He was so sweet, as there wasn't much money around in those days. He wouldn't have gone and got another one for himself.

***

I turned 13 in January 1963, and thought that meant that I was all grown up. Gosh, did I have a lot to learn. The three months after I got home from my operation must have felt a lifetime for my parents. The plaster was heavy and I was in a wheelchair. Caring for me was constant for them, although I was able to hop from the wheelchair to the toilet or the chair.

Grandma Andersen and Auntie Bet were a wonderful help to our family, and were always there to look after me when Mother and Dad were working.

Staying with Grandma and Grandpa Andersen was interesting, as they didn't have an inside toilet—they had an outhouse. The back door had steps, and the wheelchair couldn't go down without Grandpa's help. Grandpa was away fishing a lot, and when I needed to go to the toilet it was a marathon event. My dear grandma would have to dash me down their long hallway in the wheelchair, through the front door entrance and down the one step onto the veranda, and then one more step down to the path, then along the path to the gate in the picket fence that led out onto the street. We then threw a left along the footpath, then another left down the long driveway, which was unmetalled and full of potholes that Grandma had to avoid. We would go all the way down the long length of the side of the house to the backyard, which was also dirt, then across the back of the house over to the far side of the backyard, to where the outhouse stood. Grandma would open the door for me to hop in, and would stand outside, catching her breath. Afterwards, I would hop out of the toilet and back into the wheelchair. At this point of the journey, Grandma's job then was to reverse the process all the way there and back. She would be making fun of the whole event and we would laugh and laugh.

My dad was very strong, and had no trouble picking me up and carrying me, so this was only something that happened at the weekends, when my parents worked at a catering company to earn extra money. Both Grandma and Auntie Bet were always there when Mother and Dad needed them. They gave me their love, care, and time. I am so very grateful, and have always had a deep love for them both.

When the long plaster up to my thigh eventually came off I was put into a plaster from just under my knee, down to my foot. Not long after I got home from having the new cast fitted my leg reacted to me moving it, which caused a huge spasm. As my knee was very stiff from not being moved for three months, a sudden pain shot through me. I grabbed my leg, still bent at the knee, and held it against my chest. Unable to move, my scream alerted Mother. She raced in, and we realised that we had a situation—my leg was stuck in that position. Mother rang the hospital and it was decided that an ambulance would collect me. At the hospital they anesthetised me and my leg was loosened. I recovered well. As the plaster had a special base I was able to walk on the plaster, and I got around well.

When that plaster came off I was so very excited, as my right foot no longer spasmed in towards my left foot but just stayed like a normal foot, and I could walk well.

At the next appointment with Mr White, he said those magical words I had been waiting for, and which I know he had been looking forward to saying, 'You no longer need a caliper and you can wear normal shoes.' I just stood there for a minute and then the excitement welled up within me. Mother was quiet, but had a huge smile. Oh! I was so very excited, as if I had won a million dollars!

My wish was to throw the caliper off the end of our local jetty at Henley Beach. Mother told me I couldn't do that because it would go rusty and it wasn't good for the fish. My dear mother was caring for the environment in that moment in a time when every house had an incinerator in the backyard and could burn anything at any time.

I remember the first day I went to school without a caliper. I was so very happy. The student teacher, Mr Bennett, who I had a crush on, was in the school courtyard. As I walked out of the big building into the courtyard I went up to him first. Mr Bennett made such a fuss of me. The kids came up to me and asked me questions about it. I felt like the popular kid in the school for that short time, until everyone got used to it.

Over the years, Mr White also operated to correct my hand with several operations, as it originally spasmed quite a lot when I got nervous, forming into a fist and turning in towards my body.

As a child, when I was running around and not thinking, my right arm would have a mind of its own and wave freely around up in the air until I got control of it with my left hand. So, more operations were to be performed by Mr White.

The first operation fixed the waving in the air part of the problem, but then there was the problem of my hand forming into a fist. The wrist would spasm downwards, and my hand would go into a fist. An operation was performed that stopped the wrist from going down, but it then began to spasm upwards, much more violently. Mr White suggested that a bit of my left hip bone could be taken and placed into my right wrist. This worked to secure the wrist from moving.

***

When I was 14, my Auntie Bet and my cousin Paul were still living with her dad. There was also a boarder, named Lora, living with them, She worked with Auntie Bet, and they were friends. My parents agreed that Lora, who was so caring and friendly to us all, could chaperone me to a disco dance night at the St Claire Centre in Woodville. I was so excited. This was what I'd had all the operations for, and it was finally happening. I wore brand new shoes and my best dress. I remember a boy asking me up to dance. I was so excited as I walked onto the dance floor. However, my new shoes hit the polished floor and I slid on the dance floor with my feet going from under me. It seemed as though I was sitting on the floor with everyone standing around looking down at me for a long time, but it was probably only moments. Lora rushed over and helped me up. I felt a bit embarrassed getting helped up, but once on my feet I was too excited to worry. Lora then took me outside and we scratched the soles of my shoes on the rough asphalt footpath, then went back in to the disco. I had the best time. I was totally hooked on discoing. At that stage I never thought of what my hand and leg looked like. I have always been very grateful to Lora for taking me.

Because my schooling was constantly interrupted by my behaviour, as well as all the time I missed having operations, important information was lost to me. After I turned 15 in January of 1965 I started attending Thebarton Technical High School. I was excited, feeling all grown up, until I realised that I was among the youngest group, who were only in Year 8.

Our allotted classroom was upstairs, and I loved being upstairs. I was looking forward to 'home ed', learning how to cook and look after a household. Our home ed teacher, Mrs Hayden, looked like someone's very angry grandmother. I didn't really learn anything, as she was so boring that my mind would wander. I really wanted to learn to cook so that I could match my mother's wonderful cooking. Because Mother liked to cook our meals by herself, I never learnt from her.

In our home ed room the cooking stoves were back to back, in a row. One particular day we were going to learn how to fry onions, which seemed simple enough. We had the chopped onions all ready, and the frying pan was on the stove. I put my butter in the frying pan, and holding onto the wooden spoon whizzed the butter around the pan as it melted. We were then instructed to get the plate of onions in our other hand and scrape the onions into the frying pan with the wooden spoon. All was going well, and I put the wooden spoon down while I prepared to put the plate of onions into my para-abled hand. So I lifted up my thumb and balanced the plate in between my thumb and the side of my curved pointer finger. I was pleased with myself. I then got the wooden spoon to scrape the onions off the plate. As my onions hit the hot frying pan, it gave a loud sizzle and my right arm immediately did a spasm, sending the remaining onions everywhere except where they were supposed to go. I looked up to see the other girls standing like statues, totally shocked. They looked so funny with onion in their hair, on their faces and on their clothes. I had been taught at home to take these problems lightly and in good humour, and so I started laughing. I learnt fast that this was not considered acceptable behaviour in the classroom. Mrs Hayden was furious with me, and demanded the whole class stop while the disaster was sorted out. I had to clean up my own mess. I have to say, even now, that the memory still makes me laugh. I really believe that Mrs Hayden didn't want to be there. She always seemed to be either grumpy or sad.

Another incident occurred when a student teacher, a very nervous young woman named Miss Jennifer, joined Mrs Hayden for a lesson on how to make mashed potatoes. Miss Jennifer put the potatoes on to boil. As they were boiling she delivered a speech. Gradually, the boiling water changed to a sizzling noise and then smoke started coming up instead of steam. I was looking at Mrs Hayden, who just let Miss Jennifer go on without warning her. I felt so sorry for Miss Jennifer; she was visibly distressed but tried to hide it with a forced smile. I realised that Mrs Hayden had not cared about her feelings.

I started that academic year with real excitement and a genuine interest in cooking, but I soon lost my enthusiasm. I doubt that was the purpose of the class.

The headmistress of the school was Miss Williams, who was of the same religion as my family and a dedicated regular churchgoer. I heard the older schoolgirls talking about being sent to her office because they had played up. One girl was expecting to be told off, but instead Miss Williams asked her not to do it again and then they prayed to God to help her, and that was all that happened.

One day when it was lunchtime I noticed that one of the older girls looked prettier than usual, and I told her she looked pretty. She smiled at me and said she was wearing makeup, and asked me if I would like her to do my makeup. Well, I didn't have to be asked twice, although I was aware we weren't supposed to wear makeup at school. I walked out of the girls' toilets feeling special, and thanked her.

A while later Miss Williams came walking by and noticed me. She said, 'Jan, you are such a brave girl.' I looked at her puzzled until she said, 'You look so sick, but I am sure if you go over to the taps and wash your face you should feel much better.' Oh! Gosh! She knew I was wearing makeup.

'Yes, Miss Williams,' I said, and immediately went to wash my face.

When Miss Williams came back she said, 'Oh Jan, you look much better now,' and gave me a beautiful warm smile.

The other lesson I learnt to hate was dressmaking. I struggled through every lesson. Exam time came, and I really had no idea what I was doing. I was so glad when the horrible exam was finished. The next thing I knew, I was being sent to Miss Williams' office. I was trying to work out what I had done wrong, but that wasn't a worry, all I was going to have to do was participate in a prayer and I was out of there. Well, none of it went to plan. Miss Williams told me to sit down and then said, 'Jan, you were so brave to do your dressmaking exam when you must have been so unwell.' She continued, 'We have decided to give you the exam again so you can improve your marks.' Oh no! This was my worst nightmare! I struggled through the second exam, and never heard what my results were.

The class I really loved was typing, and my teacher, Mrs Snow, was thoughtful enough to find a typing instruction for using one hand, and it was for a left-handed person. I sat at a desk just like the other kids, with a big typewriter in front of each of us. I enjoyed tapping three letters and repeating over and over, then moving on to the next three letters, my fingers rested on the 'f g h j', I worked from that base, stretching my fingers out to the keys that I could reach. Then there were the further-away keys that I needed to only keep one finger on the base, either the 'j' or the 'f' stretch. We progressed to having a board up, so we couldn't see the keys. That was called touch-typing. Those wonderful lessons have served me well all the way through my life, to now writing this book on my laptop. Of course, the autocorrect is wonderful for checking my spelling. It only occasionally doesn't know the word I am trying to use, so I then go online to look up the word the way I think it should be spelled and the internet will help me by giving close examples, and often I can recognise the word.

Once I had moved to Thebarton High School, Christine and I would mainly catch up at Christmas or birthdays, but my friendship with Di remained strong. We would often get together at her home or mine. I liked going to her home. Her parents were very welcoming, and there was the added bonus that her brother, Terry, might be there. I remember being thrilled getting placed next to him at one of Di's birthday parties. The photo taken shows my infatuation.

Di and I had great fun together. She never worried about my parability, and I would forget about it until someone mentioned it or spoke the six most stupid words I knew, 'You can't do that, let me,' instead of asking the four most intelligent words, 'Can I help you?' and respecting my answer and my right to independence.

Di and I enjoyed the wonderful freedom that the children of today are not able to have. We rode kilometres down to the beach and all through the suburbs on our bikes. As long as we were home by the time we were told to be, we could be gone all day if we wanted, and we loved it. There were no mobile phones, and so there was no way of contacting us. I remember being late home once, and we were in big trouble. It was an easier time then, as there was far less traffic on the road and everything moved at a slower pace. I had sleepovers at Di's home. I can remember their cats playing chasey over our beds in the middle of the night, which shocked me, as I was not used to being with cats.

As teenagers, Di and I got interested in the Adelaide Channel 9 Telethon charity appeal, back in those wonderful days when all our state media was Adelaide-based. We loved the hilarious pantomimes with all the local stars dressed up and performing such classics as *Little Red Riding Hood*. The special guests for the Telethon would be actors flown in from interstate, from Australian TV shows such as a police show called *Division 4*.

To support the Telethon, we decided that we would walk from

my home at Brooklyn Park to Adelaide Airport, then into the city, and on to the suburb of North Adelaide where the Channel 9 studios were located. On the way, we knocked on people's doors asking for money. Nearly everyone gave what they could. When we arrived at the Channel 9 studios we presented our collection tins to be counted. We had raised just over $100, and were very pleased with ourselves. Some people got interviewed, but we didn't. Di and I then walked back into the city and caught the bus home.

When I was 15, my immaturity was a worry. I was two years older than the other girls in my class, and acted younger than all of them. My parents were advised to get some help concerning my future options. They dutifully organised a meeting, and there we were in a big office with a man looking important sitting behind his big desk. He talked to my parents, rather than addressing me. That behaviour was common in those days, and sometimes still is. It was as if I was invisible, until I heard the following words come out of his mouth, 'She is paralysed and will never do anything with her life, so take her out of school. There is a rehabilitation centre she can go to at Payneham.'

I stood up and yelled, 'You have no idea what you are talking about, I am not paralysed!' and then sat down again. I was so angry that I don't remember the rest of the meeting.

My parents and I talked over the idea of me going to a rehabilitation centre, and they asked me to try it. The thing was that I was me, in a 'normal' world. I was the only para-abled person I associated with, and I liked my life like that. Other than Dad, I had control.

My only other encounter with a para-abled person was a girl I once met who had polio. One of her legs was affected, from the knee down. I was invited to her home so that we could get to know each other. When I arrived, her father took me into the kitchen by myself and said in a menacing way, 'You be nice to Ruth or you will have me to answer to. Don't you hurt her!' Talk about an overprotective parent! I felt like I was being accused of doing something I was never going to do. Feeling so hurt, I decided I never wanted to see her again, and didn't.

Now I had to go to a rehabilitation centre, with not only a whole lot of people I didn't know, but they were all para-abled. I didn't want to go! It was arranged that Uncle Darcy would drive me out to the St Margaret's Rehabilitation Centre on my first day. We arrived, and I thanked Uncle Darcy. I was looking at a huge 1900s red brick building. The driveway was long, and swept around a large tree in the centre of a larger lawn area. Uncle Darcy parked right in front of the entrance.

I gingerly walked in through the door to find a counter to my left. A very efficient office lady asked my name and got me to fill out a form. Then she called a man named Ron, and asked him to take me down to the sports hall. Ron looked healthy. He was tall with a round waist. He introduced himself by his first name as he walked with me down the long corridor. Ron asked me what had happened to me and I rabbited on about my leg, hand, and lung. When he was just about to open the door I asked him if he was one of the workers. He laughed a hearty laugh and said, 'No, I am here just like you. I have wooden legs and they are going to put hair on them soon to make them look real.' He pulled his trousers up to show me. I was shocked! He then swung the door open wide, and there before me were about 20 people. I just stood there stunned. I was seeing people without a leg or an arm. Many looked okay, but I was to discover that, like Ron, there were hidden or internal parabilities.

One guy I spoke to who looked okay told me he had been driving a big, long transport truck, taking goods to deliver to an interstate company. All of a sudden he had to swerve to avoid a huge ship that suddenly came out in front of him at the intersection. Of course, he did explain to me as I stood there believing every word, that he was high on a drug they called 'uppers' at the time of the accident, to keep himself awake while he was driving, but that the drugs had made him hallucinate. The accident was very serious, and he was at St Margaret's Rehabilitation Centre to recover from severe head injuries.

After meeting everyone I settled down to the daily routine of rotation around the different sections, such as adult education classes and woodwork, which changed every hour. One of the activities was basket weaving, which I surprised myself by enjoying. The 'chip on the shoulder' attitude I'd had when I arrived melted away as I got to know the people there with me, and the wonderful caring staff. Another goal of being at the centre was trying to improve my education. Mother and Dad had tried to convince me to live in, as the centre had on-site accommodation, rather than having to catch two buses to get there and two buses to get home. I liked being at home, though, and I am glad I had that precious time with my parents. After six months I was offered a job and felt excited, but also sad to say goodbye to everyone at the rehabilitation centre.

I gained employment at the Queen Elizabeth Hospital, working as a switchboard operator. I felt ecstatic! I was working full-time and got trained on the job. It was a cord switchboard. I was enjoying it at the start, as the girls I worked with were great. At Christmas time some of the doctors would come down to say hi. One doctor had a full plaster on his leg and hobbled in on crutches. Apparently the night before he had got drunk—his mates told us quietly that they'd put the plaster on while he was a little worse for wear, and then when he sobered up they told him he'd broken his leg while he was drunk. We got such a laugh out of it when his mates said he'd believed them.

I wasn't at all thrilled when instructed that if there was a fire in the building we must keep working, as we only had a one exit. We were in the basement, along with the morgue. On one occasion I got a call on the switchboard from a doctor wanting me to put a call out on the PA for a senior doctor. As there was no response the doctor rang back and said that if I didn't find the senior doctor soon that the patient concerned would die. I took it personally that I could cause this patient to die, and became frantic and hysterical. The girls helped me to calm down, explaining it wouldn't be my fault. Another time I took a call to say the nurse's apartment building lift was on fire. I rang the fire brigade. However, I felt worried—had I made that call fast enough? After three months I was a wreck and having nightmares of the cords coming out and strangling me. I talked to my parents and handed in my notice.

I was starting to feel self-conscious. I loved disco dancing and wanted to have dates. Eventually I wanted to get married and have babies. I was starting to be aware that I may not find it easy to achieve these things with my parability. Having been at the rehabilitation centre with a lot of people who were all para-abled in different ways, I thought people would judge me.

When I was 16 I joined the YMCA (Young Men's Christian Association). I mean, what girl would choose to join the YWCA (Young Women's Christian Association)—they wouldn't let men in, while the YMCA would let girls in. I was happy with my choice. It was always well run and there was a wide variety of activities.

On one occasion we all went away on a camp together, and I had an opportunity to have a go at water-skiing. I got the skis on and held the hand-bar with my left hand, but kept letting go as the boat started off. I didn't have the strength to hold the hand-bar with just my left hand. I kept trying again and again until the organiser had a talk to me and suggested it was too much for me, so I had to forgo the opportunity. I always thought I would get a chance later in life, but it hasn't ever happened, although I did get a chance to go skiing in the snow.

I had the best time at the YMCA, and I met a guy called Joe. In hindsight he was a wild soul, and I think others were worried about me dating him. I know my parents were not thrilled about him, especially when he knocked over my mother's very special 'lady and the towel' statue that she had made into a lamp. We were mucking around, throwing lounge pillows at each other, and Joe knocked the lamp off the bar onto the floor and it broke. It really upset my mother. She got it fixed, but it was never as perfect at the back as it had originally been. I now have it in our home and I love it, because it reminds me of my childhood and my mother.

The Y's organisers planned an educational course for us girls. We had lessons on how to be ladies—deportment, nails, makeup, and so on. I found the lessons very helpful. I got talking to the girl who came to teach us how to do our makeup, and I started selling the makeup products as well.

The night came for us to do the fashion parade on a red carpet platform. We were dressed up—we had casual wear and evening wear. I had the perfect figure for a 17 year old and felt wonderful all dressed up. Our families and friends were there in the audience, and also my new boyfriend, Glen Marshall.

I was absolutely petrified when my turn arrived. Standing in my casual clothes—a lovely blue blouse and bright orange bell-bottom slacks with paisley material sewn into a flap at the bottom—the head of the YMCA saw that I was really scared. He took my left hand and said, 'Go, you can do this.' He had a huge confident grin as I stepped out on to the catwalk. My right hand spasmed and so did my right foot in my new shoes, but I started to relax a bit as I walked up and down, doing all the things I'd been taught; turns, stopping, and then walking on. I wasn't aware of it, but no doubt I would have been limping. I loved my outfits. No-one knew they were second-hand, as they looked brand new.

By the time I had been on the catwalk in my evening wear I didn't want it to stop, I was loving every minute of it. We were presented with our certificate as the evening drew to a close, and it all became a precious memory.

Glen and I continued dating, but I broke up with him after three months. He was a lovely guy, but I didn't feel love. Years later I was at work and had to ring a company, and a person by the name of Glen Marshall answered the phone. I said that I went out with a Glen Marshall once, and he said it was him. We were both surprised to realise after all those years that we were connecting, and we talked for a while. I asked him what I was like in those days. He said that I was very self-conscious about my parability.

When I was 16 I was dating three different guys at the same time. I saw them as friends really, but they still didn't know about the other two guys. It was working well until I had to go into hospital for a small operation on my foot. When they rang and enquired as to when I was coming home, my mother told each of them the same date and time. After I arrived home I was in the kitchen talking to my mother when the front doorbell rang. My mother went to answer it and promptly came back with Brian following behind her, holding a box of chocolates for me. Brian gave me a kiss on the cheek and sat at the table with me and we chatted. The doorbell rang again, and my mother went to the front door, this time returning with Kim, carrying a bunch of flowers for me. The intros were made and we sat there chatting. Yet again the doorbell rang, and this time my mother returned with Mike, and another box of chocolates. Introductions were made all round, and Mike sat down to join us. There I was, sitting at the table with my three boyfriends. As it was a hot day, Mother asked them if they would like a soft drink and they all thought that was a great idea. They sat there with their drinks, politely chatting to each other, while I just sat listening. Thank goodness none of them thought to ask how we knew each other, although my face probably told that story.

There was one other occasion when I was dating two guys at the same time. I had met a lovely Swiss guy named Neil, and one afternoon he arrived at my house unannounced. I welcomed him into the lounge. However, I was expecting another guy named Matt. Matt was intense, and I was starting to be unhappy about our relationship. I knew I shouldn't have invited Neil into our home, but I didn't want to make up a lie. Neil noticed that I was nervous and realised that something was worrying me. He was such a lovely, caring guy. I ended up getting upset and telling Neil what was happening. He immediately said, 'It's fine. Your mum is in the kitchen and I am a friend of the family visiting your mum.' Then, with a smile on his face for me and seeming to be quite happy, he headed for the kitchen, before quickly coming back into the lounge to say, 'I am wiping up for your mum, she has the cakes in the oven', before exiting the lounge again.

Moments after, I heard Matt's car pull up, and then the doorbell rang. I opened the door and we sat in the lounge room talking for a while. We agreed I would get a drink for us, and I went out to the kitchen. My mother and Neil were laughing and munching on the cakes just out of the oven. I got the drinks and Neil offered to carry the drink and the plate of cakes in for me. I looked stunned. Neil said, 'Come on, you take your drink and I'll take his drink and the cakes.' I followed along behind him, still stunned. Neil entered the lounge with a smile and introduced himself saying he was a friend of the family, and put the drink and cakes down on the coffee table. Matt and Neil shook hands, and Neil went back to the kitchen. We had our drinks and cakes and then I talked to Matt about my feelings. We both agreed not to see one another for a while. After Matt left I went out to the kitchen and couldn't thank Neil enough.

When I was 17 I met a mate of Di's brother Terry, called Ben English. He was good-looking, tall, and had a lovely voice. He and his family were religious, good-minded, and lovely people. We dated for a while and I really liked him. I felt so comfortable with him. He was about three years older than me. Because I liked him I wanted to let him know that I really cared about him. So I asked the advice of a girl I knew who was a couple of years older than me. I wanted to use the right words and thought this 'helpful' older, more experienced girl would know what to say. She told me what I should do, and I took her advice.

At this point I was so ridiculously naive, and had no idea that the words I used didn't have an innocent meaning. Ben had taken me on a date to the movies and had driven me home. He was always the perfect gentleman and, as we normally did after a date, we sat in the car chatting. His car didn't have the gear consul in the centre of the front seat so I could slide over next to him. I felt so comfortable resting my head on his shoulder as we chatted. When I felt it was time, I looked up at him and said, 'You know Ben, I would do anything for you.' I meant that I would exercise with him, or go to a movie that he would like to see, but that was not how it came out. Once those nine words left my lips, Ben suddenly told me that he would walk me to the door. When we got to the door he told me that he wasn't like that. I asked, 'Like what?' We never dated again.

Mother always caringly put my hair up in rollers and styled it for me when I was going somewhere. I kept getting an itchy nose every time my hair was done. I couldn't help it. Perhaps it was a nervous reaction. The more I tried not to, the more it happened. Mother would get annoyed with me because I would move every time I scratched my nose.

One day I got grumpy and told her that I would do my own hair. Mother smiled and said, 'Go and try.' My first effort was a complete disaster, bits of hair stick out every which way. When we were going out somewhere very special Mother and I would go to Carter's hairdressers. I watched intensely as my hair was put in the rollers, and then practiced at home. I would grab my hair in my good hand and with my other hand in a tight fist I would pry my right thumb back with my left thumb and forefinger, put the hair in, then let the thumb of my right hand clamp down and hold the hair. Then I would put the roller up to the hair and secure it with my left hand, winding the hair around the roller like the hairdresser did. After many, many months of practice I became very good at fully styling my own hair. By clamping a small mirror in between my thumb and my fist and lining it up with my good hand I could then see the back of my hair in the other mirror. This worked well—unless there was a sudden noise, when my arm would spasm out of control, shooting up in the air with the mirror in a firm grip—then I would have to repeat the process of lining it up. I felt so proud of myself achieving what seemed so difficult. I enjoyed every part of the process, even when there was an unexpected bang.

I also watched the hairdresser style my hair 'up' in a formal style. Once again, I practiced, and gradually began to be able to achieve a similar style. I would tease the rolled hair up, then gently comb sections of hair into loops and fasten each loop with a bobby pin.

In 1968 I turned 18. Oh my gosh! I was so very excited! I was legally allowed to go to licenced discos. I felt grown up, and couldn't wait to get there. I quickly learnt I had a major problem with my parability, and it was annoying me. My hand would spasm and my leg would tense, making me look awkward as I walked—all because I was nervous. It was a completely ridiculous situation and I had to think of a remedy.

I worked it out. I had arranged with my girlfriend, Sue, that she and I would get to the disco very early. We went to the Fiesta Villa Disco at the Findon Hotel. We were the first in the queue. Although getting there early meant that we had a long wait, we really had no problem with that. When the doors opened we would make a dash for the best seats in the disco. It was important to see the band, and also see the dance floor. Seeing the dance floor was important as we would check out everyone's dance moves to figure out what we thought worked and what didn't.

Once Sue and I were seated Sue would go up to the bar and get our drinks; Bacardi and coke for me, and whatever she was in the mood for. We would sit there and enjoy the rush of people coming in, checking out the good-looking guys while sipping on our drinks. In time, Sue would get us each another drink. I would drink it slowly, and when guys came up to ask me to dance I would refuse because I wasn't relaxed enough. By the time I was ready to dance the guys had thought I was playing hard to get. I became a challenge to them, which inadvertently worked well for me. The dance floor was full, with people crammed shoulder to shoulder, so I felt as free as everyone else to disco away. Between songs we would introduce ourselves and chat. The guy would get to know my personality and my disco ability. At that stage, crammed in like cattle on the dance floor, this was all that was important.

Looking the best I could at the discos was also important to me. I soon realised that the older girls had lovely sized breasts, while my breasts were like fleabites. I decided to stuff cotton-wool balls into my bra. So there I was, in the middle of the dance floor, swinging my arms around, discoing to my heart's content. Gradually one cotton ball appeared, then the other cotton-wool balls started to pop out, as if they were being shot from a cannon—I wished I could magically disappear at that moment.

I would accept a ride home with a guy only if we'd had a good amount of time to talk to get to know him and ask him some loaded questions about himself. I had a feeling one guy was married, so I asked how his wife was. He was so shocked and asked me how I knew her. If I met a guy that I liked at 10:30 pm or later, I would give him my phone number but would decline a ride home with him.

We went to another disco as well—The 20 Plus Club. It was great, as it had a disco and an upstairs area with a quiet section where we could sit and chat. One night, about an hour after we left, it burned down. It was completely ruined. I believe the fire started in the kitchen. I was so sad, as it was my favourite disco.

At the discos I was now on a serious mission to find 'Mr Right.' Mother spoke often to me as a child of me growing up and meeting Mr Right, getting married and having children. It was always an optimistic conversation which allowed me to assume that it would happen. I am very grateful to her for those chats. I still use the same principle of dreaming that my parents taught me from the age of three years old—to dream the biggest, wildest dreams and believe that they can become reality. When my dreams came true my parents would celebrate with me, and when my dreams didn't come true they would hug me and talk about the fact that I tried, and they would encourage me to find another dream. It was wonderful because it kept my mind full of happy thoughts.

I wanted the fairytale of getting married, being happy, and having children. I never thought it wouldn't happen. If I broke off a relationship, that was fine, and I would move on. If a guy broke things off with me and I liked him, I would be totally devastated. Even so, I never thought, not even for a minute, that it was because of my parability. I would eventually move on. I still had no intention of having sex with any of them until I was married. There were some boys who suggested, 'It will close up if you don't use it' or, 'It's a muscle and should be exercised.' I stuck to my guns and said a definite, 'No.'

One of my dates was with a guy who I met at a singles ball. I had paid for the ticket and filled out a questionnaire about my personality and what type of guy I was looking for. I was seated at a table for six, along with a guy called Adam, and we started dating. On one of our dates we went to the beach, and after a while we decided we would get a pizza. We went into the pizza shop and ordered a Hawaiian pizza. It arrived at our table and tasted great. The service counter was to the left of the table where we were sitting, facing the entrance door. The floor in front of us was clear, with tables around the edges of the walls. I wasn't concentrating on my right arm, and had it resting on the table across my body. All of a sudden someone out the back dropped a tray and my right arm spasmed and flung itself out the only way it could—across the table— collecting the pizza on its way. The pizza became airborn, like a frisbee. It flew out to the centre of the room, turned itself upside down, and landed in the middle of the floor with a splat! You could have heard a pin drop, and for what felt like forever we sat in stunned silence. Once I'd found my voice I apologised to Adam and to the waiter who came running out. I was taught that accidents happen, and to make light of a bad situation, so I just smiled and said, 'Wow!' This wasn't appreciated at all. Neither Adam nor I had any other money, and so I explained that to the waiter that it was an accident and that my para-abled arm had spasmed when the tray was dropped. I asked if we could have a replacement pizza. Adam was still sitting in stunned silence. I probably mucked it up by making light of the situation, because they flatly refused to replace the pizza. This meant we had to do a walk of shame to the door as fast as we could. We decided never to return to that restaurant again.

Adam and I didn't last, and when I was between dating guys I was invited to a friend's wedding. As I didn't have a boyfriend at the time a date was arranged for me. He was a guy with the parability of deafness. I had learnt to have a different perspective about people with parabilities at the rehabilitation centre, so I agreed to meet with George. We got along well, and I learnt how inventive he was. His mother invited me into his room to see how he had rigged up his alarm clock so that the light flashed on and off. He owned his own car, and at that stage I wasn't driving, so it was great. We went to the wedding together, and carried on dating after that day, enjoying each other's company. Going to a disco with him was fun. He had some great moves and danced in time with the music. He explained that the vibration through the floorboards gave him the beat. George was a great driver, but I realised that he often drank too much to get behind the wheel, and I felt unsafe. I talked to him about it. He got really angry, accusing me of not treating him like a 'normal' boyfriend, and broke up with me.

I loved the process of getting to know my boyfriends, and it hardly bothered me to break up with many of them. I was looking for Mr Right. Philip was interesting. He seemed to be a nice, attentive guy, but we only had three dates. We met at a disco. He came up and asked me to dance, we discoed together and then he drove me home. He was a nice guy and a gentleman. Our first date was to the movies. I used to carry my handbag with my right hand tucked under the bag. My hair was perfect, my makeup correct, and I felt confident.

We enjoyed the movie and then went for supper at a coffee lounge. The second date was to another movie we both wanted to see, and we again enjoyed chatting at the coffee lounge. Then came the third date. We went out to dinner, and started the night with a drink in the adjoining lounge. I sat on a stool and put my bag on the floor, which left my right hand exposed. He looked at my hand with a puzzled expression and said, 'What's wrong with your hand.' I told him with a smile that my hand was para-abled. Philip said with a laugh, 'No it isn't.' I have to say that I wasn't expecting that reply. He said, 'I am very observant, and if your hand was para-abled I would have noticed.' I went on to tell him that my leg was para-abled too, and briefly explained my history. He told me I was lying, straight out lying. By this point I had the giggles, which made him even madder. He said he would drive me home. And that, my friends, was the beginning and the end of our third date.

Then there was Jim. I nicknamed him 'the octopus'—you know, arms everywhere. One night he took me out to dinner by taxi, because he wanted to have a few drinks. We had a nice time and enjoyed the meal. When it was over we caught a taxi, which would drop me off at home before going on to Jim's house. I was wearing a mini dress, and my legs weren't bad looking. The dress was royal blue with a white collar and small fiddly white buttons down the front. We were sitting in the back seat of the taxi and he had my right arm tucked behind him. As we were going along he started to undo the fiddly buttons, from the top down. He was concentrating hard, and gradually getting there. I sat quietly, and when he had struggled down to the fifth button I started to do them back up, one by one, but without him noticing. He decided he had accomplished enough and went in for the plunge, only to discover there was no opening. In the flickering of the streetlights I could see the shocked look on his face. I just smiled sweetly in return. He turned away and looked out of the window for the rest of the journey. Not a word was said. When we arrived at my home he got out, opened the door for me and said, 'Good night.' I thanked him for the meal and said goodbye. When I got inside my parents and I had a good laugh.

Although I could dress up to look great, style my own hair very well, and do a great job with my makeup, I was extremely immature. Two things happened that affected my dating process.

The first was a friend who got divorced when I was 18 years old. I realised the heartache of that happening. There were no children involved, but their dog's home needed to be decided. To watch what she and her parents went through affected me. In the late 1960's divorce was hushed, but it shocked and worried me. From my perspective she seemed as though she'd had the perfect life, so I was very frightened of the fact that I could well end up having the same thing happen to me. I decided that I must be very careful, and try hard not to have the same experience.

A girlfriend suggested that I talk to a psychologist, because I was being very picky about the wonderful guys I dated. She said it wasn't normal to date such wonderful guys and then break up with them after three months. It seemed fine to me, as things would only get serious after three months. I had no feelings for them other than as friends. So I agreed to visit a psychologist.

After a lot of talking and several appointments the psychologist suggested that my friend's divorce had scared me, and that I had created a picture of Tony as the perfect person, so that no-one else could live up to that ideal. The psychologist told me not to worry, and that one day I would meet Mr Right. He said it would all work out for me. He also suggested that I try to find Tony and meet up with him to have a chat. I did try to find him, only to be told that Tony had been killed in a car accident. When I was told I was devastated, but hid it the best I could. My parents couldn't understand why I was sad, but I couldn't tell them. My feelings for Tony were my secret. I told myself that perhaps he wasn't dead, that I had heard it wrong, and decided to believe that it had been a mistake. That way, I could cope.

I only knew that his name was Tony and that he was possibly Italian. I didn't know his last name. I just had the memory of such a caring person. In my childhood years he was my invisible friend who helped me feel safe in the dark, and helped me to be as brave as I could through all my operations. Mother had a photo of him in her drawer in their bedroom that Auntie Marie gave her to give to me. I would go in and look at it. In the photo Tony looked tall and slim, and he had dark hair in the style of Elvis Presley. One day the photo disappeared. Mother must have thrown it out. I came to the realisation that I would just have to wait to meet Mr Right.

I was on a mission to find out what went wrong with divorced people's marriages. So every time someone shared that they were divorced, even if I had never met them before, I would ask them what happened, and what went wrong. I learnt that they had got married too young, hadn't experienced enough time away from their family, and that the strong quiet type of man will never be a good communicator. Also, they had given up on their dreams of work and travel in order to settle down. My thoughts were that trust and communication were essential.

At this point, I must apologise to all the wonderful, respectful guys that I dumped after three months through my teens and 20's—it was definitely me. I feel absolutely dreadful about one guy that I went out with. He was such a lovely guy, and had a really wonderful family. They were extremely lovely people. At the three-month mark I felt friendship with him, but not love. I remember years after I was waiting at a bus stop and he spotted me. He offered to drive me home, and was so very thrilled to see me. He looked different and it took me a while to remember his name. We chatted, but he seemed quite disappointed with our conversation. I asked him to come in, saying that my parents would love to see him again, but he wouldn't. I thanked him for the ride and he drove off. I found out years later that he had committed suicide. I fear it may have been my fault. If it was, I am truly sorry.

I loved my teenage years. I felt so free. Almost every teenager I met was happy to chat. We were all interested in our own path in life. If asked about my leg and arm I would explain in a short matter-of-fact manner and we just happily went along from there.

* * *

In 2019 I was able to contact Auntie Marie and Uncle Maurie's daughter, Tricia McQade, and her husband Len. I explained I wanted to research Tony's story. My husband, son and I were invited to stay in their lovely home in Mount Gambier. They were wonderful and made us feel welcome, as Tricia's parents had welcomed Mother, Dad and I in 1954. I am grateful for the help of Colleen Hammet of the South East Family History Group in Millicent and Neville Bonney, as I was finally able to solve my mystery about Tony.

Tony Harrup and his family had emigrated from the UK. His parents ran a bakery. Unfortunately, on Christmas Eve 1960 (at the time I was 10 years old), Tony, aged 19 years, and his only sibling, Georgina, aged 15 years, were killed in a car accident at Glencoe, near Millicent in the south-east of South Australia.

We went to the Tantanoola cemetery and located Tony's grave, which was next to his sister's. Their parents' graves were there too. I placed flowers on Tony's grave and started to sob uncontrollably for the passing of a young, caring man I had loved for 65 years and who had helped me so much. The three of us hugged.

CHAPTER 5
Getting a Job

After my first job at the Queen Elizabeth Hospital didn't work out, I started babysitting—which in reality was child minding—for children aged from two years old all the way up to teenagers not much younger than I was.

In addition to my babysitting I wanted full-time work. For a while I worked for Wadlow's Timber Merchants at Port Adelaide, where my dad was the head saw doctor, caring for the huge saws used to cut the wood. I was the switchboard girl at Wadlow's, and also had to balance the petty cash tin. I could never get the petty cash to balance. In wanting to make my dad proud of me, I was so nervous and timid that it didn't work out, and I was asked to leave, after working out a week's notice. I did a great job for the rest of that week, and the managing director, Mr Keith Wadlow, called me into his office and in a caring way asked me why my work had improved so much. I didn't have an answer, so I just said I wanted to leave. Looking back, I had been so fearful of letting my dad and his company down that I couldn't concentrate on the work. Once I knew there was nothing to lose, all the pressure lifted and I was easily able to do the work.

I then volunteered at what was then called The Woodville Spastic Centre. I had hopes of showing them that I was capable of doing paid work, but I didn't achieve that goal.

A large department store was advertising for sales staff, and I stood in the queue with all the other hopeful girls. A woman walked along the queue, and as she approached me I must have moved my feet. She stopped, looked me in the eyes, and asked, 'Did you limp?'

I replied, 'Yes, but … '

She interrupted me, saying, 'Move out of the queue and leave now.' I opened my mouth to try to discuss her decision, but she just repeated the word, 'Now' and pointed the way out.

I walked quietly, feeling devastated, and dissolved into uncontrollable crying. I eventually caught the bus home, and shared the story with Mother and Dad when he got home from work. With love and caring they talked me through the situation, and then we focused on what I could try next.

When I was 17, a job as an assistant housemother became available, looking after ten children with the parability of deafness. I applied, and was given the position. Mother, Dad and I had agreed that if I didn't have a job by the time I was 18 I would go on what was then called the invalid pension. I really didn't want to go on the invalid pension, which made it so important for this job to work out. I loved working as an assistant housemother. It was a live-in job and I had my own door, just like a flat. I had been spoilt at home, so I didn't know how to do housework or how to cook much. The head housemother had a negative conversation with me about my parents not teaching me how to do housework properly. I was upset that she would try to make my parents feel bad about themselves, but I felt powerless to say anything to her. We did have a cook, but at weekends we did the cooking. One day I had to soft boil 26 eggs. However, the head housemother soon realised that I had cooked them too long. She still made us eat every single one of them. The children were not at all happy with me.

It was important to me to be accepted by the children. I learnt one-handed signing, and the children grasped that fast. They had also devised a third communication method between themselves, so that they could talk about the housemothers in front of us and get away with it.

I would wake at 5 am, so I could gradually wake up, get dressed and have breakfast by myself, as I liked having breakfast just after I got out of bed. At 7 am I woke the ten children. My job was to supervise them getting dressed, making their beds, sweeping their bedroom floors, and ensuring they were ready for breakfast. When the children ate their breakfast I had to join them and eat a second breakfast. Those children were lovely, and although the work was hard I loved it. I would walk the children to school after breakfast. Then I returned to the home to complete the jobs I was allocated. Once they were done, my time was my own.

My lung disease was causing infections, so I would go to my room and do my postural drainage. In those days I didn't have the help of the puffers I have now, but I did my best because this job was important to me. I was getting run down and taking longer and longer to do my chores. I was also still quite immature, and struggled with the routine of work. My afternoon shift started at 3 pm, when the time arrived to collect the children from school. I then worked until 8 pm.

The day I got fired from this job was horrendous, as I knew this was my last chance for financial independence. I had collected the children from school—they were chatty, and it was all very busy. It wasn't until I got them home, which was about a 20-minute walk, that the housemother asked me where their schoolbags were. Their bags were still at the school. That was the straw that broke the camel's back, and I was immediately dismissed.

I went to my room and sobbed, because I had to be true to the agreement with Mother and Dad. Now I was committed to going on the invalid pension. I felt that I was a failure.

It was evening by then, and I decided I would go for a walk to look for a church. I looked for an Anglican Church, as that was the faith of my family. I passed several churches which showed signs of people about, but none of them were Anglican. I came across St Thomas More Anglican Church in Glenelg. I walked in, tears streaming down my face. The St Thomas More Amateur Theatre Group was rehearsing. They were so caring, and called the minister for me. He arrived and sat with me while I told him what had happened. The minister's only words were, 'Do you go to church?'

'No,' I replied.

'God is punishing you. I'll pray with you,' he said, before reciting a quick prayer and showing me out to the street.

I was told later that the minister had been dismissed from his duty. I walked the streets in utter distress for a very long time, and then eventually went back to my room in the children's home. I called Dad and he picked me up. I was going home to loving and caring parents.

***

I had been saving to go to England. Having to go on the pension put a spanner in the works, but I never wanted to give up that dream, and still put money away from my pension, but just less than I had been setting aside before. I was floundering, and Mother and Dad could see I was feeling lost. Mother discovered that an Anglian Church's kindy needed an assistant. They couldn't pay me, but I didn't care, as I just wanted to feel useful. I loved every bit of the two years I worked at the kindy. The children called me 'Miss Jan.' Marina Aston was the headmistress, and we got along so well that we are still friends to this day.

One day, I was telling the children about my love of animals—I had an Australian terrier dog named Trixie and a guinea pig named Guinea. One child said, 'Where is Trixie?' and I said, 'At home.' Some of the children starting laughing. I asked why, and one child said, 'You live here!' She was serious. I asked, 'Where do you think I sleep?' The answer came back, 'You hide your bed.' I then realised their perception of me. In their world I was the kindy lady, nothing more, nothing less. That was my total existence in their minds. So we had an educational excursion to my home. Mother made morning tea for them, they saw my bedroom, and met Trixie the dog and Guinea the guinea pig.

I loved doing artwork. Marina was fantastic at organising, and we put on plays, which I got to do the artwork for. One play Marina produced was Mary Poppins. It was well organised, down to the toys on the floor magically jumping into the box. Each toy had a piece of cotton attached to each, and they all came together in the box with a hole in the back. When it was time, I would pull all the cotton strings and the toys disappeared into the box. I had fun painting the formal lounge room, particularly the 'painting within a painting', portraying a country scene, which 'hung' in its painted frame above the mantelpiece.

For the Nativity play, I created a palm tree out of our bird stand. We did have challenges with a couple of young angels getting stagefright and wetting their pants. Also, there was the year baby Jesus had been left in the crib after the dress rehearsal. The children were waiting on stage for the performance to begin and the audience were already seated. Marina and I were trying to work out how to retrieve Jesus. We decided to get the most mature angel to pick Jesus up and bring him off stage. Well, our little angel did it by grabbing baby Jesus by the legs and bouncing his head on the floor all the way out. The audience had a good laugh.

I really loved my job, but I wanted to get paid work so that I could save more money towards going on my trip overseas. I finally found a job in the pet shop at the local shopping centre, which was within walking distance of my house. It was part-time work, which I was allowed to do on the pension. I loved that work, except for the mice. When I first started working there they were a huge worry. I hated them. On one occasion a cute little boy walked in and said that he wanted a black one. I had been told that black mice bend over and climb up their tails and bite your fingers, whereas the others don't. I told him if he wanted the black mouse he must get it himself, and gave him a stool to climb on. I eventually got used to dealing with the mice, and had a photo taken with them climbing on me—but just the white ones. My dog ,Trixie, would walk down with me each morning to help me open the shop. She would check all the cages, and if the kittens were in with the rabbits she would bark. Trixie once caught a canary in her mouth, as the owner accidentally let the bird out. We shut the front door and were attempting to catch it, when Trixie thought she was helping and caught it in her mouth. The owner started hitting Trixie on her head with a rolled up newspaper. I asked her to stop hitting Trixie, and then asked Trixie to drop the bird, which she did. The bird was unhurt. Trixie would sit under the counter until lunchtime. As this was still in the days when dogs could roam free, she would then walk herself over to the draper's shop nearby, where Mr and Mrs North, the owners, would share their lunch with her.

The children from the kindy would visit 'Miss Jan' at the pet shop, and their parents would leave them there while they did their shopping and then collect them on the way back home. I enjoyed my time there so very much.

It was 1969, and in those days a pure-bred boxer sold for $20—a lot of money back then. One day, I was in the middle of doing the sales pitch for a boxer when a child started tugging on my jacket, saying, 'Miss Jan come and see!'

I told the child that interrupting was rude behaviour, and carried on with my sales pitch. The child persisted, thank goodness, and I excused myself to deal with the child.

There was an emergency in the middle of the shop, where the fish tank stood. In amongst all the fish was a large six-dollar fish with an 85-cent fish wedged in its mouth. I forgot the sale of the boxer dog and ran into the chemist next door. I asked for tweezers, saying I'd pay later, and raced back to the fish tank. I grabbed a stool, stood the child on it, caught the large fish and gave it to the child to hold, while I dislodged the 85-cent fish, which had died, but we saved the six-dollar fish, although it was groggy for a day or two.

I arrived at work on the morning of the 20th July 1969, when the barber came visiting from his shop, a couple of doors up, to say he had hired a TV to watch the moon landing, and invited me to close the pet shop and go and watch with him.

There I was, sitting in the barber's comfortable chair, the shop packed with people, and everyone's eyes glued to the black and white TV screen. We were mesmerised by the extraordinary event we were witnessing. After the broadcast had finished I thanked the barber and went back to work, the images of Neil Armstrong and Buzz Aldrin stuck in my head. It was a first for our world.

Not long after, a huge male rabbit called Peter was brought into the shop. He had been fighting with the other male rabbit that the people who had bought him owned. He was so big that I put him in a cage by himself. I was told he was a New Zealand crossbreed rabbit.

The European women would come in to feel how much meat he had on his bones. I put a sold sign on the cage to stop them from buying him to eat. Eventually, the shop owner, thinking he genuinely had been sold and that the people who bought him had changed their minds, told me to take the sold sign off if he hadn't been collected by the end of the day.

I was so worried about his welfare that I found a big box, and at the end of the working day I closed up the shop and put him into the box. I really struggled, not only getting him in the box but also carrying him, as he was heavy. I rested the box on my right forearm and held it with my left hand. Thank goodness he sat still as I headed home, with Trixie trotting along behind. When I got home I put the box on the kitchen table, and showed my mother. She thought he was beautiful, but I was worried that Dad was going to be the problem, as he didn't like rabbits—except for eating. I hoped that once he saw Peter, the giant silver-grey rabbit might melt his heart.

Dad wasn't at all happy once he discovered what was in the mystery box. He stood over Peter and said, 'No way.' I said, 'Dad, if I take him back tomorrow I will have to sell him to the people who want to eat him.'

At that moment, Peter looked up at Dad and their eyes met. Dad's heart melted and Peter was welcomed into his new home. He was lonely, so I brought a cute white rabbit called 'Andy' home. Of course, I knew that Peter couldn't be with males, and Andy was in fact Angie. She quickly had babies. Trixie couldn't figure out how they go there. Peter was a great dad. I didn't know I should have separated him from them, but he dug the birthing burrow and took the cotton cloth down for Angie, and everything was fine.

***

In 1971, I celebrated my 21st birthday at home with family and friends. Mother and Dad created a lovely spread for supper, with the help of relatives. My parents had paid for a lovely outfit to be made for my birthday. A light-green jumpsuit with a matching skirt to make it look like a slack suit. It was beautiful material, with silver flecks all through it. At 21 I had a figure I would love to have today, and felt so very special. Peter and Angie's baby rabbits were a great attraction, and we found homes for all of them in the following weeks.

After the years of working part-time at the pet shop I was offered a job working part-time for the dress shop on the same block. I enjoyed the job and was thrilled that the money for my trip was growing. My goal was to save up $2,000. $1,200 was to pay for the return sea voyage to England, and would cover all my meals during the voyage. The remaining $800 was spending money for when I was in England.

In later life a different sort of job came my way, a Master of Ceremonies for a wedding. I offered to be the MC for my friend Leona Bentley.

I googled and found a person who could give me a Skype private study class on how to be an MC. I learnt what I needed to do to achieve a professionally presented MC.

Leona and I had a meeting with the wedding organiser prior to the big day. The organiser told me that she was very impressed with my organisation skills and continued to say that I was one of the most organised MCs she had met. (Ha-ha! I was stunned, as in my whole life no-one had said that word organised and my name in the same breath.) I told her it was all thanks to the private study class.

There I was, dressed in a black suit and a light blue shirt. I had all my paperwork in order of the process. The wedding took place in the garden and then the guests, of 60 people, went to the beer garden to have drinks in the beautiful warm weather.

It was time to round everybody up and get them seated, which was my first shock. People just wandered in gradually. It took a while.

Once I had introduced the newly married couple standing at the podium, I continued confidently through my job as their MC.

After the main course I lost the bride, Leona. No-one knew where she was. Eventually, I discovered that she had to take the long way around to the toilet.

Now I had the bride and groom back together again, but one whole table of guests were missing. I decided to proceed without them. Gradually the lost ones wondered back in. As that table was at the back near the door, there was no disturbance.

Everyone seemed happy with the wedding reception. I was pleased and relieved. Being in charge of such an important event was a nervous experience. I was glad my gift worked.

CHAPTER 6
Overseas Trip

From my first pay packet when I was just 16 years old, I started banking money to save for my trip to England. I would daydream about being on the ship. It wasn't an aimless dream, it was an 'I know I can do it' feeling. I didn't need that new dress or that lovely handbag—the money went straight in the bank. England was always a magical place in my mind. It was part of my family history, and I wanted to see where my favourite band—The Beatles—had started, in Liverpool. I hated flying, so I decided to travel by ship.

My dream had grown from early in my life, when Grandma Gardner spoke of England. It was her home, and she always missed it. She came from a country village called Bishop Stortford, where she knew most people. While I was in Grade Two I heard two schoolteachers talking about their overseas trip. I walked up and shared my dream with them, telling them that I would go overseas when I grew up. I was laughed at, patted on the head, and told to go out and play. I remember standing outside the classroom feeling so very hurt and confused, and wondering why were they being so mean. I wondered why they didn't believe me. My parents did. I decided it was okay, and when I was going on my trip I would tell them. This helped to make it a mission to be fulfilled in my future.

After eight years of saving I was still $800 short of my goal. I had saved diligently for all that time, and just kept putting the money away, watching it slowly grow. The more money I had in the bank, the more excited I became. In October 1974 I became worried, as I realised it was getting too close to summer to plan my trip for the next Australian winter the following June, July, and August, which would be England's summer.

One Sunday morning in October, Mother came in with a cuppa for me and gave me the Sunday Mail with the paper opened at the star signs page. I read it while Mother was with me—it said I was coming into money. Mother asked me to get up, because visitors were coming in for a cuppa. Not thinking anything of it, and feeling very grumpy as I'd been out the night before, I crawled out of bed. Uncle Keith and Auntie Bet had called around for a cuppa. In my sleepy state it didn't seem odd to me that they were all standing and leaning against the kitchen benches. Another relative, Charles, was also there. I didn't know that Charles had recently won a lot of money on a horse race. As I entered the kitchen, he walked over to me and handed me $800 in cash, saying, 'You are going to England.' With tears running down my cheeks I hugged him and thanked him. I just stood there open-mouthed and totally stunned, looking at my fistful of money. I had never held that much money before. My dad said jokingly, 'Shut your mouth Jan or you'll catch flies.' I shut my mouth, but continued to stare at the money. It was such an amazing feeling. I now had enough to book my fare and have spending money for the whole trip. Uncle Keith and Auntie Bet had come over to the house to witness the event and share in the joy of my lovely surprise. I was very thankful. It was a wonderful gift.

Charles had won his money by putting 50 cents on a ticket called a 'quadrella', which required picking four horses from four different races. In order to win the bet, all four horses had to come first. The first three horses won, and then came time for the final race. The last horse had odds of a hundred to one. The horse won by a short nose, and Charles won a lot of money!

Once Charles had given me the $800, I immediately started planning my trip to England. My dream was happening a year earlier than I had thought possible.

I made an appointment with the manager of my bank, at the head office in Adelaide. During the appointment, the manager told me that in case I lost my bank book I should write down the bank book number and keep it on me. Well that confused me.

'How do I keep it on me?' I asked.

He stared at my bust and said, 'You wear a bra, don't you?'

I was even more confused by this remark, but answered, 'Yes.'

'Well', he said, 'shove it down your bra; it will be safe there.'

My theatre friends heard about my trip, and were surprised I was doing it. One guy wanted to share his advice. He said, 'I understand that you are still a virgin.' Well, I was stunned that it was common knowledge. He went on, 'So it is very important that you start taking the pill before you go.' That shocked me even more. He continued, 'You may leave a virgin, but you won't come back a virgin.' I politely thanked him, although I had no intention of following his advice.

However, I began to wonder if I should have listened to him when, on the ship heading for England, I came very close to thinking I had lost my virginity. I had been drinking with a group of friends, and one very charming chap had enticed me to his cabin, by telling me he wanted to 'show me his alligator.' Yes, there was such a sight to be seen! The poor stuffed alligator stood eight inches tall, and held a little suitcase and an umbrella. I was quite tiddly and don't remember anything more of that night. A couple of years later I had to have some tests. The doctor just assumed I was not a virgin. He did what he had to do and I reacted to the pain he had caused. The look of horror when he realised that I was still a virgin reassured me that nothing had happened that night on the ship.

Back in Adelaide, before the alligator incident, my bags were packed. At the time I had no idea of the stress I was putting my fantastic parents through, as they kindly kept their thoughts to themselves. I was so naive, but they went along with my excitement. We only lived five minutes from the airport, and so once my bags had been put in the boot of the car we were there before I knew what was happening. I was to fly to Sydney to connect with the ship. Oh! I hate planes, but at that moment I didn't care. I was going to prove to everyone that I could do this—I was going to go overseas by myself. Sitting on the plane it suddenly dawned on me. As this was 1975, it was still possible for people to stand close to the plane before take off, and although I had an aisle seat, I could still see my parents, Auntie Dawn, and other relatives through the little window.

They were chatting and smiling, with no hint that they were so very worried for me. I suddenly felt a state of overwhelming fear. I thought, *What do I think I am doing, going for seven months!* I realised I wasn't doing this to prove to anyone else that I could do it—I wanted to prove it to myself. Suddenly, I was petrified. The plane doors were locked and I was trapped. As the plane was rolling along, the sight of the security of my family slid away from my view. I started crying uncontrollably, sobbing my heart out very loudly. The hostess didn't know what to do with me. The bored businessman next to me suddenly wasn't bored on that flight. He was lovely, and did his best to talk to me and calm me down. In the end he offered me his seat, which was the window seat. When I was all cried out, I just stared out the window. It was getting dark, and I told him I could see a fire down on the ground. He asked me what it looked like and I told him it was a small red glow. He said gently, 'Look', and I turned to look at him. He was smiling and gently said, 'If that disappears we are in trouble. That is the red light on the wing of our plane.' I was 25 years old, and had never been anywhere by myself. The aeroplane eventually landed at Sydney airport, to the relief of that dear businessman, the hostess, and especially me. When I got to the terminal, Charles suddenly appeared in front of me. I was determined that I was going to look cool, calm, and collected.

Charles decided to board the ship with me, as visitors could in those days. The ship was the *Northern Star* and she was on her last voyage, as she was going to be scrapped once she got to England. She was a beautiful ship in my eyes. Everything was so nice. Charles got a boarding pass and helped me find my cabin. It was a four-berth cabin, and the three other girls that I shared it with were in there already. We chatted, and I thought they were wonderful. I finally thought, *I can do this.*

The ship's main engine wasn't working properly, so we ended up not leaving for two days. In the meantime, Charles was having a great social life. He phoned his bank manager and arranged a ticket to travel on the ship, and sailed with us to New Zealand. I had saved for nine years to make my dream become a reality, and the day that the ship left I felt so proud of myself. I was busting with excitement. Dreaming is wonderful, and with help and time they can come true.

Charles and I stood on the deck, watching the streamers being thrown from the wharf to the deck of our ship. We attempted to catch them to throw them back to the wharf again. Loud sea-themed songs played on the PA system, and the atmosphere was electric.

The ship slowly started moving. I stood motionless, watching the streamers held between loved ones on the ship and the wharf break in two, before the people on shore shrank with the distance. I watched people crying farewell, and others excitedly laughing, and I turned to share the happiness.

My plan was to have a good social life on ship, and that was Charles' plan too, but we both wanted our independence. He was good-looking, and single, as were many girls on that ship. I was leaving Australia in our autumn, and heading for England where it would be springtime. I was escaping our winter, not realising how wonderful that would be for my diseased lung and general health.

Charles was in his element. His new wealth and his good looks made him very popular with the girls on the ship. I got to know the girls in my cabin, and we enjoyed exploring together. I loved standing out on the deck and just gazing at the sea. I was in awe of being there, living my dream. Being an extrovert, I enjoyed meeting people, and there were a lot of people to meet!

We sailed into Auckland, New Zealand, and Charles disembarked—but was not forgotten at all. From that moment on I was met with smiles and comments such as, 'Oh! You're Charles' relative, aren't you?' Auckland was wonderful to explore, and I felt sad we didn't have a longer stay there.

As the *Northern Star* set sail out of Auckland, once again the streamers broke, people cried as they farewelled their loved ones, and the music died down as the people on the wharf appeared to become smaller and smaller as we moved away.

Then, twenty-four hours after we left, we were told by the captain that we would have to limp back to Auckland, as the ship's engine was not working well. We arrived back, and a huge cheer came up from the wharf as we stepped off the ship. There were many hugs for people from loved ones who had not expected to see them again for a very long time—if ever. Charles had by this time flown back to Adelaide, to the disappointment of many of the girls.

We were given free bus trips and fed on the ship for the four extra days we were in Auckland. It was great! Some people had to arrange to fly on ahead, as their time was limited. Finally, the ship's engine was fixed, or at least patched up, for the *Northern Star's* last voyage. We were ready to sail, but this time it was different. There were no streamers and no tears. As we got out to a point that the ship's horn was blown we were far enough away that the people on the wharf looked as small as ants. As the horn blew for the third and final time, there was a huge cheer from the wharf. All those people who were so sad the first time they said their goodbyes were now thrilled that we were finally able to depart.

I was having a fantastic time on the ship. The four boys in the next cabin had their musical instruments with them. Their names were John, Paul, and George—but not Ringo. They genuinely were their names, although I have no idea what the fourth guy's name was. In a letter home on the 8th of April 1975 I wrote, 'I am lying in bed listening to George in the next cabin playing his flute.' I also wrote, 'I go to the tavern almost every night. It is much like the Fiesta Villa disco at the Findon Hotel but doesn't cost anything to get in.' In the same letter I wrote, 'I went to a discussion group and debated pollution and cars.' Wow! Back in 1975! Alongside all the activities, one of the highlights was that we got invited to the captain's cocktail party—it was open to everyone who wanted to go.

Rarotonga in the Cook Islands had shallow water, so our ship stayed out at sea and the islanders came out to us on boats. They came with big smiles and flowers decorating their hair—and with things to sell. I bought a hula skirt. It was the real deal, not plastic.

Tahiti was a disappointment, as it was so commercial, but in a postcard I wrote home I said it was fantastic. I was probably reflecting on the amazing scenery. It was beautiful, along with the wonderful warm weather. The dancers on the wharf had shiny plastic imitation grass skirts. They walked away after they had finished dancing, and while still in view of the ship just took off the skirts.

I loved stopping at different ports, to sightsee as much as I could. The mood was completely different in the Port of Cristobal, in Panama. We were instructed to take off all our jewellery, and to go on shore in groups of at least ten. The National Guard was there to protect us, as we bought our souvenirs and walked through the main areas of the city. There was a wide main street, with a medium strip down the centre. My group walked along, and we got up to where the guards were standing, spread across the street and footpaths. They told us they couldn't protect us any further than that point, as there had recently been trouble in that part of the city. Maurice, one of the guys in the group, never left my side, so I felt extra safe. He looked in one food shop and saw two big rats. I was glad I hadn't been looking! We went into one shop where the shopkeeper told us that many people had been knifed recently, and that there had also been quite a few shootings. We could hear sirens. One guy in our group wanted to go on, but the rest of us didn't. He decided to turn around with us and head back. As we were walking we realised that the six guards following us back had their holsters undone and their hands on their guns. It was a very poor area with lots of local people just standing around. It was so sad—they really needed us to buy their goods. I realised how life was so good to me, and back on board the ship I wrote home to say that in those people's eyes, I was rich. Not just financially, I was rich in opportunity from living in Australia.

I loved Barbados. It had recently gained independence from the British, and the people were lovely and very happy. We toured a sugarcane factory, and in the warm peace of the evening we stopped for drinks at the Hilton Hotel. I drank a cocktail from a hollowed-out coconut. I have always thought that I would like to go back again.

I enjoyed going into the ports, seeing the different landscapes and listening to the different languages. I was a little sad that I couldn't speak to the locals, but I smiled a lot and got lots of smiles back. Now, as I think back, some may have been able to speak English. I didn't have any trouble walking, even though it was so much more than I did at home. I limped, but I was used to that, and never a bother.

Very early one morning, a member of the crew knocked on our cabin door, as arranged. I threw my clothes on and headed upstairs. I stood on the deck. It was only around four o'clock in the morning. I was a long way from the security of my home. Standing there with tears in my eyes I saw the lights of England. I felt as though my heart could explode with excitement. I stood there, totally mesmerised, seeing the many small lights in the far distance that seemed to be blinking. It was magical. It was time for the next chapter of my dream. It was scary to leave the safety of the ship, but it was time to do some more growing up.

I was very sad to be leaving the *Northern Star*. All the staff were wonderful, and getting an extra week free of charge was a bonus. Our ship docked in Southampton. We said our goodbyes to one another, with plenty of hugs all around.

There was a bus to take me to London. Once I arrived, I booked into a hotel for the night, before taking a cheap bus tour around the city. I was overwhelmed to be in London, staring out the window, so in awe of being there, amongst so much history. I wasn't at all worried about being there by myself. I felt safe, because there were people everywhere. If I needed help, I felt that all I had to do was ask. The bus driver was giving a commentary, but I was only vaguely aware of what he was saying.

The next day I made my way to The Walkabout Club to find accommodation. The club had a great atmosphere, and plenty of friendly people. There was a room available, but I decided to take the cheaper option of a share house.

I was driven to the share house, which was about a 20-minute bus ride out of central London. I shared with some Australians, a New-Zealand guy, and a chap from South Africa. The accommodation had both guys and girls. Looking back, I think we were overcharged, but at the time I was so naive I was oblivious to that fact.

The share house was in an area that had street after street of identical housing, all with a street level and two upper floors, and bay windows facing the street. As we walked in through the front door, to our left was a door going into the lounge room and then through to the kitchen. Walking past the first door to the left were a number of bedrooms. On the right, as we walked through the front door, there was a staircase to take us to the second floor. That floor had another kitchen, a bathroom, and more bedrooms. The third floor had bedrooms and a lounge area.

A lot of children of different nationalities played in the street where we lived. At around five o'clock each night the windows of many of the buildings would be opened, with mums yelling to their children to come in for dinner.

That share house was my base. From there I would walk up the street and chat to any neighbours I would see. The laundromat was in the block of shops at the end of our street, and I found it to be a meeting place of the nations, with everyone chatting to each other. There was a public phone in the laundromat, and when someone made a phone call it would be discussed by everyone afterwards, including the person who made the phone call. Any and every conversation was open for discussion. I wasn't bored for a minute. I loved talking to the locals wherever I was. After getting to know the next-door neighbour she gave me her telephone number, which came in very handy later.

I caught buses to sightsee, and also used the underground trains. At first, the underground was confusing, but I gradually loved that form of travel. On one occasion, I got lost on the streets of London and a taxi driver asked me if I was okay. I didn't have much money, and after explaining my situation he drove me back to my apartment for nothing. He just asked me to pay it forward when I got back to Australia.

My relative, Charles, had flown over and rented a room, not

realising that he was in the same share house as me, but upstairs. We both liked our independence. All the men liked their beer, and enjoyed sticking together. We got together for barbeque meals in the backyard, which was a lot of fun.

Charles and I bumped into each other in the bank one day, and he asked if there was somewhere I would like to go. I wanted to see the Royal Edinburgh Military Tattoo, and he arranged to transfer money into my bank account so that I could make the trip to Scotland. It was lovely of him.

I took trips from the share house every day. I would go out by myself, as most of the guys were loud and rude. I enjoyed travelling by myself, as I could meet up with people and, if I wanted, I could move on without a problem. If I went away on overnight trips, I would keep paying rent while I was away.

I met a girl called Vivian, and we decided to take a trip to the southwest by bus, and to sleep at bed and breakfast accomodation. I wrote in a letter home on the 22nd of May 1975, from a lovely bed and breakfast place, 'I feel like I am living in a doll's house. We have a twin room, with pink sheets, blankets, and pillows, and pink flowers on the wallpaper.' I also wrote in the same letter, 'We have been so lucky in Torquay. We found a room, and the owners, Helen and Bob, fussed over us. It cost £1.60, and the breakfast was beautiful with a free cuppa thrown in. This morning when we received breakfast Helen gave us an extra-large helping, as she knew we were watching our money.'

Well, there we were. Me, a spoilt and very immature 25-year-old, and Vivian who was very young, probably about 18 years old, and also used to having her mum help her. We got on well, but I do remember one occasion where we had to pack our bags, and Vivian asked me to help her. I agreed, thinking that she would help me after. As we were both totally disorganised we left our packing until last thing at night, and we had to get up early next morning to catch the bus. I helped Vivian, with the pair of us fumbling through the process. Finally, she was packed, and it was my turn. Vivian fell asleep and there I was, trying to get organised, with everything everywhere and tears running down my cheeks.

***

I took an aeroplane to Denmark on the 1st of June 1975. I was going to be staying with relatives I had never previously met, and felt so nervous, as I would be with them for a month and was worried that they might not like me. My mother's father was Danish, and I was staying with a cousin of my mother's, and her family—Kirsten, her husband Finn Deleuran, who was a major in the Danish Airforce, and their daughter Karin, who at the time was 16 years old. They had another daughter, Lisbeth, who I would meet later. The moment I met them I felt so at ease. They were warm, loving people and made me feel so welcome. They were wonderful, took me sightseeing and introduced me to other wonderful relatives. Lisbeth took me to the kindy where she worked. Karin and I spent a lot of time chatting together.

Saying goodbye at the end of my visit to Denmark was horrible. I was devastated and cried a lot. I loved them. They are family we are still in touch with.

I got back to the flat in London and realised that it was nice to be back with my flatmates. It helped so much with the sadness of leaving Denmark. Not long after I arrived back, Johnny, one of the guys in the share house, had his work schedule switched from day shifts to night shifts. On the night before the changeover, we all decided to stay up with him to help him. We had a great time, and he successfully crossed over to nightshift work.

In 1975, London was in the grip of terror of random bombing by the Irish Republican Army (IRA). On one occasion, I was sitting on a red double-decker bus, and as we pulled up at a bus stop a man dressed in a white hazmat-style jumpsuit was standing there, holding what looked like a steel broom handle attached to a round disk. The conductor told me he was looking for bombs. Just then I heard a siren and looked out of the window to see a van speeding along on the wrong side of the road. I was told by the conductor that it was the bomb squad. I felt absolutely petrified and told the conductor I would go to the tube train. He said, 'You can if you want, but that is how they transport the bombs.' I stayed on the bus.

Johnny came home one night, and his face was as white as a ghost. He explained that he was on a bus and a bomb went off close by. They were all ordered off the bus and told to get on the ground with their heads down. There was always a worry that a second bomb was set to go off. It didn't happen in this case, but it had been known to happen in the past.

I started to worry about the bombings, and spoke to one flatmate about whether it was safe to leave the flat. The flatmate pointed out that it was possible that they could bomb the apartment, and from that moment on I just went out as normal. Nothing happened to me. It did surprise me how I adapted. Mother always referred to the words, 'Whatever will be will be' from the Doris Day song, *Que Sera Sera*. Yes, 'Whatever will be will be.' I was comforted by those words.

Next on my agenda was a group camping tour around Europe. I had bought a sleeping bag while I was in Denmark, when Kirsten and I had gone shopping together. I chose a multicolour sleeping bag and a cotton jacket—I still have both. I bought iron-on 'London' patches to decorate the off-white jacket. When the day of the camping trip arrived, we all met at the bus station and introduced ourselves. Of course, I immediately forgot everyone's name, but there was plenty of time to get to know them. We went across to mainland Europe on the ferry, and then the adventure began.

The tour covered seven countries in 16 days—The Netherlands, Belgium, Germany, Austria, Italy, Switzerland, and France. I really enjoyed all the different countries, and I had a story for each one. The Netherlands story is a particular favourite.

In Amsterdam, we were driven to the world famous Red Light District. I was so naive that I had never heard of it. I walked into a street with the others, but then we all parted ways. At first it looked like a street of shop windows. Well, they actually were shop windows, but of a different type. All of a sudden I saw what was in the first window—a naked woman on a seat. And there it was, window after window, woman after woman. Some were empty, as the woman who occupied that window was presumably working. Men stood at the door, and just like a shop, they talked to the woman—probably negotiating services and price.

I was so surprised, I just wandered the streets. It was like a village. Then I suddenly realised that I was lost—in the Red Light District in Amsterdam. I froze and looked around for a familiar face. Eventually, I found someone from our bus who was also lost. Together we found more people from the bus, ending up with three quarters of the group back together. It was a relief not to be alone, but we still worried about how to get back to the bus. We eventually found the way out and saw the bus. As we walked closer, the bus started up and drove ahead. We walked faster, worried that the driver would take off. Eventually we were let on—the driver was laughing at our expense. Then off we went for dinner at a restaurant, all 40 of us, and we had a wonderful time.

On the last night in Amsterdam we went for a cruise on seven of the 81 canals. It was so fascinating, like streets of water. The sides of the canals were crammed with homes, shops, apartments and people.

I arrived back in Australia in October 1975, after seven months in Europe. My lung had improved, as I had been away in the warm air of summer all the time. I had grown up too.

CHAPTER 7
Meeting the Beatles, Minus Ringo

I first heard of The Beatles in early 1963. I was 13 years old and in Grade Six at Thebarton Primary School. As I arrived at school on a cool overcast morning, Elaine Haines, my girlfriend, came running from the direction of the transportable classrooms, yelling, 'Jan, have you heard of the new band called The Beatles?' Elaine had become my best friend after I arrived at the school that year. She was the shortest student of her age, and I was the tallest in my grade.

The next day after school we rode our pushbikes back to Elaine's place and listened to a wonderful 45rpm record of 'She Loves You.' We were so excited listening to that one song over and over. Elaine was a very happy girl, full of fun. She could tell joke after joke, all clean, and had me laughing hysterically. She had soft, short, curly blonde hair, and always had a smile for everyone. Elaine's father was English. I remember him as being quiet and serious. Her mother was Spanish. I remember her being very happy and full of life. Elaine had an older brother, Allan, whom I saw from time to time. Elaine adored him. He always treated me well.

We started to talk about our dream of one day meeting The Beatles, and thinking about how we would act and what we would say to them.

Elaine and I became Beatlemaniacs. Paul was our favourite, and he was the best looking from our point of view. At 14 I was struggling at school, and not happy with myself. I was the classic awkward teenager, and Beatlemania was a total distraction for me.

I loved their sense of humour and their melodic Liverpool accents just as much as I liked their music. They were funny, which made me laugh and continued to give me a feeling of inner joy long after the TV interviews or songs had finished.

We loved The Beatles, but many of the kids at school were Elvis Presley fans. We could never agree. The personalities seemed so different. Elaine and I listened to The Beatles' music and watched them on TV at every opportunity we could.

We couldn't work out why all the girls constantly screamed when they saw The Beatles in person or in the films, so we decided to do some research, by going to a Beatles movie. We went to see 'A Hard Day's Night.' We agreed that we would scream all the way through the movie to see how it felt. So there we were, screaming and giggling our way through the movie. We thought it was crazy to be screaming, because we couldn't hear the movie. The girls around us were screaming, with serious looks on their faces, and some were crying. We came out of the theatre exhausted and with sore throats. We agreed that we still had no idea why Beatles fans screamed. Paul McCartney once described the noise as sounding like seagulls continually squawking, and I agree that is a very accurate description. It was to be another 30 years before I saw and heard the movie in full. Sitting at home in my armchair, and loving every minute of it.

My dream was to meet Paul McCartney. I am definitely a glass half-full person and there was no question in my mind that it would happen—I would meet and talk with Paul McCartney. I believed that dreams come true. Actually, back then, I believed that *everyone's* dreams came true.

Elaine's parents took her on a trip to England, and on her return I asked her what it was like to meet our wonderful Paul. Being dedicated fans we felt like a part of him was ours. I was genuinely so shocked when Elaine said with a startled look, 'Of course, I didn't meet Paul!'

I followed with a very naive, 'Why not?' Well, I was just 13 years old after all, and had no idea how many people lived in England and how totally impossible it would have been to get near The Beatles.

The following year, we heard on our favourite Adelaide radio station, 5AD, that The Beatles were coming to Australia. We were so excited, but our euphoria soon turned to despair when Bob Francis, a DJ at 5AD, and Adelaide's top radio announcer, broke the news to us all that The Beatles would not be coming to Adelaide. Bob then announced that he was going to do all he could to get them to change the agenda and include Adelaide on their tour. He contacted The Beatles' agent, but couldn't convince them to come to Adelaide. So this wonderful DJ announced that he was starting a petition. He encouraged his audience to sign the petition, telling them where they could go to sign it.

Bob Francis collected a huge amount of signatures, and again contacted The Beatles' agent. The signatures spoke for themselves, and thanks to Bob Francis, The Beatles were now heading for Adelaide. Bob Francis and the Adelaide Beatlemaniacs had changed the course of Adelaide's history!

The girl next door, Jill O'Toole, worked at Adelaide Airport. One night, a few days before The Beatles were due to fly in, there was a knock at the back door. Mother opened the door and there stood Jill. She came in and asked if I was excited that The Beatles were coming to Adelaide. Of course, she knew the answer, and then she asked if I would like to meet them. Well, I was stunned, but not enough to prevent me from giving a quick answer of, 'Yes please.' That definitely was not a moment to forget manners.

Jill had asked her manager at the airport if it was possible for me to be at the airport when The Beatles arrived. All teenagers and adults, except for airport officials and the media, were banned from being anywhere near the airport when The Beatles arrived. Officials were scared of a riot, but because I was para-abled, the manager made an exception for me. His chauffeur came to collect me in his car to drive me to the airport. At the time that didn't mean anything to me, because I had my own chauffeur—my dad. The only difference, in my mind, was that this driver had a uniform and an official-looking hat. Mother seemed to be pretty excited about the driver and the car, though.

On arrival at the airport I was immediately taken up the stairs that led to the office section on the first floor and told to wait in a very small room, about the width of a small toilet but about four times longer, with a bench seat along one side. I now think it must have been a room where they put problem people until the police came, but that day it was used for a special purpose. Someone brought me a multi-coloured soft-drink with the green, red, and white spiralling around the glass. I was given two books of photos of The Beatles. One book I still have today, the other I gave to Elaine. I was told to stay still and quiet until Jill came. It was definitely a time to behave myself, but that wasn't too hard, with my two new books to look at.

Jill came up a long time later and collected me. She took me through the foyer. There were faces of media people I had only seen on TV. I was excited to see them. Jill and I got into the airport manager's car and were driven out to the tarmac, where the plane was to stop. The airport management wouldn't let the plane go near the main terminal building with The Beatles on board. There was the special car parked on the tarmac, with their names printed all over it. The car was supplied by Australian Motors, and was to be used for them to travel from the airport to the city. Once The Beatles were seated in the convertible they were only allowed to stay on the tarmac for a maximum of three minutes.

I actually got to touch the car and got a photo taken standing in front of it. Although Ringo had his name on the car, he wasn't coming to Adelaide as he'd had his tonsils out, and would be meeting up with the others later. Jimmie Nichol was filling in for Ringo.

I was wandering around waiting for the plane to arrive. There I was, the only teenager allowed to be at the Adelaide Airport. It was a huge honour. It was very peaceful too. There were small groups of reporters, film crews, and VIPs just quietly chatting. What I find interesting now, when I look back on that day, is that not one of those reporters came and asked me if I was excited to be there or which Beatle was my favourite. I seemed invisible to them. I have to admit, I was a tall, skinny 14 year old, and looking at the little bit of TV footage that I have seen I looked very unwell because I had a lung infection and it was very cold. It didn't worry me that the reporters didn't want to talk to me that day, because to me they were just a bunch of old people waiting to see The Beatles. Now, as an adult, I know that people ignored people with parabilities—it's the 'don't look, don't stare' attitude.

As I stood there waiting I was totally oblivious to the thousands of people lining the roads between the airport and the city, as well as the thousands of people gathering in the city—children who were playing hooky from school, and teenagers and adults who had walked out of work. All for one reason—to catch a glimpse of The Beatles. It was reported in the media that one third (350,000) of our South-Australian population at that time were in the streets that day. I believe that there were no reports of bad behaviour.

It was a long wait, and as I was wandering around, away from the media and officials, I saw a truck. It had a canvas flap at the rear which was clipped up, and men in suits were standing in the back. One of the men asked me, 'Which is your favourite Beatle?' I shyly answered, 'Paul is my favourite.' He said, 'Come here and you can hold Paul's guitar.' Now, even though these men were in suits, in my mind they were standing in a truck, so they were truck drivers. As well as that, The Beatles plane hadn't landed, so in my mind that guitar was definitely not Paul's! As I refused, they told me to take a picture of one of them holding the guitar. So finally, to keep the peace with them, I took the photo.

Many years later when I showed that photo to The Beatle impersonators called 'The Fab Four' here in Adelaide, they told me who the truck drivers were. Those truck drivers were in fact The Beatles' management, and I had passed up the opportunity to hold Paul's guitar.

At 11:45 am on the 12th June 1964, the plane with The Beatles, minus Ringo, plus replacement drummer Jimmie Nichol, arrived. I was waiting at the bottom of the boarding stairs on the left side, looking up. They stepped out of the plane and there they were, standing together at the door at the top of the stairs. I must have been told to behave myself because I just stood quietly. I was probably in shock. As John and Paul came down the stairs together, Paul was looking the other way, which was too much for me to bear. I called out, 'Paul!' He turned around. By now, they were almost at the bottom of the stairs, so I took a photo of them both and John Lennon said, 'You're a bit young to be a photographer, aren't you?' I had both John and Paul smiling at me in the photo I took. I don't remember saying anything to John, but in the TV footage from ABC Adelaide of the moment just after I took the photo both John and Paul are laughing. I was there to see my favourite band, and to have one of them saying that I was too young, I am sure I would have replied, 'No, I'm not!'

They got into the car. I was at the front right of the car, and as I was getting in the way of everyone I moved and ended up near the back of the car. Jill came over and asked me if I'd asked Paul to sign my autograph book. I hadn't, so I asked Paul for his autograph. He held out his hand and just as I went to hand my autograph book to him the car drove off. He looked at me sadly and I felt so very sad. I didn't get Paul's autograph, and in those days Paul had no power to have the car stopped. There I stood, so happy to have been there, but sad that I didn't get his autograph. I took the roll of film into a chemist shop, from where it would be sent off to a photo developing company. The form was filled out, and I was given a ticket with the date of collection. I had to wait two weeks for the photos to be developed. When I did collect them I was so very excited with the special photos I had taken.

My parents wouldn't let me go to The Beatles concert. I think it had more to do with their money worries than worries about what would happen at the concert. Anyway, I had been so fortunate to have been given access to The Beatles when they arrived that I wasn't upset at all, just excited.

In 1975, when I was living in the share house in London, not long before I returned to Adelaide, I suddenly realised that I hadn't been to Liverpool, The Beatles' hometown. So I got myself organised and caught a bus into central London. A couple of people from the share house were on the bus with me and asked what I was planning to do that day. 'I'm going to Liverpool', I announced.

'What, Liverpool Street Station?' they responded.

'No. Liverpool—the city. To see where the Beatles started,' was my reply.

I had no idea how far away Liverpool was, no idea at all. Not only that, but we had no TV or radio at the share house, and I hadn't seen any papers, so I was very ignorant and uninformed in every way.

I finally found my way to the station that would connect me with the train to Liverpool. 'I'd like a ticket to Liverpool, please', I said calmly with a smile.

'Which train do you want? The one that is leaving now or the 4 pm train?' The ticket man asked.

'The one that is leaving now please,' I said in a relaxed tone.

His tone changed to panic, saying, 'See that train moving? That is your train. Here's your ticket. Get on, and walk through to Second Class.'

Running in my special style, my right leg not fully co-operating with my left leg, I made it in time to get on before the train started to move too fast. I walked through, smiling happily that I had made it onto the train. I walked far enough to believe that I was in the right area. There, to my left, facing towards me, was a girl in her early twenties. She had shoulder-length brown hair and was trying to zip up a bag, but a little white dog kept popping its head out. I asked if I could sit down, and with a bright happy smile and a very broad northern accent she said, 'Oh! You're Australian. Sit down, I have a boyfriend who lives in Sydney.' Her name was Anne, and she explained that if she kept Pippa, her dog, in the bag and the conductor didn't know, she wouldn't have to pay for her. We chatted for a while and then she asked me why I would be travelling to the 'ends of the earth—Liverpool.' I was stunned at the description, because I always had thought of Liverpool as the romantic magical city that had produced The Beatles.

Anne listened as I explained about being a Beatlemaniac. She told me that she would take me around to where the Cavern once stood, telling me that now it was just a car park. Finally, the train pulled into Liverpool station, and we made our way to the door. As we stepped down off the train, two of the most handsome men in smart suits came up to us. One spoke to Anne and the other came up to me.

'Good morning, I am Detective Gary Wallis', he said sternly, but in the most adorable Liverpool accent. 'What is your name?' After I told him, he continued, 'I want to know where you're from, why you've come to Liverpool, and what your association is with Miss Anne Baxter.'

'I'm Australian, I'm 25 years old, and I am a Beatlemaniac,' I replied, and then explained that Anne and I had met on the train, because of her dog.

Detective Wallis then stunned me by saying, 'I know you didn't get on the train with her.' Shocked, I asked how he knew that we didn't board together and asked what she had done wrong. He explained that they suspected she had been involved in a mysterious but tragic incident, and that drugs were involved. The detective went on to explain that they had been following Anne. So I explained to him about my arrival at the station in London, and how I was fascinated with Anne shoving her dog into her bag.

Detective Wallis seemed satisfied with my answers and then asked, 'Who is your favourite Beatle?' After me telling him that Paul was my favourite Beatle, he stunned me again by asking, 'Would you like to meet him? Paul and his band Wings are doing a show here in

Liverpool tonight, and I am one of his bodyguards.' Then he asked, 'How long are you staying here?'

'Paul McCartney has a home somewhere in Scotland. I believe he is probably there, so I'll stay here long enough to prove you wrong,' I answered curtly.

'You're on!' he responded with a smile. 'I'll meet you outside the Punch and Judy coffee shop at 7 pm tonight.' And off he went with the other detective.

Anne seemed not to be worried at all about the chat with the other detective. As we walked off she told me her thoughts on her future. She said that she intended to work her way up the social ranks of London and marry a wealthy man. She took me around to the spot where the Cavern once stood, and where the world-famous Beatles started their career. It was just a car park by then, but oh, to have been standing there in 1962! Above the door on the building across the road was a very small plaque stating that The Beatles had played on that spot.

After that, Anne had to go. She didn't say where, so I thanked her for showing me where the Cavern used to be and we parted. I hope her life went well for her.

I asked my way around Liverpool and found the theatre in the mid-afternoon. There was a big poster on the outside wall—'Mel Bush presents Paul McCartney and Wings, Monday the 15th of September 1975.' Across the poster was a sign on an angle—Sold Out. I just stood there a little stunned, and then took a photo of it, not realising that people were stand in front of part of it. My camera had a reel of film, so I couldn't check it until it arrived back from being developed. I had no way of knowing if it was a good shot or not.

There were a lot of people milling around the front of the theatre. A young teenager came up and asked if I would like to buy a program. He was pushy and not nice, so I refused to buy one. I was then approached by another teenager, who was polite. He asked if

I would like to buy a poster of Paul holding a guitar. I bought the poster. I went for a walk around the docks and the city, and decided to ring the lady who lived next-door to the share house in London. She had given me her telephone number and said that any time I wanted to get a message back to anyone in the share house that I could ring her and she would pass it on. Well, I rang her with a message that confused everyone, instead of easing their minds. I asked the neighbour to tell them that I was in Liverpool, that I was going to meet Paul McCartney, and that I would be home when I could. Apparently they decided I might have been kidnapped. They didn't know I knew the lady next door. Thinking that my message couldn't possibly be true, they decided they should call the police the next morning.

I eventually made my way back to The Punch and Judy coffee shop. I sat down, had a cuppa, and listened to the accents that surrounded me—everyone sounded like The Beatles. I was in the centre of their home city and I was busting with the excitement of being there. Years later I learned that The Punch and Judy was the coffee shop where they signed their contracts with their manager, Brian Epstein. At 7 pm I went outside and waited for Gary the detective to arrive, half expecting that he wouldn't come. Then I saw him, walking up the street towards me. Dusting off his trousers, he explained that he had been in an old dusty building as a part of his job.

He walked with me to the theatre and took me around the back, where there were hundreds of teenagers and a canary-yellow Rolls Royce. It was Paul's, and it looked huge. We stood on the footpath, and Gary raised his arm in the air. The policeman up against the wall of the theatre spotted us. Gary, together with the other policeman, yelled, 'Make way for the lady.' The crowd parted, like the Red Sea in the Bible. I was wearing a long, light-blue coat, and as Gary walked me through, I could hear comments such as, 'Who is she, anyway?' and, 'I don't know her!' It was a weird feeling, and I was thinking, *Who the heck am I? Nobody! This is amazing!*

We got in the door and Gary looked around, saying, 'Where is he?' On our left was a red telephone box. 'Oh! There he is, in the phone box.'

Shortly after, Paul walked out of the phone box and Gary introduced me. 'Paul, this is Jan, she's from Australia.' Paul stood there and looked surprised, then said, 'I can't believe this.'

I was too stunned to speak, but thought, *You can't believe this? No, that's my line!* Then he said, 'I've just come off the phone, I was talking to a Sydney radio station promoting our tour next year. I don't know when I spoke to an Australian last.' Gary reminded me that I had a poster. Unfortunately, he didn't think to remind me that my camera was hanging around my neck. I handed Paul the poster and asked him to sign it. 'Of course, I will. Which city in Australia are you from?' I said, 'Adelaide.' Paul signed his name and then wrote Adelaide underneath. There it was—his autograph, 11 years after I first asked him. Paul just stood there talking with me. I have no memory of what we talked about. As I stood there I glanced up and saw Linda, standing upstairs, quietly looking down at me. After a while Paul said he had to get ready to go on stage. I thanked him for the chat. He was so relaxed and friendly, and I felt relaxed too, even though I realise now how overwhelmed I must have been.

Gary then asked me if I would like to see the show. Of course, I said, 'Yes please', and he led me into the audience. He explained to me that there were no seats left, and that I would have to stand up the back. He said that he couldn't stand with me because he was there to work. Gary asked me if I could find my way home. I told him the train for London left at midnight, and that I would grab a cab to the station after the show. I sincerely thanked him for all he had done for me. I smiled, he smiled, and off he went. I took some pictures when the show started. Then, during the show, the band left the stage and Paul returned on his own, with a bright yellow three-legged stool and his guitar. He sat down, and the audience went quiet. Then he sang 'Yesterday.' Oh! It was absolutely wonderful. I just stood there staring and listening. I never thought to take a photo. Thoughts crept into my mind. I started to realise what had just happened—I just met Paul Mccartney, and there he is singing 'Yesterday!' I was wide awake but if felt like it was all an amazing dream. While he sat and sang, my thoughts turned to my yesterdays, in Adelaide with Elaine, at Adelaide Airport in 1964, and then the journey to Liverpool on the train just a few hours earlier.

Realising it was a million to one possibility, I suddenly thought, *This is it—I've been given a huge gift by God, the Universe, or my guardian angel.* One of them, or all of them, had made this materialise for me.

Paul finished the song, the band came back on, and the show went on. I started thinking that perhaps my life would end when I left the building, and that this was a parting gift. I started shaking uncontrollably. All of a sudden, there was Gary in front of me. 'What is the matter with you?' he said in an angry tone. 'I don't know', I said. Of course, he had met me in the company of a person in a questionable situation, so the way he reacted was quite understandable. With a very stern look on his handsome face, he then said in that lovely Liverpool accent of his, but filled with anger, 'You listen to me, when this show finishes you stand right here and don't you move, I'm coming to get you.'

'Yes, okay', I said in a very shaky voice.

He went back to his job as Paul McCartney's bodyguard, checking the audience. As I stood there shaking I thought, *This is it. I'm going to die.* I really believed that at that moment. I gradually stopped shaking, as I got lost in the wonderful music of Paul McCartney, with Linda playing the keyboard, and the rest of the band. It was a great show, and I'll always be grateful to Gary, wherever he is now.

The show ended and, as promised, there was Gary by my side, again with his stern voice. 'You've stopped shaking', he said. I explained that I had probably gone into shock. He told me that he would have to check the crowd, that I was to stay there and he would come back for me. I watched as the crowd gradually made their way to the exits, and looked at the now empty stage where Paul, Linda, and the band had woven their magic. The noise of the crowd gradually subsided and it became peacefully quiet.

As Gary finally walked towards me I could see he was still very angry at me. He took my arm, and as we walked to the exit I said, 'Gary, I don't think you realise what an amazing experience and gift you just gave me.' I sincerely thanked him again for making this wonderful experience materialise for me. He obviously realised that I must have been in shock.

He asked me if I would like to go to the police bar with him, and I told him I would like that. On arriving at the bar Gary bought me a drink. After chatting for a while he was satisfied that I was not on drugs and drove me to the train station. We were a bit early, so we sat chatting for a bit and then—yes—he kissed me! WOW! What a wonderful way to end my amazing visit to Liverpool. Just before the train arrived, Gary got out of the car to open my door. While he was walking around I noticed a 'Police' sign on the floor, so I put it up on the dashboard for him. When he opened my door he noticed the sign. 'Oh no! Was that up', he asked with a panicked voice, and was so relieved when I told him I had just put it up. What a wonderful, handsome, and caring man Gary was. Lots of people called Liverpool 'the ends of the earth' back then. But my description of my day in Liverpool was a magical, amazing experience with a hint of romance.

On the train ride back to London I sat quietly thinking, *Gosh, that kiss!* That little dog popping her cute head out of the bag had started a string of the events which materialised into a stunning day, to be treasured forever. I got a taxi to the share house. At 4 am I unlocked the door and walked in. Everyone was sound asleep, but I was wide awake. There I was, having experienced one of the most exciting days of my life, and I had no-one to tell my story to. Anyway, would they believe me? Oh, of course! I had the autographed poster of Paul.

I couldn't sleep. Morning eventually came, and I told my wonderful story, only to get the reaction, 'Well, we're glad you weren't kidnapped!' Then the very dramatic flat mate from New Zealand, who was training to be a lawyer, examined the signature, asked me questions, and decided that I really did meet Paul.

Thinking back to the time when Elaine Haines first introduced me to The Beatles in 1963, to meeting The Beatles, minus Ringo, at Adelaide Airport in 1964, and then my encounter with Paul McCartney in Liverpool in 1975, I smile, and am extremely grateful.

In the 1990's I was listening to the radio one morning, and heard that the Adelaide Beatles impersonators, a group called The Fab Four, were going to get on the rooftop of a building in Rundle Mall. They planned to re-enact The Beatles final rooftop performance in London in 1968.

I decided to go along, and see if anyone would be interested in seeing my photos from 1964. There was a truck, and a woman standing near the truck. I asked if she was connected to the group performing on the rooftop. She was, and so I showed her the photos.

'Oh!' she said, 'The guys would love to see these.' So she invited me up to where the group was having publicity shots taken. They were very busy, sitting on those big exercise balls, and smiling away as the photographers clicked their cameras. Then when the shoot was over the woman told the guys about my photos. They came over to have a look, and were absolutely amazed. It was a funny moment for me, because there I was showing these Beatles impersonators, dressed in full Sergeant Pepper costumes, photos of The Beatles. They were so excited to meet me and see the photos because I had met The Beatles, and each of those boys would have loved to have that same opportunity.

I was invited to stand up behind the band on top of an Adelaide building, while they played the same songs as The Beatles had sung on the London rooftop all those years before. I leaned forward at one stage, to steal a glimpse of the people below. As with the film from the real Beatles all those years ago, the people below were looking around and then up as they were walking through the mall.

As I never got to meet Ringo, when I heard he was coming to Adelaide to perform I contacted the ABC TV station and spoke to the producer of the *7.30* show and said that seeing I was there to welcome The Beatles minus Ringo in 1964, it would be great to welcome Ringo to Adelaide all these years later. The producer thought it was a great idea, and advised me to contact Michael Smyth on ABC Adelaide Radio. He interviewed me about Ringo and tried to follow up. He rang back to say that he was running into dead ends. He said he couldn't even find out what time Ringo was arriving in Adelaide. Apparently he was ushered out of Adelaide Airport the back way, to avoid the press.

I went to Ringo's show with my Beatle-loving friend, Jill Pownceby, and her husband, Jeff. Jill and I managed to get down the front. I quite enjoyed the show. I took some photos, but they were blurred. Before going to the show I wrote a letter to Ringo asking if I could meet him, to welcome him to Adelaide as I had welcomed John, George, and Paul in 1964. I took it to the back entrance of the theatre, and handed it to an official. A truly Beatlemaniac thing to do, but to no avail.

CHAPTER 8
Q Theatre

My love for acting and the Q Theatre started at an early age. In 1960, when I was ten years old, Mother, both my grandmas and I went to see 'My Fair Lady.' That first early experience stayed with me. It was like going to the movies, but when the curtains opened, instead of a screen there were real people playing the characters. There was action, beautiful backgrounds, beautiful costumes, music, songs, and a wonderful story. I was mesmerised. It felt like I was part of the story, and no-one around me existed at that moment in time. I had been magically transported into this wonderful experience, and it was absolutely amazing for me. Then the curtains closed and my reality returned. We clapped and clapped. Then it was time for us all to head home and back to our everyday lives.

The magic of theatre hit me again in 1962, when Mother took me to see a play at Australia Hall in Angas Street. In fact, it was the building adjacent to where The Arts Theatre was built in 1963.

This all came about because my mother was working for a catering company, Maynard Catering. The Maynards' son, Mervin, was acting in a play, along with his mate, Ian Rigney. I'd recently had major surgery to my right foot, and had a plaster from just above my toes right up to my thigh, which I had to keep on for three months. By this time, the pain had gone, it was very comfortable, and I was just left with an impressive white plaster that no-one could miss. After the amazing stage show had finished, Mother and I stayed seated, just waiting for the audience to leave. Unlike with the performance of 'My Fair Lady', the magic continued after the end of this play. Ian and Mervin came down to where Mother and I were sitting and carried me backstage, with Mother following. The magic of the stage turned to the magic of backstage. I met the people from the play, who had walked off stage and transformed from the characters into the actors who had played the parts. Wow! It was amazing for me—they were real people, and they were talking to me! They made me feel so special. I am so grateful to Mervin Maynard and Ian Rigney. After that, the theatre bug well and truly bit me.

In 1972, when I was 22 years old and in a rut, Mother realised that I was quite bored. She found out about an amateur theatre group that conducted a workshop for 'would be' actors. After a bus journey and quite a long walk, I arrived at the foyer door of the Q Theatre for the very first time.

Don and Betty Quin owned the repertory Q Theatre—commonly known as the Q. Betty Quin had worked in advertising and been a playwright before. She was short and slightly stooped. She wore no make-up and had straight brown-grey hair pulled back in a bun. I never thought she looked plain, because she was such a special and caring person. Betty was gentle and kind, one of the sweetest ladies I've ever met. She was a quiet achiever. She could act and was a great playwright—a very talented lady. After the Q, Betty wrote scripts for Australian TV dramas that were performed interstate. Betty had empathy and compassion for all.

Betty brought a professional actor's level of expectation into her theatre, even though the Q was for amateur plays. I remember my first day, walking through the side street entrance to the Q front foyer. There were rolled up carpets at the foyer's entrance which we all had to step over to get through the door, which had formed part of the set of the show that had closed the night before after its six-week run. The foyer was an absolute organised mess. We were all ushered in to the auditorium.

A chap called Barry Hill, who I was to learn was the musical director, spoke to us all about the Q workshop and asked us if we had any questions. Barry was a talented pianist and a lovely person, but at that point I felt overwhelmed, timid and wide-eyed. I sat there speechless and just listened.

My pleasant—but seemingly impossible—dream was to be an actress. I was trying to be realistic, though. I found out that I could be a part of the theatre community, and help out by selling programs. I became obsessed when I realised that if I sold programs I got in to see the show for nothing—what a deal! I sold programs four nights a week plus the Saturday matinee, and then sat in the front row, first seat to the right (no-one wanted to sit there) for each and every show. I watched intensely. I loved it. I always felt like a square peg in a round hole, though. It definitely wasn't anyone at the Q making me feel that way, it was entirely me feeling inferior.

I was a bit socially naive when it came to the live theatre way of life. Everyone called each other 'darling' in loud confident voices, and gave one another dramatic hugs. They truly were wonderful people, and always included me in their after-show parties. I couldn't comfortably call anyone 'darling' and never attempted to do so, for fear that I would not do it as well as they did. It has only been recently, in my late 60s, that I feel comfortable enough to call my Graham 'darling', and others that I feel a close connection with, but nowhere near with the gush of the theatre group.

As was the thing with going to after-show parties, if you went to the toilet there was the possibility someone might gossip about you. One night I'd had a couple of red wines and nothing much to eat. I had a great figure that I wish I had today. My outfit was the bright green jumpsuit with silver flecks all the way through the fabric that had been made especially for my 21st birthday. The jumpsuit had a zip right down the front, and a removable skirt, which, when added, made it into a pant suit. It also had three fiddly little buttons at the wrist, covered with the same fabric as the jumpsuit.

By this point in the evening, many people had already left, and I excused myself from the small group sitting and chatting, in order to go to the toilet. Thinking it wouldn't take long, I started to undress. Off came the skirt, and I hung it on the door handle. I then unzipped the jumpsuit, and started to take it off. I was quite tiddly, and not thinking, I undid the buttons on my right wrist with my left hand and pulled my arm out. I then realised that I couldn't use my mouth to undo the buttons on my left wrist, as I did with other outfits, as they were very small and fiddly. So now I was in a situation where my right hand didn't work and my left hand was stuck in the inside-out left sleeve. I couldn't go to the toilet, and I got the giggles so badly that I was scared I would wet my pants. I struggled to get back to being fully dressed. Eventually succeeding, I went back down the passage to the room where the small group was chatting. I then asked if someone would undo my buttons on my left wrist. I then left the room after saying a shy 'thank you', walked down the passage and repeated the whole process again. This time with success, but still giggling at the predicament I'd got myself into. I gave them plenty of time to chat about me that night, if they'd wanted to.

All of the workshop people were younger than me, and some had a lot of confidence. In the main theatre troupe was a group of girls who always made me feel included. I felt very comfortable in their presence. Many years later, at Betty Quin's funeral, someone told me that those girls were lesbians. I knew about homosexuals, because Mother had explained that to me, but I don't believe that Mother knew there was such as lesbians. It wouldn't have ever worried me if I had known. I think we all have the right to be who we are, but I was so naive. They must have realised that I had no idea about their sexuality, and I had a great time chatting and spending time with them.

One Saturday afternoon, during a matinee, I was in charge of front of house. The show was in progress and there was silence in the foyer. The props girl from backstage had a thing for the guy in the lighting box, and used to sneak up to the lighting box during the performance. It never worried me, until that day, when she stepped in the wrong place and fell through the ceiling into the foyer. Her fall was broken by a coffee table, and she didn't hurt herself. I felt sure I would be in trouble because I was in charge. I immediately called Betty Quin, who came straight in from home to assess the damage. Betty calmly said that she would sort it out, and to just leave everything to her. She was a one in a million lady.

One day Betty Quin saw me slouching on the front of house counter and said, 'Jan! Actresses don't slouch. Stand up tall.'

I belly laughed and said, 'Betty, I'll never be an actress!'

In a calm voice, she replied, 'You never know.'

It would be great, I thought, a dream come true. I realised it would stay a dream, because when I got nervous my right hand would spasm into a fist, my right leg would spasm, my toes would curl under, and having one leg shorter than the other, I limped. I had a lung disease as well. An actress, who, me?

I recently watched a documentary on a stage show with a cast of people with parabilities and thought of how lucky I was to have had the Q experience and Betty Quin in my life. These days, I see people with parabilities appearing on television, and think society is gradually, hopefully, starting to recognise our abilities and to look past the parts of us that 'loaf off.'

Of course, from the moment Betty told me to stand up straight and that actresses don't slouch, I made a conscience effort to stand tall to please her. One day, Betty came up and asked me to help her. I would have done anything for her. She needed someone to help her with a rehearsal, reading for a person who hadn't arrived. I was a terrible reader, but most of the words were not big, complicated words, so I could manage them. Cold reading was another matter altogether. I had to put my left pointer finger at the spot that I had just read and read ahead to quickly find my future line and check the words, and then get back to where my finger was to listen to where everyone else was up to, so that I could follow them. I would then read my line when it came to my turn, before repeating this process as fast as I could. There were words that I couldn't understand or pronounce, but once they told me the word, I'd have it. I didn't realise at the time that Betty was actually auditioning me.

Not long after, Betty said there was a part in a workshop show that needed a grandma to sit in a chair, not saying or doing anything, but just be present on stage. Without me realising, this was Betty's way to get me on stage. It was an amazing feeling, sitting in that chair for the first time. Sometime later I was told that Betty had written the part into the play especially for me.

After the workshop show, there was a major production called, 'For Art's Sake.' Betty asked me to audition for a minor part, and once again I said yes to that request.

I arrived for the audition, and took a seat in the auditorium, about six rows from the back. Others came and sat around that same area. A guy called Tom Clarke was there to audition as well. All the speaking parts were taken, and then came the casting for the none-speaking parts. The producer thought Tom and I looked good together, and cast us in the second act.

As the curtain came up for the second act, I was seated stage left, looking towards the audience, but not focusing on them. Tom entered from stage left. He was to come and get me, and together we would walk over and look at the artwork on display. We were always at the theatre from the start of the first act, and had nothing to do but talk until the second act, and then again until the curtain call. Tom was married and had a young daughter. He was very good-looking and I enjoyed our time chatting. The play ran for six weeks, and of course I fell in love with him.

I was 23 years old, and I wanted to wait until I got married before I had sex. I also didn't believe in dating a married man, and Tom was definitely married. We did spend time together around other people at the Q. To my mind that wasn't wrong. Tom would drive me to the after-show parties. I remember going to a party at the home of one of the actresses. She was a lovely lady, and happily married. When we arrived at her home it looked just like a normal middle-class Adelaide brick home. As we walked in through the front door we were amazed at what we were seeing. Everything was first-class antique. Everything! The hallway floor was highly polished wood and the lounge room where we were shown into had white carpet. It all looked magnificent. She was a great hostess, so relaxed, and told us to make ourselves comfortable. Fortunately, for Tom and me, there was only one seat left—so I sat on Tom's lap. We were given a drink, and I didn't know where to put it. Thinking I couldn't put it on the antique table I put it on the floor.

'Oh!' she said, 'The table is treated for stains, but our white carpet is not!'

Tom and I never crossed the line. It was hard work not to. Tom was adorable and a true gentleman, and I loved every minute we spent together. He was a photographer and I wanted some publicity photos taken. So he picked me up one afternoon and took me to a riverside spot to take the shots. It was so peaceful. Tom smoked, and I remember thinking, 'What style', as he leaned up against the tree, one leg bent, with his foot on the tree as he lit his cigarette. I had dressed up in a blue shirt and trousers. The photos were taken. The last time I saw Tom was when he came to deliver the photos. He wouldn't take any money for them.

Another workshop play I auditioned for was Jane Eyre. I went up for the part of Lady Lyn. Lady Lyn was a bossy older lady, and I had to burst onto the stage and yell at Jane Eyre. One particular night I was on stage and my parents were in the audience. When I burst onto the stage, a man sitting in front of my parents said to his wife, 'Isn't she a bitch!'

Immediately, my dear dad leaned forward and said to the man, 'That's my daughter.' I was delighted when Mother told me about the incident.

Another time, they were getting organised to do a workshop production on a play about Indigenous Americans. I was given the choice of playing one of a number of squaws or of taking a lead role. There were two lead male roles. One role had already been cast, and so I took up the other role, playing a man who became a chief in the closing scene. I bought a black wig and had a shirt made for me. In those days I was so slim and didn't have a bust to speak of, so it looked fine. I was on stage rehearsing, oblivious to the fact that Betty was sitting in the back of the theatre. I was told that Betty commented that the actor with the round neck shirt was doing well, and asked who he was, as she had not seen him before. She got a shock when she realised it was me!

I loved the workshops and worked very hard. After the Indigenous American workshop a major production was being planned, called 'Thunder', a play that was based on the Brontë family—Charlotte Brontë, her sisters, Anne and Emily, and her brother Bramwell.

Betty asked me to audition for the part of Emily. Another girl was auditioning for Emily as well. When I arrived for the audition I was handed a script a short time before the audition started. When it was my turn to read my part I was absolutely terrible, because I'd had no time to work out the words. I couldn't read the script properly and sounded like a sad child trying her best. It wasn't until years later that I found out that my reading level at the time was that of an eight-year-old child. I knew, of course, that the other girl who was also reading for the part of Emily was a brilliant reader. All of a sudden a voice boomed out from the back of the blacked out auditorium. 'Jan!'

'Is that you Betty?' I called into the darkness.

'Yes!' she answered sharply. 'When were you given that script?'

'Just before the reading,' I replied.

Betty walked up from the back, and was fuming. She told everyone that the auditions were cancelled and to come back the next evening. Then she turned to me and said, 'Jan, take the script, study it, and be here tomorrow for the audition.'

I told Betty that I would definitely do that. Once I got home, I put every minute I had into working on it. The next evening we were back at the theatre again. I read Emily's role and got the part. I felt for the other girl, because she was a lovely girl, but I think I looked the part. The Brontë family didn't get much food to eat in those days, and I was really skinny.

This was a very special moment, in that Betty Quin treated me as an equal in every respect. So many people these days seem to think they need to feel sorry for me, or have this silly attitude that I am not equal to them. I know all minority groups get treated that way, but it is such stupid behaviour. It was great in the 1970's, as most people I mixed with were far too interested in their own thing, and just let me get on with my life.

I was so very excited about playing Emily Brontë—it was a huge opportunity for me, and I remained very, very excited until I was handed the full script. Then my excitement turned to absolute horror. The script was huge, and the print was tiny! There were so many pages that the staples couldn't hold the entire script together, so it had been divided into two parts.

I went straight to the director, handed her the script and told her I couldn't possibly do it. She gave the script straight back to me, and told me that Betty Quin wanted me to play Emily. She told me that I would be Emily unless the time came when she felt I couldn't handle the role. Then she instructed me to study, study, study, and give it my best shot.

There I was, with the huge responsibility of bringing Emily to life on stage. I made my mind up to do my best, no matter how daunting it felt. The play had a cast of six actors in total, and 42 characters. In addition to playing Emily, I had six cameo-speaking roles as various characters from the Brontë sisters' books.

I got home and read very slowly through each page, stopping when I got to a word I didn't understand. I would try to work it out and, if I couldn't, I would ask someone and repeat the word over and over until I was able to remember it. I would then read on until I got stuck at the next word and so on. When I had done that, twice through, with the whole huge script, I moved on to the next stage.

I marked a red line under each person who was speaking before one of my lines, and then underscored all my lines in blue. After this came the hard part—studying my lines. I did it in blocks of several pages, overlapping each block with the next block. As a group, we went away for a study weekend. I was still so timid about the part, but we did a lot of talking over that weekend and it really helped me.

I had a fearful time in the first week of rehearsal. I had a hair appointment, and in a rare moment of spontaneity, probably because I felt so afraid of the play, when the hairdresser asked me what style I wanted I decided on an Afro perm. So I walked in to the hairdresser's with straight, shoulder-length hair and walked out with short, tightly curled hair. When I got outside I realised with horror what I had done. Emily Brontë didn't have an Afro hairdo!

We had started our six weeks of rehearsals, and I wore a cap to hide my hair. The director told me to take my hat off while rehearsing. I said, 'Before I take my hat off, I can undo this for the play.' By this time all the other actors and crew were looking at me. Most all of them were around 19 years old, and I got the feeling they saw me as very old and boring at my age of twenty-six. As I took off my hat there was stunned silence. The director finally broke the silence, saying that we must continue with rehearsals and she would deal with the issue of my hair later. Further research revealed that Emily had naturally curly hair, and so in the end I had the easiest hairstyle, as my perm grew out of the afro into looser curls by the opening night.

As I was working at Samuel C Richardson in the CBD at this time, I would drive to the West Terrace Cemetery each lunchtime and walk around, imagining the feeling Emily would have felt out on the moors all those years before. When I was acting, I tapped into the sense of isolation and peace that I imagined Emily would have felt on the moors.

When I was performing in other plays at the Q, I hadn't thought about my limp. I did what I was told—move to there, sit there, get up and walk over there, just as the other actors did. The Brontë play, however, was huge and I was suddenly conscious of my limp.

I was pretty sure Emily Brontë did not have a limp. I told Betty that I would get my shoe built up to stop my limping. I was told that I had never limped while I was on stage in character, only when I was off stage. I couldn't quite believe it. That sounded weird to me. I never tried not to limp—I just felt the character I was playing and got on with it. It became automatic in the end. My cameo parts were all done downstage right, some sitting reading poetry and some standing. The rest of the time I was walking around the stage. I walked confidently with no limp, and the lace cuffs on my blouse covered my clenched fist, so my parabilities were not visible to the audience.

We rehearsed for the six weeks, with full-dress rehearsals for the final week. On opening night I was so involved with my performance of bringing Emily to life that when the play finished and the audience of two hundred people clapped, I jumped with fright. The show went well for its run.

One night, a group of people from work came to watch. Of all nights, the pencil rolled off the little table to my right. I got a shock and looked at it, which was so wrong. To bend down and pick it up wasn't going to work, as my right hand didn't work. To swing around and pick it up with my left hand would have looked so wrong, so I just sat reading the poetry. Back at work the next day I was asked by Geoff Simms, one of the guys in the office, why I didn't just pick it up. I smiled. He had forgotten my hand didn't work.

During the run I only lost my words once on stage, and was saved by one of the cast. Earlier that day I'd had an argument at work with my boss, Vincent Jackson. Although I would never show my emotions in front of him, it had affected me after I left work. I let it get to me. I was so angry with myself for falling down on my line.

One of my cameo-speaking parts was quoting a poem. I enjoyed having a captive audience, with everyone quiet as a mouse as I delivered my words. One night, with the spotlight on me and a blacked out stage, I delivered a slower performance, just loving the moment. In notes from the director after the performance, I was asked not to do it again. I didn't.

A few months after *Thunder* had closed, we were asked to perform it again for the Adelaide Fringe Festival. The actress who had played Emily's sister, Charlotte, wasn't available, so Betty asked a good friend, Pam Western, if she could help out, and she agreed.

I was so excited meeting Pam Western. As a fan of a TV show called the 'Channel Niners', I had watched her many times. She was such a warm and friendly person. Pam treated us all as equals, but because I was a bit older than the others I felt closer to her. We spent time together. I have loved her since that special time. Rehearsing with a professional actress, I learnt so much from her. I will always be grateful to her. Not only was Pam an internationally successful professional actress, but also the recipient of two Logie Awards.

Pam had been trained as a method actor in Dublin, Ireland, in a professional theatre where she did many improvised sessions. Graciously, Pam worked with me, teaching me so much. On one occasion we spent a whole Saturday together at the theatre doing impromptu work, with her teaching me the principles of method acting.

I contacted Pam in 2019, all those years after working together on Thunder. I was so thrilled to be in touch with her again. It felt like time had stood still. Pam reminded me of our impromptu work together outside rehearsal hours. She said, 'I wanted our characters to be really believable as sisters. To have a closeness, due to a shared history.' In another part of her email she wrote 'In the play we really felt like sisters. There was more unplanned hand holding and touching on the shoulder. Things that close sisters would do.' I just remember the feeling of loving her as a sister. Pam said that she didn't remember I was para-abled until I told her why I was writing this book. She remembered me as a person who worked hard and was a good actor.

We were to perform six nights straight for the 1978 Adelaide

Fringe Festival. We had rehearsals for six weeks, and we all had a study weekend away together, which was wonderful.

The play opened, and I stood there as Emily Brontë, next to Pam, who was standing on stage as Charlotte, my character's sister. At the end of each night the audience clapped loudly. I loved that sound. We had good write-ups in the press. It was an absolutely fantastic experience!

A few times, after I walked off stage, I started shaking. I was to learn later it happened because I had come out of my character as Emily to return to myself too fast. I was at one with Emily, thanks to Pam Western's method-acting lessons.

Although I had been told that I didn't limp on stage, it really only came home to me one night after the play. We had joined the audience for champagne and a chicken supper. I had changed, and was going through the auditorium to the foyer. A lady, who had watched the play, congratulated me and asked me as I walked past her if I had hurt my leg. I said, 'Yes, I just bumped it', and that was that.

On New Year's Eve, the Q group had a fancy-dress party. As I love a party and dressing up, I decided to go as a hippy—the wig, the flowers in my hair, the bohemian clothes. Added to that, I wore full makeup—the works. This was the 1970's, when hippies were still a trend, but I went all out, transforming myself from the girl next-door image—which was the real me. I arrived at the party and knocked on the door, to be met with the words 'Sorry, this is a private party.'

As the door was closing on me I said, 'My name is Jan Gardner. Could you tell Betty Quin I'm here.'

I was finally allowed in, to comments of, 'Is that really Jan?' and 'Wow! Jan! I didn't recognise you!' It was a great party. My boyfriend and I ended up at the twenty-four-hour Pancake Kitchen in the early hours of the morning, and the looks I got made us laugh.

Betty had started an agency, which made it possible to get TV work. Of course, I was interested. Betty called me to go to an audition at the studio at Channel 7, for a pilot TV show called *Emergency Line*. For the audition there would be a panel of four professionals, including a doctor, a psychologist, and so on. I would be auditioning for a one-off appearance as a young unmarried mother, whose partner wouldn't provide any money to care for the baby.

I arrived at the audition early and sat in the waiting area full of other people. I had no preconceived ideas about whether I would succeed or not, and asked the girl sitting next to me what happened in the audition. She just told me that I would find out when I was called. After that, I sat quietly, waiting for my turn to go in, with no idea what was ahead of me. Finally, I was invited in and asked to sit down.

The interviewer, Thomas, sat in a big leather chair behind a big desk in a large office. All of a sudden he said, 'What is your problem?'

I sat there staring at him and then took a deep breath. As I took that breath I realised that he was expecting me to respond as the charater, so I looked at him and said what I remembered about the character description.

'I'm a single mum and I have a little baby. My boyfriend won't give me any money.'

He looked at me and asked what my boyfriend's name was. Wow! I hadn't thought of that. So I used the name of my current boyfriend, James. Then he asked me what my baby's name was. Again, I hadn't thought of that either. I just said the first girl's name that came into my head, Amy.

'Okay,' he nodded. 'Tuesday. Be here at the studio at seven in the morning for the makeup call.'

I just sat there glued to the seat staring at him. Then I said, 'Does that mean I have the job?'

With a bored voice, he said, 'Y-e-s, shut the door on the way out.'

Well, I was in shock!

I hate early mornings, but at seven o'clock the following

Tuesday I was there bright and early for my makeup call. After the makeup was done I was shown into the studio and seated in a comfortable lounge chair with a standard lamp behind me. It was to look as though I was talking on the phone at home. I had the phone to my ear, and out the corner of my eye I could see a panel of people sitting at a desk. Filming commenced. Everyone had their jobs—cameramen and other people were moving around, looking important. The panel people then asked their questions, just as I was expecting. It was really quite an enjoyable time.

When the show was aired on TV, I sat at home with Mother to watch it. Dad was at work, as it was an afternoon show. It was strange watching myself on TV. All I can remember is Mother telling me that I didn't look sad.

I had one other part as an extra for the same TV show. I was a hippy dressed in the outfit I wore to the Q Theatre's New Year's Eve party. I realise now that Thomas had hired me for my speech, my delivery, and for being able to think quickly.

I felt so very happy with my stage and TV work, and looked forward to future plays and possibly even to more parts in TV shows.

One day, while walking in the city, I met up with a woman called Julie Preston, who ran an acting school. She said that she was very impressed with the part I played in Thunder. I'd had good comments in the paper, so I took her words at face value. She asked me to have a meeting with her, so I did. I was made to feel special, and a video was taken of me doing different bits and pieces. She told me that I had a great face that the camera loved, and that I should do a course at her acting school. It was to cost $12, which I believe at that time could feed a family of four for a week. Julie told me that all the course participants would be helped to get work in the industry at the end of the course.

She also told me that while I was doing the course I was not to go to the Q Theatre at all, and I agreed. I believed that Julie had my best interests at heart. I did the course. I struggled with the time that we had to cry real tears. For the life of me I couldn't achieve those tears at all. After I sat down, I was so disappointed with myself that I started crying.

The course ended, and all the others had been given the opportunity to get work in the industry except me. So I rang Julie and said that the others had got work and I hadn't yet.

Her voice turned cold and said, 'You're crippled. Who the hell do you think you are?'

I checked up on Julie, and found out that she had never been to the Q Theatre. The reason she told me not to go to the Q Theatre while I was doing the course was because the people there would have warned me not to have anything to do with her.

After that, someone advised me that I should go to another agency and be proud of my achievements. I took a deep breath when I walked into the next agency, and behaved as though I was some well-known star. The people were lovely, but I blew the interview. After that, I was far too embarrassed to go back to the Q Theatre.

Some years after, I got a phone call to go back to the Q Theatre to be a part of a get-together function. However, my housemate had been involved in a car crash and had just got out of hospital, so I declined the offer.

In the early 1990's I heard that Betty Quin had passed away. I went to her funeral. It was so sad, but lovely to catch up with some of the Q gang again.

I will be eternally grateful to Betty Quin for her belief in me. She saw my passion, and her encouragement helped me to achieve what seemed to be an unreachable dream. She was able to stretch me way out of my comfort zone to achieve more than I thought possible. Betty, Pam, and Thomas at Channel 7, all believed in my abilities. To have that belief in someone with parabilities was uncommon in those days, and can still be uncommon these days.

I hope that in the 21st Century people with parabilities can be included for our abilities, our professionalism, and our passion, in every form of media and live entertainment, as well as all forms of business. I hope that Betty Quin, Pam Western, and Thomas at Channel 7, who helped me in the last century, will be followed by thousands upon thousands of people in prominent positions who give everyone respect, and the opportunity to show their strengths, wherever they are in the world.

The pathetic attitudes, held by people such as Julie Preston, which represent a mindset that belongs in the 18th Century, will, hopefully, disappear completely.

CHAPTER 9
Employment

When I returned from my overseas trip I wasn't quite as skinny as I had been before I left. The warm sea air on the voyage home had helped my lung, as well as all the walking I had done while I was in Europe. I felt and looked healthier, and enjoyed being at home again. Once I had settled back in I started to think about applying for a job. I talked about it with my parents. Although they were concerned about me losing my invalid pension, they also knew that I needed to advance my future.

At the government employment office I was offered two jobs. I wanted to apply for both and then decide, but I had to decide sight unseen. I took the second job that I was offered. It was really a 'sliding doors' moment. I often wondered what I would have experienced if I took the other job. The job I decided on was part-time and I made the incorrect assumption that it could become full-time.

On the 11th of February 1976 I arrived early at Samuel C Richardson, a distributor of electronic components. I was interviewed by the company's accountant. The hook for them was that they would receive part-payment of my wage for three months from the federal government. I got the job, and was introduced to my elderly work partner, Mr Redding, a short, grey-haired man with glasses and a stoop. He was quite deaf and seemed very old, like a grandpa, but as I was only 26 years of age, I may not have had an accurate view.

I saw the job as another dream come true. I'd always dreamt of getting a job with a desk and a swivel chair, and now I had exactly that! I gently sat down, and with the biggest smile on my face spun around in the chair, then leaned gently against the back rest. I was thrilled. Mr Redding then took me around the office to introduce me to the others.

I was now employed as a credit controller. My job was to ring companies who were overdue with their payments. I was trained for this work while on the job. Mr Redding had been there a long time, and taught me the role. I felt confident I could carry out my role well. There was also another smaller company connected to Samuel C Richardson, whose director was called Mr. Tim Smith. I was to handle a portion of the accounts for Samuel C Richardson and all of the accounts for Mr Smith's company.

I felt so isolated at first. All the other girls knew each other well. Gradually I was included, and they were lovely girls. Different girls would ask me to have lunch with them from time to time. The lunch hour always went too quickly.

Mr Redding was steady as you go with his work, but I was out to keep the job and also work my way off the invalid pension. I worked very hard. The harder I worked the grumpier he got. I think he was hoping I would leave, but I wasn't going anywhere. As time passed, I was told I had achieved getting more money in for the company than anyone else had. But the internal newsletter only ever praised the sales people's achievements. I wasn't ever mentioned. Tim Smith's only comment to me was that I should try harder.

I found it difficult to cope with Mr Redding's constant negative behaviour towards me. It wasn't at all easy. I went to the managing director, Mr Mark Davidson, and asked him if we could talk. He invited me in to his office. I told him that Mr Redding had become impossible to work for, but that I loved the work I was doing. Then I said either he goes or I will. Mr Davidson told me that he didn't want either of us to go. I asked that a manager in the company be put in charge. He asked me if I was sure that was what I wanted. I assured him it was. I was naive about the pros and cons. Mr. Davidson said that once the change was made it couldn't be reversed. He then said that Mr Vincent Jackson, the head of accounts, would be in charge. I had no idea that Mr Redding was actually my best option.

Vincent, a tall dark-haired man of medium build, took over and things started off okay. I was still doing well. However, I think Vincent wasn't thrilled about Mr Redding losing his independence, which was fair enough. They had both been there long before I arrived. Mr Redding no longer caused problems for me and I could get on with my work, but he had a lot of chats with Vincent.

I started to realise what Vincent was up to at Christmas time. There were two dates for Christmas leave. There was the choice of working up to Christmas Eve and coming back later in the New Year, or taking leave earlier and going back straight after the New Year. Over the years, I noticed that Vincent would always give me the opposite of the dates I requested, so I began asking for what I didn't want. It worked like a charm for a few years, until I got tiddly at a Christmas party, and revealed what I had been doing.

The company Christmas parties were fully paid for by management, and consisted of a free two-course meal and all that you could drink. I always felt uncomfortable, because the other girls wore beautiful dresses that I couldn't afford.

The year that I was 29 years old, one of the guys at work, Frank, asked me to the Christmas party. I really liked him, so I got a long, sleek, low-cut black dress, designed to impress him. I felt a million dollars. After the party, we were invited back to the beautiful home of the general manager, Randall Bennett, and his wife. I was a little tiddly and accidently spilt red wine on their beautiful white carpet. I felt absolutely terrible. I never asked him if it came out. I was scared to, in case he said no.

Frank and I left after a while and went back to his place. I always said I wouldn't lose my virginity until I turned 30, but that night, at 29 years old, my timeline changed. Back at work I got palpitations every time he appeared. Eventually, I realised that it was a one-night stand. I was devastated, but had to act normal. No-one picked up on the fact that there was anything wrong.

Vincent was never positive about my work, even though I was

doing well. He would have little digs at me. Some of it was fun and some was stinging. Sometimes it felt like he was flirting, but not in a serious way. When it was stinging, I really felt it. He was having a difficult time in his life, and I felt like I was getting the brunt of his anger.

After I had been with the company for a few years, Mr Redding left, and a man called Dennis Potter took his place. Dennis was a tall, slim man, who would have been good-looking in his younger days. He always asked unusual questions, such as, 'Why are you still single at your age?' Dennis was the only person in my life who asked me directly if I was a lesbian. Although we worked quite well together, I would change the subject when he asked questions.

I did make the occasional mistake registering a received cheque into the wrong account. I knew others had made the same mistake, and it was easy to fix. However, Vincent would storm down and yell at me in front of everyone as if I'd killed someone.

One day, Vincent stormed down to my desk and yelled that I had made a mistake entering a cheque. I went to lift the pages of the book to check what I had done. He slammed his fist on top of the pages, yelling, 'Don't you dare do that while I am talking to you.'

He was so loud. I sat and looked into his angry eyes until he had finished. After he'd gone I checked the entry. It happened on a day that I had been off sick, and Vincent had done my job—it was his handwriting. I lifted the huge entry book and carried it down to his office, which was in the main area. I didn't, at that stage, care who heard me. I said, 'Excuse me, Vincent, is this your handwriting?' He looked and confirmed that it was. I then explained to him that I was away that day, and it was his entry that was wrong. He didn't respond.

Vincent often had lollies on his desk. If he had grumped at me, when I next needed to go down to his office about work I'd casually say, 'Oh, you have another lolly there! Who is crawling to you today?'

I realised later there was a structure to the office environment. In this case, the managing director was Mister Nice Guy. The general manager, Randall Bennett, was the opposite, because he had to follow the managing director's orders and dish out the mean stuff. I had seen Mr Bennett walking past my section with his face as red as beetroot. I was informed he'd kicked the waste paper container clear across the large, open-plan section of the office in a fury on more than one occasion. Vincent, the head of the accounts department, seemed to get on well with the office staff. I was the only one I ever heard him yell at.

One day, my dear dad was in the city and decided to come and see me at work. As I was talking to him in the foyer, Vincent came down the stairs. I introduced him to Dad and they shook hands. Vincent was smiling but looked shocked. Later he said to me he was surprised. He said he had imagined my dad to be a short man with a slim build, but he was met with a six-foot man of solid build.

I inherited my strong personality from my dad. My loving, caring ways and communication skills came from both my parents. As for being disorganised—well, that was just me.

It came time for Samuel C Richardson to change and connect the business to the computer age. Vincent looked delighted when he came to me to say he was going to have to show me how to work the computer. My internal reaction was one of absolute horror.

I spoke to my best friend, Graham Cocks, telling him how scared I was. He offered to help me, as he was already using a computer at his work and also had one he used at home. He was wonderful. I would go over to his place and he would gently talk to me about the fact that a computer is just a machine, and when you know what to do it will feel easy. I gradually got over my horror of using a computer, as Graham taught me all I needed to know.

I hadn't said anything at work about Graham's help with the computer. One day, without warning, Vincent approached my desk and said to go with him to learn how to use the computer. I followed him and we sat down in front of the screen. He said, 'You press this button to start, then this button does this,' and so on, until eventually he said, 'Okay, you try.'

I proceeded by doing what he had said with internal confidence, quietly saying along the way, 'Is this right?' and, 'Is that right?' Stunned, Vincent replied, 'Yes.' He never once said, 'Well done!'

I enjoyed talking to the clients on the phone, and had a good response from them, with my positive attitude. Some would say, 'I have your cheque on my desk, I was waiting for your phone call.' They would like to have a short chat, and then the cheque would arrive the next day.

During one call, the client said they were looking for a credit controller and that they were impressed with my work. He asked me if I would be interested. I was very interested. He asked who my manager was and I told him.

A while after, Vincent appeared at the door and told me not to wait to hear back about the job. No call ever came back from the business who had been interested in hiring me. That was the end. I wasn't going anywhere. At one stage I went back to the employment agency, asking to get another job. I was told, 'You have a job, be grateful.'

I was constantly getting lung infections during winter, but unbeknownst to me my lung disease was silently becoming a bigger problem. The only noticeable effects were tiredness and a lot of coughing. I was not doing my postural draining at all, and I should have been doing it every day. Mornings were the hardest for me, as I would struggle to get to work on time. Vincent would sometimes be at the clock-in box, looking at me and then at his watch. He would constantly check my work, and would only ever be negative about it. I felt harassed. On the days when I arrived at work to find his car was not there, it was like a weight being taken off my shoulders. Yes, I had slowed down with my work since my early days with the company, but there was a reason for that. Inside my lung was a hidden trauma. If it was a visual trauma, such as a very deep cut on my arm, it would have caused a huge reaction.

I had a deal with the sales manager, Colin, who was a wonderful man. He worked with me to get goods to clients. If a company wanted goods, but owed too much money, I would phone them and try to come to an agreement that meant if they paid a reasonable amount of the money owing, they could have a reasonable amount of the goods on credit. It worked every time. I had wonderful communication with the people at the various companies we worked with.

Unfortunately, I made the great mistake of letting it be known that I had been working at the company for nine years. The managing director heard me, and decided to dismiss me before I reached the ten-year mark, as ten years of part-time work meant I would be entitled to long-service money. Things changed from then on. Vincent banned me from working with the sales manager. He had become more difficult. I wanted desperately to save my job, and started having nightmares about Vincent yelling at me and banging my desk. I would wake up in a fright and not be able to go back to sleep. The constant negative strain between us was taking its toll on me. My desire to do my best was starting to diminish to the point that I wasn't putting in as much effort as I should have. So I decided that I would do a communications course to try to work it out with Vincent.

One Friday afternoon I got a phone call from Vincent to come to his office, and not to bring my credit control book. I sat down in his office and he told me that the company was reorganising the credit department, and with a smile on his face told me that I was being dismissed with a minute's notice. I assume the minute's notice was their way of protecting themselves from anything I might say to the clients I spoke too.

I am sure Vincent was expecting me to stand up to him, yelling at him, and demanding to keep my job. Stunned, I just sat there. It felt and sounded like my head had suddenly been invaded by lots of noisy mosquitos, making my brain feel weird. I just sat there, staring into his brown eyes, unable to move. Then, gradually, the odd feeling in my head travelled through my body.

Suddenly, I could see Vincent was sliding a blank piece of paper over the desk to me announcing the fact that it would help me until I got back on the invalid pension. I was puzzled, and turned the paper over to see a cheque for $2,000. I just sat there, stunned, staring at the cheque. Time seemed to stand still. Quietly, I asked if I could go and thank the managing director, Mr Mark Davidson. He told me that I could, but it wouldn't make any difference. I quietly told him I understood.

As I walked passed the desk of the managing director's secretary, Joanna, I quietly said, 'I've just been fired.' She laughed, and I assured her that it was true and said that I had been given a minute's notice. I knocked on Mr Davidson's door, and was invited in. I thanked him for having me work for the firm and allowing me to work off my invalid pension. I asked if I could speak to the general manager, Mr Bennett, and was given permission. I gave a similar speech to him. By the time I got back to Joanna's desk she was furious. She stormed past me and started yelling at Mr Davidson for all to hear. Everyone in the office was stunned. I then went downstairs to my office and rang my friend, Graham. He said that it would take a while for him to get into the city, because he would have to catch two trains to get home from his office, so that he could pick up his car and make his way to my work place.

I had packed my personal belongings, and sat quietly in the foyer. I hadn't been emotional at all. I was in shock, but didn't realise it. Hannah, the switchboard girl and receptionist in the foyer, was very caring. Gradually, the staff came down to wish me good luck. Joanna asked how I was coping. She was so caring, and also informed me that she had told her boss what she thought of him. At the time I felt sorry for him, and fully blamed Vincent.

Joanna came down again later to ask if it would be possible for me to go to the local pub after work, as the staff would like to have farewell drinks with me. I said I would ask Graham what he thought when he arrived. Graham eventually arrived, and said it was fine with him for us to meet the others at the local pub for farewell drinks. Hannah, the receptionist, rang upstairs to let Joanna know we would meet them at the pub. Vincent came down the stairs after Graham's arrival. They shook hands and Graham said something to the effect of, 'Well, this is far from a pleasant situation.' I don't believe there was a reply.

We sat at the pub, waiting for everyone else to arrive. Graham was so supportive and caring. I was glad he was with me. At about 5:20 pm the staff started drifting in. We were so touched that they took the time to have a drink with us. Joanna and Hannah walked in with a huge arrangement of flowers for me—they were magnificent. Everyone seemed as stunned as I felt, as I had worked at the company for nine years. I was in the social club at work, and it was customary to give a parting gift to members of staff who belonged to the club. I asked Geoff Simms, who ran the club, if I could give a speech at the office presentation. He was happy for me to do that.

We eventually left the pub and headed to my parents' home. I wanted to tell them in person what had happened. Feeling numb, I spoke in a matter-of-fact way, explaining what had happened, and blaming Vincent.

They hugged me, and were so sad for me. They asked me to stay with them for a while, but I seemed to feel I was alright. Graham drove me to my flat and asked if I would like him to stay with me. I said no, and that I just wanted to sleep. He got a big vase out, filled it with water to put my magnificent flowers in, and sat it on my coffee table in the lounge room. He gave me a big hug and said goodnight. I sat down on my lounge chair and looked at the flowers. I must have gone into some sort of trance because I suddenly realised that sunlight was creeping silently into the room. I obviously hadn't moved all night.

On the following Wednesday, I drove back to give my speech at Samuel C. Richardson. It was a strange feeling, walking in. Hannah welcomed me. Joanne and Geoff Simms, the social club president, came down and gave me a hug, and then walked upstairs with me. Most of the other workers came into the office for my farewell.

I had written a speech of positiveness. I think they were all expecting some sort of a revenge speech. I thanked them all for their friendships, and I spoke of being able to have so many dreams come true. I had achieved a great deal in those nine years – renting my own flat, learning to drive, getting off the invalid pension, and having a desk with a swivel chair. I had really spent a lot of time thinking about that speech. They were all a bit stunned that I didn't mention Vincent at all. He was there listening. Geoff said that it was the best speech he had ever heard. I felt quite proud that I could leave with dignity.

In the years that followed, my nightmares about Vincent continued, but over time they became less frequent.

After a time of being lost in grief for my job, I was determined not to go back on the invalid pension. I had a good friend, Rob Walter, who used to live in a commune. I got on well with his friends, too. He worked in a government employment centre. I asked Graham to come with me to see if Rob could find a job for me. Rob got me an interview with a training business. The business was going to open a bookshop.

The interview went well. The interviewer had a phone call in the middle of it, from his son. It gave me time to think—*Until I've lost the interview, I have the job.* So when he got off the phone, I said, 'Do you know why you should employ me?'

The interviewer said, 'No.'

'You need me, that's why,' I replied.

He thanked me and told me that he would let me know. I was convinced that I'd lost that one, until I got a phone call to say that I'd got the job. I was told that I got the job because of my outburst. He said it meant that I had confidence in myself.

That job was medicine to my soul. My boss, Edward Green, was such a sweet, encouraging man, and the committee was a lovely group of people who had kind hearts. I had an office bigger than the office of my former boss, Vincent, on the ground floor of a multipurpose building. My self-esteem had been battered to pieces, but here, I was starting afresh, with a new, wonderful boss. Sadly, though, I never felt fully confident in the role—I felt that my work was not good enough, and so I worked longer than my paid hours in order to make up for it.

Graham proposed to me on his birthday—the 4th of October 1984—and the following year, on the 9th of March, we were married. My new boss, Edward came to our wedding with his wife. He took photos, which I borrowed and forgot to give back. I still have them, but I am unable to locate him. Disorganised me! I returned to work after the honeymoon.

***

Some enchanted evening—it was actually the 2nd of October 1998, 14 years after I had left Samuel C Richardson, I stood in a crowded room at the company reunion. I asked somebody if Vincent was there, but nobody had seen him. It was a wonderful night. I hadn't seen most of the people I spent nine years working with since my farewell speech back in 1984, after Vincent had given me the minute's notice. I still remember so clearly every moment of that sacking.

Once the reunion was in full swing, I felt a tug on my skirt and a voice said, 'He's here.'

My heart throbbed. I wanted to run to Graham, I felt so scared. It was silly—I had absolutely no need to be scared, but I felt safe when I reached Graham's side. My eyes scanned the crowd. Vincent was on the far side of the room. I stood motionless, then suddenly his eyes met mine. He smiled broadly. A smile crept over my face, my hand raised, and my fingers waved in response to his greeting.

I stood with Graham, chatting in the crowded room full of people I knew. I turned around to the food counter to find Vincent on the other side. He smiled and came around and gave me a greeting kiss on the cheek. He remembered Graham and we chatted away. It was all fine, of course.

I had questions to ask about my working days, but I had heard that Vincent's house in Melbourne had burnt down in the bush fires, and so I thought I would ask about that. Vincent said that he and his family had got out with just the clothes they were wearing and one car packed with items from the house. He talked of how it had always been important for him to have the best of everything, but since the fire he had changed his priorities in life. I found that all my anger had gone. I wanted desperately to have a quiet chat with him, and Vincent agreed to have a chat before he left.

He came and found me later in the evening, and we sat down together. With a big smile on his face, Vincent told me that he admired me for all I had achieved in those years that I worked at Samuel C Richardson. I had wanted him to know that I suffered five years of nightmares and went through years of hating him, but I didn't say any of that. I am so glad that I didn't. I realised that his home burning down had been a soul-changing experience. He was different, and so was I.

After that reunion night the nightmares stopped. I still had the occasional dreams about work and Vincent, but he was talking with me in those dreams. The nightmares never returned.

There was another reunion in 2013 that I was invited to. Again, it was wonderful catching up with some of the people I used to work with. There were some who hadn't come, including Vincent. The general manager, Mr Randall Bennett, was not at all happy to see me there, and I was told later that he had made the comment that I should never have been invited because I had been fired.

That is when the truth became reality. It was him, not Vincent, who had given the instruction that I be fired.

CHAPTER 10
Marriage

In 1979 I joined a singles group called 'Solitaire.' We met at Maughan Uniting Church, in Franklin Street. I'd been bridesmaid to two of my friends, and had started feeling that I was never going to be the bride. Time was moving on. I was now 29 years old, and all my friends were married. My dream of being married and becoming a mum felt like it was dimming, but I still had faith in my lucky coin.

When I was in Rome in 1975, my tour bus stopped at the Trevi Fountain. Forty-five passengers tumbled out to make our wishes. However, there were men with their trousers rolled up, collecting the coins for charity. I asked our driver if we could come back when the men had gone, so it would look romantic, like in the movie.

The driver said, 'You can stay and wait, and then meet us in the next country, or just throw your coin in now. It's your choice.'

I turned around and threw the coin over my shoulder into the world-famous fountain. My wish was for a wonderful caring man to come into my life, and that we would fall in love. Also, if I loved anyone enough to marry them, then my wish was to have a son just like him.

I got very involved in the Solitaire group, and was having a good time. The group was full of all sorts of people from different backgrounds. I found myself taking the role of a counsellor to many of the other members, without even trying. I was friendly, relaxed, and always had time for a chat with anyone. Gradually, people in the group were coming to me and telling me their heart-wrenching problems. I was a good listener, and their problems made my life seem easy by comparison.

One day I was in the church by myself, just sitting quietly. I wanted to meet a special man. By this time it was 1980, I was 30 years old, and my coin hadn't worked. Most of the men I was meeting socially were either divorced or married. I sat and concentrated on what I wanted in a man I would fall in love with. I wanted him to be loving and caring, single—but not divorced—to have a belief in God without being fanatical, respectful of other people's faiths, with a good job, and to be a good friend.

A couple of weeks after that quiet thinking time in the church, a new chap called Graham came to one of the Solitaire meetings. I was having a difference of opinion with one of the ministers who was involved with our group. I was speaking up loud and clear, explaining my point of view. I felt very comfortable with the group, and so the new guy didn't bother me. After the meeting we all went to a coffee lounge for a cuppa, and the new guy came with us. I sat next to him. We started chatting. He had lovely brown eyes and a great smile. We decided to exchange phone numbers to meet up for a coffee. Graham was of the Catholic faith, and they had a singles group too. That night they were not meeting, so he thought he would come to our group to see what we were doing.

We became coffee friends, and I enjoyed the time we spent together. He was a serious type of guy, but very easy to talk with. He was very polite and caring, had a good job, and believed in God. Time went on, and Graham and I became friends—not boyfriend and girlfriend, but best friends. There was no thought at all of him being my Mr Right or anything close to that in my mind. I was dating other guys and introducing them to my best friend, Graham. I would ask him what he thought of them and he never liked any of them, which stunned me, really.

One day Graham said to me that he had looked at our star signs and we were compatible, as I was an Aquarius and he was a Libra. I laughed and said, 'Of course we're compatible, we're best friends!'

After this, my insecurities started to creep into play. I couldn't do the three-month out-the-door thing because he was my best friend, not my boyfriend—but I felt that he wanted to be more than just friends. Even though he wasn't my boyfriend, I spent one lunchtime sitting in a work friend's car discussing how I could gently part ways with Graham, but we couldn't think of anything gentle enough.

At the same time, there was a lovely French couple living upstairs from my flat and they had met Graham. They both told me that we were made for each other and we should be able to see that. I smiled and said, 'You don't marry your best friend.' They looked at each other and then looked at me blankly.

In 1982 I decided that I wanted to have my tea leaves read. I found a European woman called Mrs Downing to read them. I was careful not to tell her anything about my life, as I was sceptical about her ability. She talked a lot about her son while we had a cuppa. As I looked around the room it was obvious she was a very religious person. Then, holding my cup, she told me that my grandma was watching over me. I had passed Centennial Park Cemetery on the way, where grandma's ashes were, and, as always, I'd call out, 'Hi Grandma!' Mrs Downing then described the front door of my flat and the view that I could see. Well! That got my interest. She was completely accurate! She then proceeded to tell me that I was going out with two men, one was from Adelaide and the other was from Queensland. I have no idea how, but she was completely right again. By this time I was sitting on the edge of my seat. She then told me that these men were no good for me, but it was okay because a third man in my life was the right one. I sat back on my chair and said that there wasn't anyone else. She wouldn't accept that and got so cross with me, saying that this person had dark hair and that he occasionally visited me, perhaps to have coffee. Then Mrs Downing said that it didn't matter, as I would figure it out sometime and that she saw wedding bells and great happiness. She said that I would be okay financially, but not great—and much, much later in life when I was a lot older I would be very rich.

It didn't enter my head at all that it was Graham she was referring to. My life went on as normal with Graham as my best friend. We would go out for an occasional dinner together, or he would come over for coffee and a chat.

I put the tea-leaf reading out of my head and focused on work. I hadn't seen Graham for a while when he knocked on my door out of the blue one afternoon. He walked in quietly. As I went to put the kettle on for a cuppa, Graham threw a letter on the table.

'What's that?' I asked.

'Read it!' he replied. I inquired as to the contents of the letter, hoping not to have to struggle with unfamiliar handwriting. But Graham repeated the words, 'Read it!'

'What, now?' I asked. He just nodded in response. I stopped what I was doing, sat down at my little three-seater table, and started reading the letter. It was written in December 1983.

> *Dear Mr Cocks,*
>
> *I have been searching for my younger brother, and perhaps you could be the one I seek.*
>
> *If you are interested in helping me solve my problem, would you contact me and let me know whether I am on the right track or not.*
>
> *Even if my assumptions are correct and you do not want to follow up, I would still prefer a negative answer rather than be left wondering.*
>
> *Hope to hear from you soon,*
>
> *Yours truly,*
>
> *Merle.*

I already knew that Graham had been fostered by two wonderful ladies in Victor Harbor, a seaside town about an hour's drive from Adelaide. They had told him that they believed his parents had died in a car accident and that he had no siblings. Those dear ladies had fostered him when he was just two years old. The ladies fostered four other boys of varying ages, all at the same time, as it was just after the war. Graham was the last to join the family, and they loved and cared for him. They cared for him so much that he was able to attend a well-respected boarding college in Adelaide. He appreciated their love and care so greatly that he changed his name by deed poll to one of the ladies' family names.

I stopped reading, swung my head around to Graham and said, 'But you were an only child and your parents were killed in a car accident.'

'That is what my foster ladies were led to believe,' he replied. He then told me that he had contacted Merle and said that he thought she had it wrong, until Merle mentioned one detail about what name would be on his birth certificate—no-one knew, not even me. He had kept that to himself, in case a situation like this ever arose.

Graham learned from Merle that he had six siblings and a dad, all living in Adelaide. His mother had died when he was two, and his father could not look after so many kids on his own.

I asked him if he had met them, and Graham said he had visited them all and they were nice people, but he couldn't understand what they wanted with him. I said, 'You are their brother. They want you back into their family!'

Graham told me that his siblings said that there were some family secrets and that he must ask his eldest brother, Lewis, for the details about them. When he caught up with Lewis, Graham was told that his mother, Gladys, was part Aboriginal and that his father, Miamo Salvemini, was of Italian heritage. Miamo's parents came from Molfetta, in Italy.

I finally made us that cuppa with a plate of biscuits, and we talked it through. It was a huge shock for Graham, as he had believed all his life that he had no living relatives. He had now discovered that he'd been taken from his very sick but loving mother at six months of age and put into care. When his mother died in 1944 he was just over two years of age, and then the foster family arrangements were made. I really wished that I had met the two ladies. Both Graham and I wished I had met his mum.

It was around this time that I was having trouble with my boss, Vincent, at Samuel C Richardson. I was advised to do a communications course. On week three of the course the tutor gave us a homework project. The project was to go to someone we knew really well and ask them ten questions that we had never been game enough to ask before.

It was a Saturday night. I was all dressed up to go on a date but I had been stood up. So I called Graham. He was home, and I told him about the questions for my communications course homework. We agreed that I would drive to his unit, have a cuppa, and then do the ten questions. I sat down at my table, worked out the ten questions, and wrote them down.

There we were, in his lounge room, me nervously holding the piece of paper with the quite personal questions. The tutor had explained the reason for the exercise. When we are not game enough to ask a person a question, we subconsciously make up a story in our own mind to fill in the answer. We then take that imaginary answer and perceive the person as though our made up answer was the truth.

I started gingerly with the first question and worked my way through the list. Graham quietly answered each question with a genuine reply. His answers showed his dedication and love for the ladies who brought him up, his love for his 'Auntie' Katie, and his love and care for his foster sister and her young sons. I was stunned by this side of Graham that I had never known. By question nine I just sat there quietly. He asked me if I was okay. I simply said that I was totally in love with him. I realised that my subconscious had been clouding my opinion of this amazing man.

Graham was shocked, I think, and said, 'Well, it is my turn now to ask you questions!' I was horrified when he asked me why I was having affairs with the guys I introduced to him. He said, 'You're not that type of girl.' I explained that I was a virgin until I was 29 years of age and I just wanted to be loved. Being a 'goody two shoes' wasn't helping me find Mr Right. I was a virgin until the year before we had met.

We then started dating. It was July 1984. Three months later, on the 4th of October, we went out together to celebrate Graham's birthday. He was acting strangely grumpy and I couldn't understand his behaviour. I asked him if he was okay and that made it worse. I didn't really enjoy the evening and we decided to leave. We had a cuppa back at his place and he wasn't acting much better.

I said I'd better go.

The next thing I heard was, 'Will you marry me?'

I immediately said, 'Yes', as I fell into his arms. We just kissed and held each other for a long time. I rang my parents and asked if we could go over to their home. We went and told them, and there was great excitement.

The story then came to light of how the separation of Graham and his family took place.

***

Lewis O'Brien, the eldest brother of the seven siblings, told Graham the family story. Their father was away working and their mother, Gladys, ended up in hospital. The two eldest brothers, Lewis and Doug, who had about 15 months' age gap between them, were in their early teens by then. Their mother had told them to look after the younger children and not to tell anyone that she was in hospital. Gladys didn't tell the hospital that she had children left at home alone because she was so very scared of the children being taken away from them. In Australia at that time, the fact that she was part Aboriginal meant that the children would be taken from her—now known as the 'stolen generation.' The two eldest boys did their best. Rosemary, the eldest girl, who was eight years old at the time, cared for six-month old Graham. He was her 'living doll' and she cuddled him and changed his nappies because she had watched her mother do it. The eldest boys fed them with what they knew—Weet-Bix and milk or Arrowroot biscuits and milk, for breakfast, lunch, and dinner. Graham was given bottles of milk. To this day, Graham's breakfast is Weet-Bix and milk.

One of the neighbours told the authorities about the children being on their own a lot. There was a knock at the door one day—it was a woman from the authorities. She checked through the house and decided that the children should be taken away. The woman came back with some other officials. All the children were taken into care, but the older children were kept separate from Graham. Graham's sister, Pam, told me she was told to distract Rosemary, not realising they were taking Graham away.

It is impossible to comprehend how the experience would have felt for them all, and the trauma of that event. The next time Rosemary and her siblings would see Rosemary's living doll again was 40 years later.

Over the years, Graham's dad Miamo tried to find him, but the authorities wouldn't allow any contact. In 1983, while researching the family history, Merle realised that Graham's surname must have been changed. The only way that she could possibly find out was to go to the Children's Welfare and Public Relief Department (now Families SA).

Merle told me that it was an interesting situation. Initially, they refused to tell her. She told them that she was prepared to sit there until they gave her his current surname. The official went off to seek advice. After a long wait she decided to give up and was going to leave, but found she couldn't move. She said it was the strangest feeling, as though she was magically glued to the seat. So she just sat there. Shortly after, the official returned. They had agreed to give her Graham's current surname. Merle then went through the phone book, found him, and sent a letter to the address that was listed with his phone number.

A short while after I had read Merle's letter, in April of 1984, a gathering was organised at the home of Rosemary and her husband, Des. This was just six months before our engagement. Graham's brothers and sisters were there, along with their husbands and wives—only one brother was unable to attend. They all got to meet me, and got to know Graham better. It was a fabulous night and I felt instantly comfortable with them all. We did a lot of chatting and laughing.

A couple of the girls and I were in the kitchen together and they wanted to know what I thought about Graham having Aboriginal blood. I told them that I was thrilled, as Aboriginal people are very special and very clever people in many ways. I learnt that Graham's great-great grandmother, Kudnarto, was the first Aboriginal woman to legally marry a white man in South Australia. She had to get permission from the Governor to marry. The authorities insisted that she must learn to read and write, and also do a course in housekeeping—all of which she willingly did. Her husband was a goat herder and was illiterate himself. After they got married she taught him how to read and write, and also taught their children.

Graham's eldest brother, Lewis O'Brien, is very highly respected in South Australia as an Aboriginal Elder. From an early age he loved reading, and a friend told him that there was a building he could visit to read and borrow books. Lewis found out it was called a library. So he went along and was stunned to discover there were hundreds of books. Lewis started reading, and one by one he read all the books on subjects that interested him. We believe he has a photographic memory, as he has so much knowledge and can talk with authority on so many topics. This was the State Library of South Australia. It now has a greeting stone by Lewis at the entrance, to welcome visitors. Lewis has a lot of community involvement. He received a doctorate from Flinders University in 2011, and was awarded The Order of Australia in 2014. Lewis has also published his memoirs, *And The Clock Struck Thirteen*.

Graham was awarded an Australia Day Medal for Achievement in 1999, for his continuous and dedicated work in the Defence Science and Technology Organisation. I am so very proud of Graham, and thrilled he was recognised.

***

Graham had two mates—Luke and Bruce. They were his only mates when we met. Luke was Irish, with a strong Irish accent. He could be described as a wild child, and still had some of that wildness in his adult life. Bruce, on the other hand, was a polished speaker, and shrewd and private in nature. When Graham and I were just coffee friends these two were okay with that arrangement. As Graham and I grew closer and fell in love, they still thought we were coffee friends. I thought it was great—the three amigos, true mates. Bruce was in a relationship and Luke was married to Pam, with a young son, Sean. Graham said he wanted us to let his mates continue to think we were just coffee friends. I couldn't understand it but agreed to follow his lead, as they were his mates.

One Saturday night we had been out and I slept over at Graham's unit. On the Sunday morning there was a knock at the door. Graham answered, and in walked Luke and Bruce. I walked out looking dishevelled with my hair a mess, dressed in the good clothes I had been wearing the night before. Both the guys were shocked. Graham explained that we were now engaged, which further shocked them both. From then on, both Luke and Bruce made it very clear that neither of them approved of me.

Mother and Dad were absolutely delighted with my engagement. This had been a dream for me—to find a good, reliable, and very caring man that I could love and feel loved by. It was also my parents' wish for me to find a man to love—and this wish had come true for them too. They had got to know Graham very well and felt secure in the fact that their little girl would have a happily married life.

I had heard of many people who had troublesome times with their in-laws. I was quietly relieved that we would not have the same problems. I totally underestimated the behaviour of Graham's two mates. It became obvious that his mates were both happy in their own relationships, but did not respect Graham's choice of lady.

If one of the guys rang and Graham asked me to answer his phone I would be met with, 'Hello, can I speak to Graham', in a tone that one would use with strangers. I would respond with, 'I am Graham's secretary, one moment please', in a put-on posh voice. Graham would get asked, 'What is wrong with her?' I had reacted as a child would, by bringing myself down to their level.

Mother and Dad held a wonderful engagement party in the big back garden of my childhood home. There was a good turnout of my relatives and friends. Graham's new-found family came, except his brother Peter who had hearing difficulties. It was the first time my parents had met Graham's new family. They warmly welcomed them, and got along very well with them.

The wedding plans were coming along on schedule. Mother showed me some material and suggested it for the bridal party girls to wear. The colour was a soft apricot, and I agreed it was perfect. We bought my wedding dress from the woman who lived next-door to me in the flats—it cost $60. It was beautiful, and I was very grateful, as I couldn't afford anything more expensive. A dressmaker altered it to fit me. She said that it would have cost over $1,000 dollars if I had bought it new. Mother and Dad sorted the seating arrangements, after asking our advice.

Luke and Bruce's behaviour was difficult for me. I should have talked to them and tried to sort it out with them, but that didn't happen, unfortunately. I was scared that the situation might get worse. They were important mates to Graham, and were both asked to be a part of our wedding party. Bruce was the best man, and Luke was the groomsman. My closest school friend, Di Harvey, was my matron of honour, and Tanya Middleton was my bridesmaid. Tanya and I also had a close friendship and often went out socially together. We both had flats in the same complex and had shared many experiences. There was a couple downstairs from me, and when I held a party they came up and asked us to stop all noise as they were meditating. Tanya and I thought that was hilarious.

At one party I held, a guy brought illegal drugs into my apartment. We found him and threw him out of the flats—Tanya is ten years younger than me, and I needed to protect her and her friends. Tanya and I also hit the discos together, and had many great discussions about boyfriends and life in general. Vikki, the daughter of my other school girlfriend, Christine, was our flower girl. Graham had his dear 'Auntie' Katie as his mum for the day, and she partnered with Graham's dad. Unfortunately, his dad was starting to get dementia, but he did very well on the day.

It came time to arrange the hire of the men's wedding suits. As is tradition, the bride suggests the colour to complement the bridesmaid's outfits. On advice from the girls, I had decided that two-tone grey suits would fit perfectly with the girl's dresses. I understood that tradition dictated that the groom didn't see the dresses until the wedding day. Luke and Bruce had other ideas. They demanded that I should not choose what colour suits they wore, and insisted on seeing my wedding dress and the bridesmaid's dresses before the wedding. Poor Graham was caught in the middle. This wasn't their wedding—it was ours. I insisted on tradition. It stressed me out so much. The guys were acting like nightmare in-laws, being so direct with their dislike for me.

There was more. Bruce, an excellent speaker, kept saying over and over, 'You wait until you hear my speech', with a devilish laugh.

It was said so many times that I became extremely frightened of him delivering a speech at our wedding. All the stress was taking its toll on me. My lung was playing up and I was so scared of a lung infection as we got closer to the wedding day. Even at the wedding rehearsal night Bruce was taunting me about his speech. We needed support from both men, and we weren't getting it. They were a main part of our wedding party. If I said anything to Bruce he would have told me he was joking. But I had known him for long enough to be quite aware that he wasn't.

On the eve of our wedding day I went back to my childhood home to be with my parents. Unfortunately, I was so worried and stressed I spent most of my time in my room.

Early that evening, on the eve of our wedding, Graham's mate Luke demanded from Graham to know where his wife and child would be sitting at the reception. We had placed them at a table with people we knew they would feel comfortable with and would enjoy talking to. Luke wanted Graham to ring me and say that they must sit at the wedding table, or where Luke could see them. Graham rang me, so that I could ask my parents. I was furious and said that they were sitting where they had been placed, and seating would not be changed at this late stage, then I hung up on Graham.

I told my parents what had happened and went back into my room. I hadn't thought how worried it would make my parents feel. Not because everything was ready for the church service and the reception, but because I had always been the runaway girlfriend. I was now 35 years old, and I think they were scared I would stop the wedding. It should have been a lovely time for the three of us, but it was totally ruined.

About 11 pm Mother gingerly knocked on my door, came in, and quietly said, 'Do you think it might be a good idea to ring Graham?'

I smiled and agreed. When I rang Graham he told me that he'd told his mates that if they created any more problems it was not necessary for them to be at the wedding. We talked for a while before saying goodnight. I told my parents, and the relief on their faces was obvious. It was a testament to our strength and love for each other. The guys' bad behaviour didn't part us, but brought us closer together.

The next morning, I had my hairdresser's appointment after my bridesmaids came over to help me dress. Mother, Dad, and I had photos taken in our back garden, and Tammy and Tabatha—our corgi-cross dogs—got in on the act.

It was an 11 am wedding, and the forecast temperature for the day was a hot thirty-six degrees Celsius. I think my dad was worried that Graham might not wait if I got to the church late. He insisted on setting off very early. I tried to tell him it was too early, but he had made his mind up. When we arrived at the church we were so early that Bruce ran out to our car and told us to drive off, because Graham was having a soft drink at the pub with Luke, and the ministers hadn't arrived. Dad had no intention of driving off—we weren't going anywhere. He demanded that the car stop. The bridesmaids arrived and came to help me out of the car. We then walked to the undercover entrance of the church and just waited and waited. It was actually a very precious time for Dad and me as we stood there, together with my bridesmaids and flower girl. We were chatting, photos were being taken, and people were walking in from the street to compliment me and wish us much happiness.

On the 9th March 1985 I married the love of my life. We stood at the steps to the altar with my Uniting Church minister, Reverend Ivor Bailey, and a Catholic priest, Father Oliver O'Brien. Reverend Bailey and Father O'Brien shared the wedding celebrant duties. My other Uniting Church minister, Reverend Phil Carr, played our song, 'The Twelfth of Never' on the grand piano during the signing of the marriage certificate.

Ivor had previously asked me what I wanted the sermon to be about, and I just said love. We were both standing there, flanked by the bridesmaids, flower girl, best man, and groomsman. Ivor started talking about the fact that we were standing there in front of him because we thought we were in love. I was shocked. I was staring into

Ivor's eyes wondering what was coming next. I could hear Graham's mate, Luke, trying to control a giggle. Ivor went on to explain that the process of our wedding day wasn't anything to do with what love is. He said that love was when there are dishes in the sink and you are so tired—love is doing the dishes. He went on to explain love in a marriage. It was such a special sermon. Father O'Brien read the special verse from Corinthians 13:4-8 'Love is patient, love is kind.'

Photos were taken on the lawns at the wedding reception venue. It was a hot day! My wedding gown had long sleeves, but when I was asked if I was too hot I suddenly realised I wasn't feeling anything but comfortable. The wedding reception was such an enjoyable celebration of our love for each other.

The MC came over to Graham and me, and said that he had a problem that needed to be sorted. He went on to ask us who he should approach to say grace before the meal—the priest or the minister. We suggested that he should ask them to decide. The MC got everyone's attention before the meal and asked Reverend Ivor Bailey to say grace, and Father O'Brien stood up and said the grace. It was their joke, and we smiled. Person after person approached us during the meal, saying they were confused over which one was the priest and which one was the minister.

My Graham made a wonderful speech, which included his three families. The wonderful ladies who fostered and loved him were represented by his 'Auntie' Katie whom we loved dearly and who was his mum for the day, and his birth family, who had found him and whom we love—his birth brothers and sisters were present with their partners—how wonderful it was to have them with us. Finally, he spoke of his new family, my wonderful and beloved parents, and thanked them for welcoming him into our family.

Bruce gave a wonderful, well-written and well-presented speech with great depth of feeling, which I was relieved to hear. Luke's speech was a brief thank you to my parents, and then he read the telegram messages. My dad gave an emotional speech about my start in life, my hurdles, and how thankful he was that I had met Graham. He got a little choked up and sat down. Finally, Mother's brother, my Uncle Keith, gave a speech to welcome Graham to the family.

We danced our first dance to 'Moon River', sung by Andy Williams—my favourite. Mother and Dad came over, and the four of us hugged and danced together.

When it had all ended I didn't want to get out of my wedding gown. I just stood in front of my full-length mirror, smiling and feeling wonderful.

Our bags were packed, and off to the airport we went. Many came to farewell us off for our honeymoon, on the six o'clock flight to picturesque Kangaroo Island. As we sat in the small passenger plane, we watched the sun set over the Gulf of St Vincent on our special, memorable, and enjoyable wedding day.

***

We arrived at Linnetts Island Club Resort at American River, and settled into our accommodation. We went into the dining room, where we were introduced to all the other guests as the honeymoon couple, and were met with cheers and claps. The dining room was lovely, with candles glowing on all the tables. We stayed for a while and then headed to our room, with people smiling and making little comments, which made us smile.

We were horrified to find that the keys for my suitcase were back in my parents' home in Adelaide. We just stood there looking at each other and the case. Finally, Graham said, 'Well, I'm not going downstairs to ask for pliers. They might assume that you have a chastity belt.' That was fine with me, so I went down and explained that we had left the keys back in Adelaide. I could see the funny side, and it gave them something to chat about. Other than the forgotten keys, our honeymoon was wonderful. The weather was cool, but we went on bus trips, and the days went by so fast.

By April 1985, Graham and I were settling into married life. I was back at work, selling training products, but not doing very well. I was still having nightmares from my time working at Samuel C Richardson, and now felt totally overwhelmed with my new job. I also felt guilty about the trust that my wonderful current boss had in me, as well at the caring men of the board. I wanted to do better at my job, but I wasn't experienced enough.

I never really stopped feeling insecure. I was doing my best, but I continually had nightmares about Vincent. He actually came to my new workplace one day. We chatted, and I could feel the anger burning inside me, but I was an actress. I said, 'Look at this—my office is bigger than yours now!' He said, 'The office doesn't make the person.' I answered, 'I've always known that, Vincent.'

A month after our wedding I had days when I would get very emotional. I thought it was because of the nightmares, or the fact that I still felt like I wasn't doing a good enough job. I would close the office and go up to see Edward. He told me that I could talk to him anytime. I would cry and talk. He would listen and advise, like a wise uncle. He was a lovely man.

I started feeling so very sick, and I said to Graham that it was one of two possibilities—I was dying of a dreadful disease or I was pregnant. Finally, I found out that I was pregnant. I rang Graham at work and also rang my parents, who were overjoyed. On the way home I went into a shop and bought a brown teddy bear, which felt lovely to cuddle. Mother told me later that she wanted to buy our baby a yellow teddy bear, and I reassured her that she could, as the brown bear was mine.

That evening, after Graham got home from work, I was all ready to celebrate (responsibly of course, as I was now growing a baby). I was thinking we could have dinner out at a nice restaurant. In the meantime, Graham had caught the bus and two trains home, which gave him a chance to think—and think deeply he did that day. He was thinking of all the responsibilities, emotions, practicalities, and financial implications. By the time he got home he had started to have a migraine headache. We hugged as he walked through the door, and then he said, 'I have a nasty migraine and need to go to bed.'

Graham had his unit and his car paid off. We were in a secure financial situation. I had a second-hand car, which was also paid off, but no savings. I wanted a home to bring our baby up in, which was such a silly thing to be thinking about. In later years, I heard that I had been experiencing the nesting instinct. Buying a house would mean the start of financial struggles that would continue well into our future. I had no understanding of the change to our finances it would cause.

I got myself dinner and spent the rest of the night ringing friends and relatives. I was so scared of losing the baby, which was probably a total over-reaction, but my fear was strong enough that Graham and I decided I would leave my job.

The name the health workers used for me at that time (behind my back) was a 'geriatric mother', meaning that, at 36 years of age, I was very old to be having a baby. I had no idea at the time. So there I was, a para-abled geriatric first-time mother-to-be, viewing life through rose-coloured glasses.

There is a greater likelihood that older mums will have a still-birth, or give birth to a baby with problems, but I had no idea of that at the time. My specialist said that because of my age I must have an amniocentesis. This meant taking fluid by sticking a needle in my stomach to see if our baby was going to have any abnormalities. There we were, looking at the monitor as the needle was headed down into my stomach. Our baby was sucking its thumb and as the needle headed closer, our little darling moved away—how clever. During my pregnancy I was so healthy and happy. I really couldn't believe it, as I had heard of all the problems that I may experience.

Mother's brother, my Uncle Keith, found a house at Hallett Cove for us to look at. We drove there, but Graham had a priority.

He insisted that any house we bought had to be no more than an eight-minute walk from the railway station. So, before looking at the home, Graham got out of the car and I drove slowly to the station as he walked. This exercise felt so embarrassing to me—I was scared someone would see us. The reality was, however, no-one knew us from a bar of soap and probably wouldn't have cared anyway. It worked out to be just a seven-minute walk, so we drove back to the house to have a look.

We had looked at other homes in Hallett Cove, but this house had a good feel to it. There were three bedrooms, but no ensuite. The bedroom which the owners used as their master bedroom was directly off the dining room. I visualised us using it as a family room. The laundry came off the dining room too. If we ever bought another house, it would have an ensuite, and definitely would not have the bedroom and the laundry coming off the dining room. We were so naive, but that is life. We bought the house in September and moved in November, before our baby was born.

After moving in, we couldn't afford both heating and cooling, so we agreed to gas heating because of my lung disease. That meant that the gas line had to be connected to our house, as there was only mains electricity when we bought it. The workers decided to cut through the front lawn. I just happened to see them out the window as they began. By this time I was seven months pregnant, but I had been continually feeding my cravings for cream buns, so I looked like I was ten months pregnant! My hair sat aimlessly on my head, I was very tired, with a permanently strained look on my face, which was free from makeup. I waddled with a limp out into the garden, and asked the gas engineer if he was planning to cut all the way through the lawn and the concrete path. He said yes, and told me not to worry about it. He was treating me as though I was a barefoot pregnant female who should have stayed in the kitchen. I threw a hissy fit, ordered him to stop immediately, and told him to get his boss on the phone. In those days, mobile phones were big bricks. I spoke to the boss, and he told me that cutting through the lawn and the path was the only way to lay the gas line. I persisted, saying, 'No', while throwing a huge fit, which would have looked far from stylish, I am sure. Finally, they decided that they could do it from the other end of the house, which wouldn't interfere with anything.

We made the house into a home with the limited funds we had, and it was comfortable. Lee was born on the 30th January 1986. He took his first breath at 3.37 pm. Many years later I realised that if you look at a digital clock when the time is 3.37 and turn it upside down, the display spells LEE. The joy of having our baby felt like winning the lottery ten times straight. Graham was by my side through it all, being supportive and caring. We had dreamed of having a son, and there he was—a healthy little baby, bringing us so much joy.

***

I was so exhausted with Lee at home. I was breastfeeding, and was not capable of doing more than taking care of Lee's needs. I had my heart set on breastfeeding Lee to give him the best possible start to his life. Graham took the first four weeks off work and was a magnificent support. My parents were wonderful, and were there for us whenever we needed help. When Lee was 16 months old I had a major lung infection and finished up in hospital. I found the separation from Lee and Graham heart-wrenching and devastating.

Graham's ability to be organised, capable, and a loving father to our Lee was so comforting. Lee felt equally comforted by us both. He was a happy baby, and loved meeting new people.

Our financial problems were a big concern, and in those days I wasn't at all good at budgeting. We had many an argument about money.

Our friends were wonderful, giving us clothes and toys that their children had grown out of. We were so grateful for their help. Lee had no idea that they were second-hand, and when he got to an age where he did, we made discovering what had been given into an exciting game.

Our mortgage had a very high-interest rate, and as we hadn't bought the house until later in life, we had to pay it off faster than younger couples, as well as paying bills, and buying food and essentials.

I once said to a friend of mine whose husband had a senior position in the public service. 'I envy you and your family. You have no money worries, a beautiful home, and you can give so much to your children.'

Her answer stunned me, as she said, 'Don't envy anyone with money, Jan. Most people live on the edge of their income, so people with higher incomes are no better off than you, they just look richer. Many have just as many worries with their money.' That honest insight was a great comfort, and did help me to look constructively at what we were achieving.

I tried to contribute by getting a door-to-door job selling Avon makeup products and other items, and used to have Lee in a pusher as I walked from home to home. I didn't do it for long. I found it didn't really help, as I was buying as many products as I was selling.

We were loving parents, and the three of us have countless happy memories. We were doing well with disciplining Lee to be polite, respectful, and obedient most of the time, but he did like to test his boundaries. We insisted on him saying 'please' and 'thank you', and if he tested us by refusing we would just deny giving him what was on offer. We never gave empty threats of punishment, we always made sure we could carry it through. This little boy of ours did test us, even though he knew the consequences were definite. We also gave him the freedom of open communication.

Over the years, Graham and I have both mellowed. Our love for each other has never broken but has got stronger with all our challenges. We worked together. Every now and then we went out with a group of people who were far better off financially. We just ordered what we could afford and paid for our own drinks and meals at the end of the night. It worked well, except one time, when it was decided that we should all split the bill. As our friends didn't have to be so careful with their money, it cost us so much more than we could afford. It wasn't their fault. They didn't understand the full extent of our financial struggles, as we didn't go around advertising our problems.

Over the years we have struggled through the sickness and crises of various friends and family members, some of which have been severe. Graham's mate, Luke, died of brain cancer, then Graham's dad died, followed by one of his sisters, and two of his brothers—who both had massive heart attacks. We loved them all. In later years I lost my parents, aunties, and uncles. Graham lost his 'Auntie' Katie. These losses of loved ones, including the ones we hadn't visited often but still loved dearly, took their toll on us. For each one we worked through the emotions together. Graham's mate Bruce has also mellowed, and is still our friend.

Over the years, Lee continued to test our parenting, as most kids do. If he wanted to go out he would tell me, 'Dad said it was okay.' So I would go and ask Graham. He would know nothing of the request. Graham would do the same, and check with me.

On one occasion the three of us were standing in the kitchen. Lee was 13 years old, and wanted to go to a concert with his mates, but we decided it wasn't well organised. Lee was insisting. We were saying, 'No', and explaining why. This conversation was repeated. In his frustration he stood there quietly thinking, before blurting out, 'You two have no idea how to be parents.'

We just stood there speechless, and then I burst into laughter. Graham and Lee joined in, and we hugged each other. Lee didn't go to the concert.

When Graham was working and Lee was at school my time was my own. I caught up with girlfriends for a cuppa at their homes or out at a café. I never went out without makeup on and my hair was almost always styled. I styled it myself, although occasionally I would just put a cap on.

While at home, I would have the radios on in the kitchen, the lounge room, and our bedroom. This meant I could hear my favourite easy listening music throughout the whole house. When Graham arrived home from work he would walk through and turn each radio off. That was fine with me, as I had them all day.

The closest big shopping centre at Marion was my favourite place to window shop and sit, enjoying a cuppa, and watching the people passing by. I would try to guess what their lives were like by the way they presented themselves, never finding out if I was correct.

When my Graham retired from work my life changed. I didn't put the radios on when he was home. I didn't miss them as he was home to talk with.

One day, soon after he had retired, our decision to have only had one car caused an interesting situation. I got dressed to go to Marion Shopping Centre, when Graham asked me where I was going. I said, 'Off to Marion.' Well, then it hit me. He said, 'Okay, I need to go to a shop down that way. How long do you need to be at Marion, five or ten minutes?' I burst out laughing—poor Graham was serious. When I calmed down, I said 'Okay I'll put the kettle on and we can have a talk over a cuppa.' We talked about the change to both our lives that his retirement had created. I apologised for laughing, but a smile was creeping on my face at the same time, as I explained at length that I had always gone window shopping and people watching while he was at work. We talked through the changes that Graham's retirement brought, compromising at times, but with communication and caring we successfully rode—and continue to ride—the happy and sometimes awkward road of retirement.

Having Graham home was wonderful. By the time he had retired, Lee wanted to go overseas for an important convention. We were able to help him make the trip possible, and also made it possible for him to visit my wonderful cousins in Denmark. They made him welcome, just like they did when I stayed with them many years before.

Our life now is great, and peaceful. We have a comfortable home. Lee comes and visits from the city, staying with us for a few days at a time. The three of us are family. We love each other and are good friends. That is more precious and more valuable to us than money.

***

The year 2020 brought a lot of challenges and upset to our world in so many ways. My lung disease meant that I had to stay indoors all winter without visitors. I actually enjoyed the experience. My doctor, who I had phone consultations with, was worried about my vitamin D intake, but I said that it wouldn't kill me missing out on the sunshine, as my vitamin D levels could be corrected by tablets if necessary. The phone was my connection to the outside world.

However, I mainly concentrated on writing and checking the manuscript of this autobiography, trying to juggle stories from the past 70 years of life, and squashing what I could into print. My Graham spent much of the time on his computer. He also did the first edit of my manuscript, which was a great help. Lee worked from his apartment, and kept in frequent contact with us. He seemed to enjoy the change in pace, and didn't mind not socialising with his friends, choosing instead to concentrate on his business and to make a priority of visiting us.

'I was on a mission to find out what went wrong with divorced people's marriages. I learnt that they had got married too young, or hadn't experienced enough time away from their family, or that some strong quiet type of men were not good communicators. Trust and communication were essential.'

Jan Cocks-Salvemini

CHAPTER 11
Being a Nanny

My childcare work started in my late teens. I had been volunteering at the local kindergarten, and one of the children's mums asked if I would like some childcare work. I took instructions about bedtime and enjoyed the time with the children. On top of which, I got paid! I thought I'd found my dream job.

Word soon spread. I found the work easy and enjoyable, always treating the children with respect and never talking down to them. The children seemed to enjoy me caring for them, and I was asked back again and again.

Among the many lovely families I worked for was a family with two children—a boy and a girl. Although they were siblings they were also the best of friends. The whole family was delightful, and their home looked like a cute dolls' house inside and out—everything was perfect. Once the children were in bed I would imagine that it was my home. It was a lovely way to pass the time. Many years later I discovered that the parents split up, and I felt so very sad for them.

As the years went by I gradually got regular childcare work. My parability was questioned by many of the children. Quite often the parents would get a shock and say, 'No, you can't ask that.' I would reassure the parents that it was fine, and that it was natural for children to be inquisitive. I would then quietly explain to the children and the parents that when I was a baby I got very sick, and after that my hand and foot wouldn't work.

It is so important for people with parabilities, if they feel up to it, to be open about communicating with children and adults, so that everyone feels comfortable. It is our job to help with inclusion. Of course, for people who have recently become para-abled, it is important to work through the shock first and so it is fine if you're not ready to talk about it.

A good strategy to deflect attention away from your parabilities is to politely decline talking about your parabilities, and then to ask a question on a different subject. For children, a random question such as, 'What is your favourite animal and can you tell me why?' For an adult, compliment them on an item of clothing, and ask where they bought it. It is also fine just to end the conversation and leave.

There are one billion people living with a parability, each one of whom is an individual, and at a different stage of working through what their parability means to them. They may be like me, completely happy and accepting of themselves. They may be at the opposite end of the spectrum and struggling to accept their parability. For this reason, it is so important not to make assumptions. That is why it is important to ask people if you can help, and then respect the answer they give.

During the time I worked for Samuel C Richardson my work was only part-time, and did not provide me with enough money to live independently. This meant that in order to keep the wolf from the door, I had to have other work. As I had successfully done a lot of childcare work during my teens, I thought that I would look for childcare work again.

In 1978 I saw an advertisment for an after-school childcare position. I met with the parents and their delightful daughter, Victoria, who was six years old. My job would consist of picking Victoria up from school and caring for her until her parents finished work. I would also prepare the basics of the family's evening meal and do their washing, when needed.

Victoria was blonde, lovely looking, and very bright. I really enjoyed working for Victoria and her family. Unfortunately, after two years, they moved away and my time looking after Victoria came to an end. We had got along so well and I felt very sad. We did catch up later in life, and Victoria spent New Year's Eve with us one year.

After I stopped working for Victoria I cared for another girl, Natalie. Natalie's dad Peter arranged the interview, and told me not to be worried when he answered the door, as he would be wearing a dress. I was intrigued about the style of dress he would be wearing. When I arrived at the house Peter answered the door wearing a kaftan, which made complete sense.

Natalie was six years old, and she was such a sweetie. The job was similar to my role looking after Victoria. I would collect Natalie from school and take her home.

Not long after, another job came my way. I now had three jobs, and they fitted together well. I would do my 9 am-3 pm credit controller job at Samuel C Richardson, then collect Natalie from school, staying with her until 6pm, when I would drive home, have tea, and then go to my next job, selling flowers at restaurants until ten o'clock at night.

One hot Wednesday afternoon in the summer of 1983, I did my usual drive from work to Natalie's school. I parked down a side street facing the Adelaide Hills, and noticed a small amount of smoke reaching for the sky. I collected Natalie from her classroom and by the time we got back to the car the smoke was pouring up from the hills.

The following is an extract from an article by Penelope Debelle, entitled, 'How Ash Wednesday Changed Our Lives':

> It is 30 years since 28 people died in the Ash Wednesday bushfires, the worst in South Australia's history.
>
> It was a Red Alert day at the end of a hot, dry spell that had scorched the ground tinder dry. Temperatures hit 43C and the squally north-easterly winds were gusting at 75 km an hour.
>
> On Ash Wednesday, eight fires ripped through the state. The Adelaide Hills fire started at Mount Osmond and roared up the freeway. Vehicles, bumper to bumper, picked their way through the smoke while the fire sped up to Crafers, on the way destroying the Eagle-on-the-Hill Hotel and the BP station opposite.

That afternoon, in February 1983, I put the radio on while I got Natalie's afternoon tea. I stood at the sink, staring out the window, listening to Murray Nicholls' report. His delivery was moving, as he watched his own home burning down. I had tears in my eyes.

I then called Natalie's mum to let her know that we had arrived home safely. I got a shock when she told me that her husband was camping in the hills, and she didn't know where. She asked me not to mention it to Natalie.

There wasn't any contact from Peter for over twenty-four hours. After that time, we found out that Peter had been having a beer in the Eagle-on-the-Hill hotel on Mount Barker Road. All of a sudden a firefighter raced in and ordered everyone out. Peter, in typical Australian fashion, said, 'I just bought this beer, and I'll leave when I've finished it.' The firefighter said, 'Just take the beer with you. In a few minutes this hotel will have burnt down. Get out or lose your life.' So Peter left—with his beer. The hotel burned down shortly afterwards. Peter was safe, but had no way of making contact with his family. There were 28 deaths in South Australia that day. Peter was reunited with his thankful family the next day.

A few weeks after, some friends and I drove through the area where the fires had been. It was so eerie. We all went quiet. All the trees were charred, the ground was black, and there was no noise at all. No birds chirping and no leaves to rustle with the soft wind blowing.

My work caring for Natalie was from 1982 to 1985. Natalie and I still keep in touch. For the next 20 years to about 2004 I did local child-sitting-work. In 2004 I decided that as I enjoyed child-sitting/ nanny work that I would see if I could join an agency as a carer. In fact, it worked out very well for me for some time. After the in-depth interview, the agency directors said that they weren't bothered about my parability and didn't feel it was necessary to let the families know, even though I told them I was very happy for them to disclose the fact.

Through the agency I got some wonderful jobs for wonderful caring parents and their children. Many asked me back time and time again. I loved the job and the families I met. The children I cared for were almost always a joy. It was also a wonderful learning process about parability for the children, and I think the parents too.

One little girl had her birthday party in the afternoon on the day I sat for her. Knowing it was her birthday, I bought her a doll. She was delighted and immediately called her new doll Jill. Every time I sat for her after, Jill would appear too.

Unfortunately, one of my jobs looking after three boys aged 4, 6 and 8 years turned into a nightmare. The parents instructed the boys that they could not use the backyard swimming pool because I would not be able to help them if they got into trouble. That destroyed their evening. They swore at me, threw clothes at me, and wouldn't do anything I asked of them.

The experiences as a nanny reflected on my upbringing and the importance of giving our children boundaries as parents. It is tough love, which can be hard for parents. The boundaries, the lessons of do's and don'ts. We gain that insight and grow to feel secure in our own lives.

CHAPTER 12
'Parking For The Disabled' Campaigns

On three occasions, with wonderful support from sponsors, I organised 'Parking For The Disabled' campaigns. The first occasion was in 1989, when I approached and obtained sponsorship from the RAA for a 30-second TV community service announcement, which I also featured in. The second occasion was in 1998, when I worked with the Joyce-Russ Advertising Agency on the 'Check Out The Parking Permit Not The Person' campaign. After obtaining sponsorships from various companies, a second TV community service announcement was made, along with a radio announcement and 21,000 car bumper stickers. The third occasion was in 2011, after obtaining sponsorship from the RAA and my local Lions Club for the production of 10,000 car bumper stickers. I also arranged for community service announcements to be made on two radio stations.

The first campaign was sparked by the difficulties I was experiencing with parking. I had a permit to use the disabled car parking spaces. Unfortunately, cars not displaying a permit often used these parking spaces. As I was finding it difficult to find a park, I started designing a poster to explain the situation. My husband Graham worked with me, and we asked our local Lions Club of Hallett Cove & Districts to sponsor the printing of them, which they did. About six months later I had a meeting with the manager of our local ANZ bank about sponsoring the printing of 100 updated posters, which they did.

I wanted to know how much the local council was charging the shopping centres to police the car parks for the disabled. The City of Marion council representative told me that it was none of my business and to leave it alone or he would make trouble for me. I then threatened to call the Current Affairs TV program, and he said to go right ahead. So I did. They sent a reporter and a cameraman to talk with me. The cameraman decided to have a look at the parking situation. He came back amazed, and phoned for another cameraman. After the interview was aired the representative from the council did everything he could to be nice to me. The Current Affairs interview helped the parking situation for a while, but not for long. I needed to generate more publicity.

I started thinking that it would be great to get a TV advertisment made to highlight the problem. I decided to ring Channel 9, my favourite TV station from childhood, and spoke to a chap called Barry Ellson. He was wonderful. He explained that ads were free to air, but I would have to pay for the production. He contacted a cameraman and scriptwriter who both worked at Channel 9. These two wonderful guys came to my home, had a cuppa with Graham and me, and we worked out an outline for the script. However, we still needed to raise the money to make the ad.

It was Graham's idea to speak to the RAA (Royal Automobile Association) to see if they would be willing to donate the $2,000 needed to produce the advertisment. I contacted the Adelaide branch of the RAA and made an appointment to see their public relations and marketing manager, Peter Smith. I explained the purpose of the ad and told him how much it was going to cost. 'Is that all you need?' he asked. I nodded and he said, 'Okay.'

He also gave me some invaluable advice. He told me to run the campaign myself, rather than getting a community group involved, as that would give me control of the campaign. I took that advice on board and have never forgotten it. He was absolutely right—I was able to do things my way without being railroaded by other people's agendas.

I let the video producer and scriptwriter know that I had the funding. They worked out the script and shots and then contacted me to say they wanted to add other aspects for a stronger delivery, and needed an additional $2,000. I burst out crying, as I didn't want to ask for more money—I was so grateful to Peter Smith and the RAA for their sponsorship. Still feeling upset, I rang Peter Smith, and he said he would put it to the RAA board. On the 2nd of May 1989, I received a letter to say that the board had approved the extra money.

I phoned around and found people with parabilities to be in the ad. Filming took all day. The producer wanted me to look as though I was not really para-abled, to show the public that sometimes a parability is not always obvious, but it was a condition of the Motor Vehicles Department that everyone in the ad was shown as obviously para-abled.

The ad made a great deal of difference. I would get out of my car and people would tell me that I shouldn't be parking in the disabled spaces, because I looked 'normal'. I would thank them for caring about the disabled parks and then show them my permit. It all worked well. The parking spaces started to be used rather than abused. I got a few dirty looks for not appearing to be para-abled, but I was at peace with that.

The campaign drew media attention, and the interviews and articles helped to get the message out, but the campaign started to become too successful. I began getting letters from people with internal parabilities expressing the trouble they were having with people abusing them for using the disabled spaces when they appeared to be fine.

By 1997, I realised that another campaign was needed. Not only were people with hidden parabilities finding themselves targeted for 'misusing' the parking spaces, but by this time the colour and shape of the permit had changed from red to blue and from square to rectangular. Everybody was a little confused.

The state government didn't want to know, so I approached the RAA again. Peter Smith had left, but his replacement, Peter Hennekann, listened to what I had to say. He suggested that I contact the Joyce-Russ Advertising Agency. I spoke to the directors,

Paul Joyce and Peter Russ, for almost an hour during our first meeting. I felt proud of myself as I didn't miss a beat. At the end of the meeting they said that they would get back to me within a week. They agreed to work with me, and they were absolutely wonderful. Together we started planning the new campaign. Peter Russ approached a number of businesses, and Westfield, CPS Credit Union, and 5DN agreed to sponsor the campaign, along with the RAA. The RAA distributed thousands of bumper stickers throughout South Australia. I arranged to distribute them around Adelaide. The bumper sticker stated 'Check Out The Parking Permit Not The Person.' This certainly helped people with hidden parabilities, so that they were no longer harassed while using the car parks.

Within a few years all the bumper stickers had been distributed and more were needed. It was now 2003. I felt that if this new campaign could be bigger than the earlier ones then it might not need to be repeated for some considerable time. I thought it was time to get the government involved. Unfortunately, the Minister for Transport refused to be part of the campaign because I was an individual, rather than an organisation.

I then wrote to Peter Hennekam at the RAA. Fortunately, the RAA was happy to sponsor a re-run of 30,000 bumper stickers. I was interviewed on the Channel 9 program 'Adelaide Today' and Channel 7's 'Today Tonight' program. The message was out and about.

I started wondering what the required number of disabled parking spaces actually was. My Graham found out that the Building Codes Board required that 2% of car parking spaces must be allocated for those with a disability parking permit. I called around and found out that the number of permits that had been approved was as follows: ACT – 13,318, NSW – 250,000, NT – 1,200, QLD – 115,324, SA – 61,723, TAS – NA, VIC – NA.

I then put in a submission to the Building Codes Board stating that there was a need to increase the number of allocated disabled parks to 3%, and recommending a two-tier parking system—wide spaces for wheelchair users, and standard-size spaces for non-wheelchair users. No action was taken.

By 2011 I felt that a re-run of bumper stickers and a new community promotion was due. However, administration procedures in the RAA had changed. Matthew Hanton, the manager of strategic communications, told me that the RAA would be happy to arrange the production of the stickers, but he suggested I get an additional sponsor who could also be the nominated campaign organiser.

The Lions Club of Hallett Cove & Districts was willing to be the additional sponsor, and would share the production cost of 10,000 updated bumper stickers. The update included the logos of both the sponsors, and also a contact address for the campaign organiser.

It is important for people with parabilities to do whatever we can to help people understand our needs. This can be done by educating them politely and with a smile. It is our responsibility, if we want to break down the barriers around people's perception of parabilities.

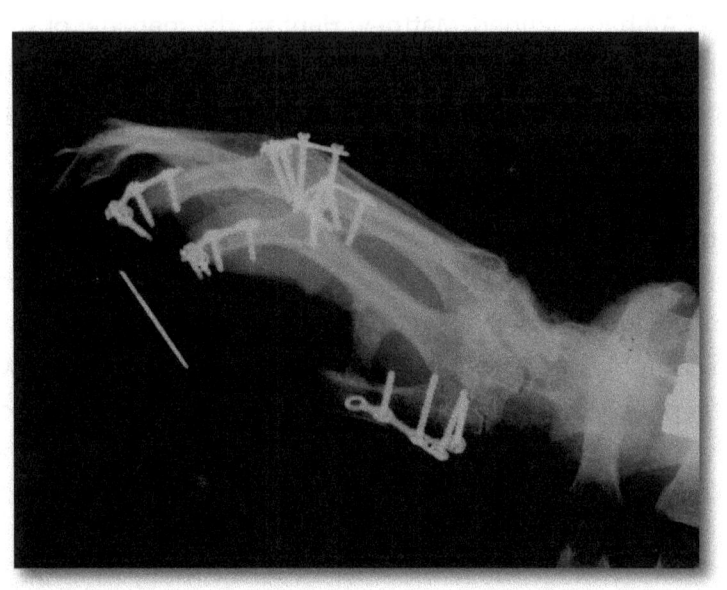

CHAPTER 13
My Hand and The Pretty Blue Screw

Many years ago my right hand started to change from a ball shape to the fingers spasming outwards. I didn't have control over it. To start with it didn't bother me at all until I began noticing people looking intently at my right hand. I would glance down and to my absolute horror my middle finger would be spasming upwards while the other fingers and my thumb were curled up. I was unintentionally giving complete strangers the finger!

I was referred to a specialist, who told me that he could make my hand look natural. It sounded good to me. After the operation I had dreadful pain because the pins that were holding the bones in a stable position were too long, and it felt like needles were sticking into my skin.

I went to a second specialist. When he put the X-ray up on the viewing screen he had a look of absolute horror for a moment, until he controlled himself. The inside of my hand looked like a cross-stitch in needlework. I had a second operation, the pins were removed, and metal caps were placed over each knuckle, secured with four little screws. The operation went well and my life got back to my normal.

Many years later, when I was staying in Cairns, the skin broke on the main joint of my little finger. I saw a very pretty metallic, silver speckled, sky-blue object peeking through. It fascinated me.

I went to a local doctor, who cleaned it and covered it with an airtight Band-Aid to keep it protected. He said he would change the dressing weekly until I went home. Gradually, as the weeks went by, I could see the wound opening more and more each time he changed the dressing.

One day the Band-Aid came unstuck to reveal the very pretty metallic-blue screw head had completely broken through. This time,

I was seen by a different doctor. He was so shocked that the wound hadn't been dealt with sooner. He said that in the tropics there was so much that could have gone wrong. I was referred to a surgeon immediately, and the screw was removed. The surgeon advised me to have all the remainng screws taken out when I got back to Adelaide, as my finger bones had fused.

On arriving back home, the rest of the pretty blue screws and plates were taken out. My only regret was that I couldn't keep one of those pretty screws to show my family. In my childhood years the medical staff would give things like that to the patient, for a keepsake, secured in a sealed container.

***

Some people I meet see me as different to them, and I think how sad it is to think like that. If I can't do something in a conventional way, I can usually find another way of doing it. Often, it is just a matter of thinking outside the square. I paint my own fingernails by holding the handle of the nail polish brush between my teeth. It works well, and is steadier than a hand. Drying dishes is easy too. I put a tea towel on the bench, put the dish on the towel and dry with my working hand using another tea towel. I can even do up shoelaces using one hand after I had my hand operations. If I ever do need help, I ask. I am very happy and content with who I am. A very happy and contented old duck.

'Di and I had great fun together. She never worried about my parability. I would forget about it until someone mentioned it or spoke the six most stupid words I knew, 'You can't do that, let me,' instead of asking the four most intelligent words, 'Can I help you?' and respecting my answer and my right to independence.'

Jan Cocks-Salvemini

CHAPTER 14
Lee

I fell pregnant in May 1985. Graham and I both wanted a son. At the age of 35, I considered it important to see a highly experienced obstetrician. The obstetrician advised me to have an amniocentesis, as my age meant there may be the possibility of having a baby with problems. The amniocentesis was done 18 weeks into my pregnancy, and we had both agreed that if they found anything wrong we would definitely be keeping our precious baby.

All the tests were done, and at the follow-up appointment we were told our baby was healthy. The obstetrician then asked if we wanted to know the baby's sex. When we said yes, we were asked why. We explained that Graham had helped his foster sister care for her two boys, and wanted his own son. I didn't want a girl because I was a naughty child and felt that with a girl I would be in for a healthy dose of karma. I loved Graham and wanted a son just like him. We wanted to know, because if our baby was a girl we wanted to be prepared to love her from the moment she arrived. If we only knew at the birth, we didn't want her to start life with us in shock. The specialist told us to go home and paint the walls blue. We both burst into tears of joy. We went home and thought of names. We decided to call him Lee. I introduced people to the bump in my stomach by saying, 'This is Lee, our son.'

Not having air conditioning in the house made it so hard in the harsh days of the Adelaide summer, with Lee's birth expected mid-January. We had a heatwave, with temperatures reaching forty degrees Celcius some days. Our lounge room faced the afternoon sun, and the temperature was often as hot inside as out. Being heavily pregnant, I would drive to our local shops, where the air conditioning only cost me the price of a drink and a cream bun, which I was constantly craving.

I believed that everyone was as ecstatic about my pregnancy as I was, and was totally oblivious to the fact that Mother thought I might die having the baby, due to my parabilities. I didn't think of any negatives during the pregnancy or during the birth. It didn't even enter my head.

Nine months came and went, but Lee was in no rush. Another week passed. Then finally, two weeks late, he decided to think about making a move. The pains started, and I had no idea that the pain at that stage was just minor. I went to a neighbour and asked her what to do. She had children and explained that this was just the start. Finally, I was admitted to hospital, but the contractions weren't close enough together for the doctors to take any notice. It was a long wait, but finally it was time. I was given an epidural to ease the pain, and Graham and I eagerly awaited Lee's arrival.

As I was a private patient the obstetrician had to ask my permission to allow a student doctor to watch Lee's birth. She was sitting up high in the viewing seats. That seemed ridiculous to me, and I asked the doctor if she could come down and join us. She came down and then the fun began.

Not having any pain, I was in great spirits. The doctor asked me to push, but the lack of sensation from the epidural meant that I couldn't figure out how to push. Everyone else was pushing for me, and we were all laughing hysterically. I was saying, 'Come on Lee, it's time to meet us.' Finally the doctor told me that Lee seemed to be too comfortable in there, and he'd have to help him out. He took what looked like huge stainless steel salad servers, which were actually forceps. I was stunned, 'What are you going to do with those?' I queried, in a total panic. The specialist explained, and I couldn't imagine that they would fit, but of course they did their job, and Lee's head appeared. At that point, I demanded that the obstetrician get out of the way so that I could see our son's crowning in the mirror. He did, and I watched Lee's head emerging into the world, closely followed by his little body. He was blue.

My expectations were that the obstetrician would give Lee to me for a cuddle, so that we could bond. In fact, he laid him on my chest, still blue, with his backbone facing me, so that my first thoughts of our precious son was that he looked just like the skinned rabbits my dad used to have ready to cook. The obstetrician then picked Lee up to start him breathing, but baby Lee averted the indignity of being held upside down and hit on his back by giving the biggest yawn, and his precious life started.

Lee was born on the 30th January 1986. The ward doctor visited me each day, asking me how we were going. I was ecstatically happy. Each day he asked the same question, and each day I gave the same reply. On day ten he came in to ask the usual question, and I was crying uncontrollable. He smiled, which annoyed me, and said, 'It was important for you to cry before you went home, you were too happy and I needed you to come down from that high. You're ready to go home now.'

The enormity of responsibility had finally hit me. I was in charge of this precious baby. The nurse brought him in that morning and laid him on the bed after he had been weighed and bathed. I stood there looking at him and said, 'You poor little darling, you have me for a mum.' Then I picked him up for a cuddle—one of thousands upon thousands that Graham and I gave him. I was determined to be the best mum I could possibly be. There were going to be obstacles because I was para-abled, but I thought I would deal with them as they presented themselves.

We were struggling financially, and a good friend gave me the clothes her sons had grown out of, as well as their pram and pusher. We were very grateful. Almost everything Lee had was second-hand, except for the gifts we received from family and friends.

Changing Lee's nappy was a challenge, as at that stage my right hand would just spasm into a ball. I put the safety pins in by putting the forefinger of my good hand underneath, so it would prick me and not Lee. When he was small he would lie still, which made it manageable, but as he grew and started wriggling, disposable nappies solved the problem—although they hurt the bank account.

My wonderful Graham stayed home for the first four weeks, which was such a help. Graham is not only a very loving husband, he is also the best dad that Lee and I could ask for him to have. I became so exhausted with caring for Lee at home. I was breastfeeding, and was not capable of doing more than looking after Lee's needs. I had no idea that my lung disease had killed off so much of one of my four remaining lobes, and that the fumes from this were poisoning me. I just felt guilty that I was being so very lazy. One of the neighbours had four children, all boys, and would often come over in the morning to have a cuppa. She would tell me that she had dropped the children at school, cleaned the kitchen, and done the washing. I would sit there with her, Lee would have a clean nappy on and have had his morning feed, but that would be all I had achieved. I felt terrible, and would burst into tears after she left. Even so, I was not alone. As well as the support that Graham gave me, my parents were wonderful, and were there whenever we needed help.

When Lee was 16 months old I had a major lung infection, and had to be hospitalised. My doctor was very angry that I was still breastfeeding, and demanded that Lee be weaned off immediately. The separation from Lee and Graham was heart-wrenching, and to be told that I must stop breastfeeding made it so much worse. I believed that breastfeeding was the best thing for a nourishing, bonding start to life.

I have heard since that if I had taken iron tablets during my pregnancy, Lee may not have been allergic to cow's milk, as was the case from the moment he was born. The day after he was born the nurses cared for him overnight, as I was so exhausted. The next morning, a nurse walked in and warned me not to be upset. Lee was in her arms, and there were huge blisters on his small body caused by an allergic reaction to the cow's milk. I was absolutely horrified to see him in that state. I was told that the blisters would go in a very short time, and they did. He grew up on soy milk.

I sang nursery rhymes to Lee, both before and after he was born. At around three years old he said, 'Stop mummy, it's awful.' We found out later that he had perfect pitch. All the way through my pregnancy, and after Lee's birth, I loved listening to easy listening 1960's music on the radio. I had a radio in the kitchen, another in the lounge, and one in our bedroom, so wherever I was in our home I could hear music, and perhaps Lee could hear it as well.

At 18 months he would sit in his play pen and watch Play School on the television, while I was busy in the kitchen. One day I lost track of time, and realised Play School must had finished. As Lee was very quiet I was worried. I looked through from the kitchen servery to see him sitting spellbound, mouth gaping, staring mesmerised at the TV. He was listening to an orchestral concert. I just stood there watching him for about 15 minutes. When Graham came home I told him that I thought we had a musically minded child. We found a music group for two-to-four year olds. When we arrived for the first session there were children's musical instruments laid out in a circle. Lee was overwhelmed and ran with delight to collect as many instruments as he could hold. That wasn't acceptable behaviour for the group. I quickly took the instruments out of his arms, put them down, then grabbed his hand. This was followed by a tantrum. We all recovered and he quickly fitted in.

By the time he was five we had found a reasonably priced music teacher. Mrs Brown instructed us to make our way down the driveway to the back shed, where, to our absolute astonishment, were two beautiful grand pianos. Mrs Brown was smiling and looking at Lee. He was standing in total amazement, as if Mickey Mouse had suddenly appeared in front of him. Mrs Brown gently took his little hand and together they got down and crawled on the floor to investigate the underneath of one of the grand pianos. Mrs Brown was talking to him about what was under there. Then they crawled out and she picked him up and showed him the inside, explaining how it worked by pressing the keys.

Lee started having lessons once a week, but we couldn't afford a piano for him to practice at home. A fair while after, we were visiting some friends who had a piano. They let Lee play and noticed how interested he was. When we said we couldn't afford one they said they would see what they could do. They found a pianola for us to look at, but only the piano part worked. It was a price we could afford, and it came home. From that day on, we couldn't get Lee off it without a struggle. He practiced and practiced. He came to me one day and announced that he was going to teach me to play the piano, and that it would help my para-abled hand to work. I sat down with Lee and we talked about my hand and leg not working as they should. He listened as I told him about me being a very sick baby. When I finished he was happy, and it didn't seem to worry him after that talk.

He could never be bothered to learn to read music—he just wanted to play. Mrs Brown suggested we just let him enjoy playing, as he wasn't having any trouble remembering the songs. That was a wise decision. He loved his music and we would constantly have to drag him away from the piano for dinner or bed.

Bedtime was not the usual, 'Get into bed and I will read you a story' routine. Because I couldn't read well, from the time he got to sleep in his big bed, my approach was to make bedtime fun. I would say, 'Okay Lee, time to throw you into bed.' He would smile happily, and I would hold his hand while walking to his room. Standing at the end of his bed I would pick him up with my left arm and then collect his legs with my right arm. Then I would count 'One, Two, Three', and throw him onto the bed as he giggled. I would then sit on the bedside chair and we would talk for a while with the light on low, then finally I would sit with him in silence until he went to sleep. I would have the dimmer light on, because I was scared of the dark. Lee wasn't though, and in later years the night came when he said,

'Mum, why do we have the light on?' Well, it was time to confess my reason. He couldn't stop giggling. He asked me not to be scared, and to try turning the light off. I agreed, and sat there petrified. I have no idea why I was scared, but I just felt I had no control because I couldn't see. I found it difficult to find my way out that night, but after that I would have the light on in the lounge and a dim light would filter through under Lee's bedroom door.

***

Our Lee grew into a very happy little boy. He was very sociable, with a wide smile. His blue eyes smiled too, most of the time. A friend was worried about me letting Lee talk to strangers, but it was important for his communication skills to feel comfortable talking to people. I always had my eyes on him, and we'd had the stranger-danger conversation. At four years old Lee started kindy, and loved it. I was constantly having lung infections so I was glad of the break, but missed him terribly at the same time.

On the 30th of January 1991, on the day of his fifth birthday, Lee attended his first day at school. It was at the local Catholic primary school— St Martin De Porres. His reception class had a wonderful teacher called Gary Pascoe. The children called him 'Mr P.' That first day as I walked Lee into his classroom I was feeling so very sad. I loved spending time with him, but it was time for him to take the next major step in his young life. I tried not to show my sadness, as Lee was so excited. We walked into Mr P's classroom to heaps of coloured decorations. Mr P put so much effort into working with the children. I chatted to Gary and asked if I could take a photo. I took the photo, and left Lee in his capable hands.

When I returned in the afternoon to collect Lee, Gary walked him to the car and told me they thought they had lost him. Just after morning recess Gary had instructed all the children to take some paperwork out and put it in their bags. After a minute or so Gary realised Lee was missing, and started frantically looking for him, as did the office staff. They searched the school, and were about to ring me when Gary thought of one more place to look. There was Lee, sitting quietly in the gutter at the edge of the footpath of the car park. Gary asked him what he was doing. Lee's reply was, 'My mummy will come and take me home in a minute.' After telling me what had happened, Gary gave Lee a big smile and told him that it was now time to go home. Gary walked Lee to the car on many occasions, and would tell me about that day's mischief. When we arrived home Lee and I would discuss his behaviour. It was quite a regular event.

I volunteered in the school canteen, just as my mother had done when I was small. I really enjoyed helping out, and the chats with the other mums helped. Over the years I became friends with Marg Gill, the canteen manager.

I spent time with a few of the mums, and became good friends with some. Annette Bugeja and I would chat in the school car park. Our friendship grew from there, as her son Peter and Lee got together a lot. Cathy Crotti and her husband Peter met up with us at church at weekends. Lee and their son James were mates. One semester, James and Lee had a school project to make a dinosaur using only paper and tape, so Cathy brought James over to our home. The boys worked on their project while Cathy and I had a cuppa. After a while, they came out of the family room with only one leg of the dinosaur made. They could hardly get their arms around it! They worked so hard, and it became a very large dinosaur which was displayed in the school library.

My friend Anna's children, David and Adele, also attended Lee's school, and I got to look after them after school, which I loved doing. They got along well with Lee, and I had the privilege of becoming their Godmother. Our friendship grew stronger as the years passed.

I willingly volunteered to help out in Lee's classroom. On the first day, standing in front of the class with Gary, I suddenly felt extremely nervous. When Gary asked if I would take a child and listen to her reading, I froze, flashing back to the insecure little girl I had been in 1957. Standing there in my adult body, with my reading ability at the stage of an eight-year-old, I forced a smile and said, 'Yes, of course, Gary.' Thank goodness I recognised all the words. That was the end of me volunteering in class. It would be another four years before I found someone to officially test my reading ability. When it was discovered that I had the reading age of an eight-year-old I attended a special course and learnt to read.

That year, Lee moved up to the next level of his music group, and also announced that he wanted to start giving piano concerts. He had learnt several tunes by this time, so I checked up at a local nursing home. They said they would love him to go and play to the residents. He had seen a program, and wanted to have a program of his tunes to hand out before starting. Graham helped him make a program, with his photo on the front and a list of the tunes he would play inside. It was an A4 piece of paper, folded in half. At the nursing homes he would hand out the programs, then climb up onto the piano stool and play the music from memory. Once he finished he would walk around and shake hands or get a kiss. He loved it, and so did his audiences.

School wasn't his favourite place to be, and he got up to mischief quite often. One day when he was in Grade Two, I arrived to find Gary Pascoe on yard duty. As I walked into the play area Lee rushed over and gave me the biggest hug. I was surprised and delighted, until Gary came over to explain that Lee had been naughty and had to sit until he was told he could go. It broke my heart to walk away, with Lee's big blue eyes staring into mine. I had to force myself to turn my back on him and let Gary take charge. I started walking away, and as I looked back I saw our little Lee sitting with such a very sad look on his face. I felt like I was abandoning him.

Lee had a strong will, and so did I. At times it meant that there was a real battle. Graham and I agreed on the structure of discipline we gave Lee. We were strongly against hitting him, and were adamant that he learnt good manners. Neither of us believed in making empty threats.

If he wouldn't do what he was told, something he loved was taken away from him. There were times I put him in his room, and as there was no lock on the door I would put an alligator strap from his door handle to the handle on the bathroom door. It worked well, until he got strong enough to pull the door open and walk out with a grin on his face. He wouldn't get anything without a please, and it was immediately taken away if we didn't get a thank you. It is called tough love, and as a parent it is so hard. Lee tried to outdo us by telling his dad I had said yes to requests he made, even if he hadn't asked or if I'd said no. Graham and I had agreed to talk about any requests together, so Lee's ploy never worked, which upset him.

***

I loved making Lee's birthday cakes. It was such a joy for me. I would decorate a basic packet cake. I learnt how to make the designs from The Australian Women's Weekly Children's Birthday Book. I made many, such as Donald Duck, a piano, a racecourse, and a rocket cake—which tried to take off and crashed on the way to the celebration (that was my story). For his first and second birthdays I made a train cake. For his first birthday, I made the cake exactly as it was in the book. By his second birthday he was into Thomas the Tank Engine. Graham and I worked on the cake together, and we were thrilled with our masterpiece. On the day of his second birthday we proudly bought out the Thomas cake. All, including Lee, were delighted with the little blue engine with a happy face. We sang happy birthday, and our little two year old was delighted. We didn't think about what would happen when I plunged the knife into Thomas. Lee's face turned to horror, and he screamed and screamed—we were killing Thomas. The cake was whisked away to the kitchen and everyone distracted Lee.

Lee didn't like school much as the years went on. It was a challenge to get him to do his homework, and became very hard getting him moving each school morning. He was given two warnings to be ready, then I resorted to the 'three minutes to my next move' routine. First I am in the kitchen for three minutes, then I move out and sit in the car for three minutes, then I reverse down the driveway and park on the street for three minutes. He would then run up and get into the car, often with his shoes in his hand and his backpack unzipped.

Although we could be tough parents, we all loved each other.

Lee had a friend called Jack who had trouble at home. When it became unbearable he would ask to stay with us. We would agree he could stay, but I would say that I must ring his mum. He was always well behaved with us. When I would ring his mum she would tell me she didn't care where he was. A couple of days later she would ring and ask to come and talk to him. She would then either say that Jack was going home or ask if he could stay for a couple more days. Sometimes we would come home to find Jack sitting on our front doorstep waiting for us.

Lee has an artistic mind, and his school was sports minded. The principal called us to advise that we should take him for an appointment with children services, due to his behaviour at school. We took him to the appointment and the three of us were interviewed. We said we were prepared to help Lee, and that any advice would be valuable. Then we sat and waited while the lady went out the back to sort through the file. We were nervous when she returned, but she reassured us all was well. It was Lee's school that was the problem—it was sport-orientated and Lee couldn't fit in. We were told when he got to college he would fit in more. I have to say I was quite delighted to report back to the principal that it was them and not Lee. Of course, Lee wasn't perfect—we were aware of his immature behaviour, and overall it was a great school.

A few years later, we applied for Lee to go for a piano scholarship to attend college the following year. He told one of his class teachers and her reply was to tell him that she'd tried for a scholarship and hadn't got it, so not to worry if he wasn't successful. He came home feeling very sad. When he got the scholarship, Lee asked me to go in with him to tell her he'd got it. I am sure he thought she wouldn't believe him unless I was there. When he told her she just said in a quiet voice, 'That's nice for you Lee', and that was that. The next year he started attending Cabra Dominician College with much excitement.

***

In the early days of college, Lee tried his hand at being a bully. The situation was dealt with swiftly by the college, which we were very grateful for, and it stopped Lee from attempting it again. He loved maths, computer studies, and tennis. His scholarship meant that he was in the choir, which he hated. When I went to watch the choir performing, I realised he wasn't singing but was miming. I realised I was to blame for that. After he told me at the age of three that my singing was awful, whenever he sang I would foolishly say the same to him. In my mind it was for fun, but of course he didn't take it that way. It was a huge mistake I made. He loved his very active time in the drumming group and playing the piano, which went some way to making up for his miming.

In his early teens he started going to the Blue Light Discos, and really enjoyed them. The discos were introduced in South Australia in 1982 to promote better relations between police and young people.

The three of us struggled through his teenage years. We had an argument one night and he walked out. It was dark, and I panicked. Graham said to let him go, but I was too worried and walked aimlessly around the neighbourhood looking for him. After a fair while we decided I should drive around and try to find him, as he was angry with his dad. I drove around to no avail. Eventually he came home and went to his room.

As Lee enjoyed giving solo piano concerts, we took him along to the Dudley Moore concert at the Adelaide Festival Theatre in 1996, and to the Victor Borge concert in 1997. Lee got to meet Dudley Moore at the Adelaide Festival Theatre on the 7th of November 1996. The English comedian and movie star had got his start by winning a musical scholarship and training as a classical pianist. Many don't know that he had a parability—a club foot. The Americans saw him as a sex symbol. In those days access to famous people was easier if you were game to have a go, and I had a genuine purpose. Lee was being bullied at school, and I had written to Dudley, asking if it would be possible to meet him after the performance. Once the concert was over Lee and I made our way to the back entrance. When Dudley appeared he was wonderful, talking to our ten year old Lee as an equal. He told Lee not to worry about not liking football, and that Lee would be playing the piano long after the other boys stopped playing football. He was happy to have a photo taken with Lee. A lovely, caring man.

The following year, Lee met Victor Borge. He also performed at the Adelaide Festival Theatre. He was a professional pianist and comedian, and combined both talents in his performances. With the success of meeting Dudley Moore the year before I made my way with Lee around to the back entrance after the show. Victor Borge came out and was quite happy to chat to Lee. He encouraged Lee to keep his music practice up and happily had a photo taken with Lee.

The contrast between Dudley Moore and Victor Borge was huge. When Dudley came out, the office lady told him his stretch limo would arrive shortly and he thanked her. He also still wore the outfit he performed in. The limo arrived and we walked out with him. He looked so very sad and lonely as we waved goodbye to him. On the other hand, Victor Borge had changed into casual clothes and a baseball cap. He told the lady to cancel the limo and asked her to call him a cab. Although they were very different, both these talented men gave wonderful encouragement to Lee, and we are so grateful to have had the opportunity to meet them.

CHAPTER 15
Poetry Performances, Radio Presentation, and Making a CD

In 1992, I became involved as a part-time member of the Celebration Concert Group, who regularly performed at nursing homes and senior-citizen groups. The members of the group had various skills. I recited poetry. The other members of the group sang, played the piano, or did some other performance. During the school holidays, Lee would come along and do a piano recital. I performed with the group until 1999.

I dislike poetry immensely, and can't sing to save my life. However, I like performing, and so poetry was my answer to singing. I have a good speaking voice, so why not? I had elocution lessons when I was 11, but wanted to brush up on everything I'd been taught, so I phoned a radio station and they referred me to an elocution teacher. He had a pronunciation accent, and was a gentle and caring person. I obtained a study grant from the Government Employment Agency to pay for a short course.

After this, from 1992 to 1995, I recited poetry on 5AA and 5DN radio for Len Somerville, adding to my skills by attending courses in technical operation and radio presentation at Adelaide University. I had the voice for radio, but I was hopeless at counting backwards, which was important. I had enough trouble with organising my life on normal time, let alone in reverse. I realised that I couldn't be an operator, but hoped to team up with someone so I could be a presenter. Of course, that wouldn't have worked, because I couldn't read well at all. I also had no confidence in myself and found it hard to communicate. It was a low time in my life.

Not willing to give up, I asked if I could have a go at doing voice-over work. It was voluntary work, but I thought I would like to have a go at it anyway. I had a feeling that they could see I wasn't prepared to accept that no form of radio was within my ability. The script they gave me was peppered with Aboriginal names which I found very hard to pronounce, and I failed the reading miserably. I asked if I could practise, and it was explained to me that the people who succeeded at that job were fantastic readers and only needed to read once, with no read-through needed beforehand. This was quite enough for me to realise that this was one of my dreams that was going to disintegrate.

In 1996, I became associated with the Classical Guitar Society of South Australia, and performed in an ensemble with one of their members, Lincoln Brady. I recited poetry and Lincoln played guitar. We performed at Carclew House during one of the Society's recitals and at the Society's spring festival and competition. We performed two pieces at Carclew House, the first based on the sixth-century Greek poet Sappho—'Strophes of Sappho' by Jan Freidlin and 'Into the Dreaming' by Peter Scuthorpe, and the second piece was an Aboriginal story about a dugong.

In 1997, I worked with a composer to perform a collection of poems written by South Australians. Shortly after this I met up with an old childhood friend, Ian Rigney, who was an award-winning theatre director. I asked him if he would be my artistic director for poetry performances. He accepted, and was my guiding light in the presentation of the poems.

By 1998 Lee was 12, and his piano playing was beautiful. I had the idea of making a CD of love poems backed by music. My Graham helped me approach poets whose work I thought was nice, to ask them to be a part of the CD. We used a recording studio in Adelaide, and the production went well. The final result was a CD entitled, *Words of Love.*

We didn't have the money to get professional media promotion. We did have a launch, but only sold a few copies. At least we'd had a dream and tried. It was time to look forward to the next challenge.

'I can't sing to save my life. However, I like performing. So poetry was my answer to singing. I have a good speaking voice, so why not?'

Jan Cocks-Salvemini

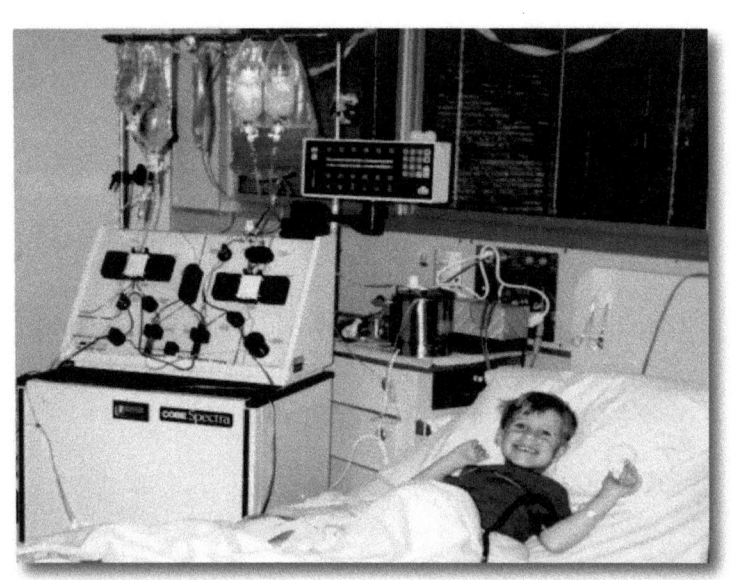

CHAPTER 16
Lee's Health Scares

Guillain-Barré Syndrome

I drove to pick Lee up after school on the 14th of December 1991. It seemed a normal day. Lee bundled himself and his school bag into the back seat of the car and fastened his seat belt. I asked how his day had been. He said that Mr P had asked him a silly question at lunchtime. He'd asked if Lee wanted to have a sleep. I thought that was so strange. I asked why he thought Mr P had said that. As Lee replied that he didn't know, I started the motor and turned my head back towards him, to make sure the school driveway to be clear. As I looked at him I could see that both his eyelids were drooped, just like a very sleepy person's eyes. I asked if he felt tired, and he crossly replied, 'No!' I explained that his eyes looked very sleepy, and that he would be able see them in the mirror when we got home.

When we got home, Lee looked in our bedroom mirror and thought that his eyes looked funny. We then had to rush off to his music appreciation lessons. I told his teacher that I was worried about his eyes and she sat him on her lap and had a chat to him. She agreed with me that I should take him to see the doctor.

When Graham got home we took him to our local doctor who thought we needed to take him to an eye specialist, so we arranged an appointment for the next morning. In the meantime, we contacted a friend of ours, Christine, from Graham's model-railway group. Christine worked with children, and she agreed that he should be taken to the eye specialist. She also gave us a name of a neurologist, just in case. The eye specialist said that it was definitely not an eye problem. We were expecting that answer, because at breakfast that morning Lee was walking through the kitchen and laughing, saying, 'That's funny, my knees just felt like there were no bones in them.' We had also noticed that his voice had a slight Donald Duck tone to it.

I asked the eye specialist if he would ring the neurologist for us, as it would be one professional talking to another in preference to a parent. He made the call, and the neurologist agreed to see us at 1.50 pm, ten minutes before his consultancy started. We arrived at the appointment and the neurologist examined Lee.

He said, 'I don't know what you thought you were going to be doing this afternoon, but you are immediately taking Lee to the Flinders Medical Centre—within the hour.'

We were told that Lee had one of two possible medical problems and both needed urgent attention. We took him straight to the hospital, and after another examination he was immediately admitted to hospital. He had contracted Guillain-Barré Syndrome.

There were lots of tests to follow. Each day he seemed to deteriorate very slightly. I remembered my parents being there for me as a child in hospital, keeping cheery for me, always positive and never talking about any of their sad feelings in my presence. So here I was, passing on that wonderful quality. It didn't matter what was going on, we smiled at every opportunity.

'Yes, Lee, I know it hurts, but only for a moment.'

' Oh! I like that Christmas tree, look at the great star!'

'What, your hand isn't working? Oh! You're just trying to keep up with me!'

He would laugh. Then, when the other hand didn't work, he would laugh again and say, 'Look, I'm winning.' It was very important for Lee that we kept cheery. Yes, Graham and I were devastated, but that was on us. It was our responsibility to keep our son as happy as we could, to give him the best chance—for all our sakes. We had no idea what was ahead of us, but for now we had to concentrate on keeping Lee happy.

At one stage, doctors came in and connected Lee to a machine which took the platelets out of his blood and replaced them with new platelets. My parents came in to visit. Dad was wonderful, smiling and joking, a repeat performance of all those years ago when he would come to visit me. Unbeknown to us at the time, Mother was in the very early stages of Alzheimer's disease, and she just sat quietly. We adults dwell on pain, but children don't. I knew that from my own childhood experience. Children live in the moment.

Lee was in a private room, with a nurse seated at the door, constantly watching Lee and the person in the adjacent private room. The person in the adjacent room died, and there was a lot of crying. I explained to Lee that the person had gone to heaven, and that the family was sad they didn't get to say goodbye.

Lee was now losing more use of his arms and legs, and he became totally paralysed from his neck down. He was now only managing to eat jelly, but he was smiling constantly, and alert to all that was happening around him. Graham and I had been sitting with him from day one. Our happiness levels were up in order to help Lee, we were living in the moment and dealing with what was immediately in front of us, rather than worrying about what might happen.

Lee's wonderful schoolteacher, Gary Pascoe, came to visit and brought Lee a large amount of cards which had been handmade by his classmates. Those cards were done with so much care, and Lee loved them. We were so pleased to have Mr P visit, and Lee was laughing and having a great time with his teacher. All of a sudden a doctor popped his head around the corner and said, 'Just got the latest blood tests back and Lee is immediately going to intensive care.' I couldn't see the urgency, because he was laughing, and I wanted that to continue, so I said, 'As his schoolteacher is here, could we wait until after the visit please?' I knew I had to keep smiling at that moment, but I was frightened at what this meant. The doctor looked at me sternly and replied, 'I wouldn't care if the Queen of England was visiting, that boy is going to intensive care immediately. His teacher can come too, but it is happening now.' Gary said he would come along, so he and I made it into a happy event.

'Hey! Lee,' I said brightly, 'You're going for a ride in your bed and we get to come along with you, but we have to walk. You get the special treatment.'

'Yah, I'm lucky!' whispered Lee.

So off we went, with a big, brown paper bag sitting on his bed with all his things inside.

On our arrival at intensive care Lee was quickly transferred to the bed. The doctor said that they had to place a cannula into his left leg. I knew this was going to hurt him and said, 'Lee, hold my hand, this won't take long.' It was no good saying, 'This won't hurt' because it definitely was going to hurt. I looked at Gary as they were getting the needle ready, and his face was drained of colour. He had such a compassionate and caring expression. Gary being there had helped cheer Lee up. He was, and still is, such a lovely man and a wonderful teacher.

He told me he didn't think he could cope with this, and I thanked him for coming and told him it was fine if he needed to go. As it was happening I wanted to cry, but I had to stay strong. After Gary left, I held Lee's hand while he cried his way through the hurt of having the cannula put in. Once it was over I distracted him with all the wonderful 'get well' cards that Gary had brought. My lungs started to play up, so the staff got me a nebulising machine to use. With the mask on and the nebuliser going, I sat there with Lee.

Intensive care was constantly noisy, with people all around— medical staff coming and going, and people visiting their loved ones. Lee was among the youngest at that time, and people were so caring about asking how he was going. I would smile and say, 'Okay', but Lee was getting worse. As well as being paralysed from the neck down, he had stopped eating and could only sip water and speak in a whisper.

Graham and I continued as we had done from the start, taking it in turns to do a bedside vigil. One day the nun from our local church came to visit and insisted on taking me to the canteen for a cuppa. I didn't want to leave Lee and felt terrible walking away. We were told later by a staff worker that the strain on our smiling faces told a story of total stress. We just needed to keep happy for Lee. We did our best.

One day, as I sat by Lee's bedside, the doctor called me out to talk to her. I told Lee that I would be back in a minute, leaving with a smile on my face. The doctor walked with me to a private room. She sat me down and told me that Lee was in a critical condition, and now had pneumonia on his right lung. She said that we may lose him in the next twenty-four hours, and that I should ring my husband and anyone else I need to. I could feel my mourning for Lee welling up inside of me. This could be it. We could lose him. I was devastated, but I knew I had to hold myself together. I thanked the doctor and walked out of the office, shutting the door behind me. Standing there outside I stopped to take some deep breaths, then walked back to intensive care. I put a smile on my face and walked straight back to Lee. I said, 'I'm just going to ring your dad,' then left the room and took another minute to myself. Lee looked so small in that big bed with the white sheets. I took some more deep breaths and went to ring Graham. He had gone home, which was about a half-hour drive from the hospital. He told me he would shut the doors and windows, and then drive back to the hospital.

I went back to Lee. We could hear the Christmas choir singing, and he smiled and whispered, 'Can they come in here, Mummy?' I told him I would ask. I went to the intensive care doctor and asked if the choir could come in to sing for Lee. The doctor looked startled. His answer was, 'Mrs Cocks, this is intensive care, we don't have music in here.' My next question was to ask if one person could come and sing to him quietly. That was okay with him. I went and spoke to the choir. One lady followed me back into intensive care. She said hello to Lee and lit her candle. Her singing was soft and so lovely. I think the carol was 'Silent Night.' It was a magical moment for Lee and me. However, I was jolted out of the moment by a nurse telling me that I had a phone call.

'Please take a message,' I implored.

The young nurse insisted, saying, 'People care about Lee.'

The phone call was from our friend, Karina Van Dok, who told me that the children were doing the Christmas nativity play at the school and were praying for Lee. I quickly thanked her and returned to Lee saying, 'All the children at school are praying for you.'

Lee whispered, 'That's nice.'

Just then the doctor walked by and saw our Lee with the biggest smiley face and obviously melted. He just said, 'Let them all in.' I moved fast in case he changed his mind, quickly invited the remaining choir in, and then returned to Lee.

As the choir assembled themselves and started singing I looked at Lee grinning from ear to ear. Again, the nurse came up saying there was another call for me. Protesting didn't work, so I went to the phone. It was Libby Thompson's mum asking if she could put Lee on a prayer list for people to pray for him. After thanking her and saying yes I returned to Lee, just as the choir was finishing. I leant over to Lee and told him that a lady was putting him on a prayer list. As the choir blew out their candles I thanked them and they left.

Lee whispered, 'Mummy, is the whole world praying for me.'

Not having the heart to say no, I just said, 'Something like that, Lee.'

I sat there, realising the enormity of what could be ahead for us, feeling so very sad that this may be my last day with my son. On my mind was the fact that I had not been able to enjoy the special Christmas music moment with him uninterrupted. It made me feel sad. There was our little boy, lying so motionless in his big hospital bed.

He whispered, 'Look, Mummy.'

I looked straight into his eyes. They were smiling, as was his whole little face. His eyes weren't looking at me but at his hand. Then I saw it. The thumb on his left hand was moving. I called the nurses and we were all so excited. By the time Graham had arrived Lee was able to move his thumb and forefinger, and he just kept bending one while the other was straight and vice versa. Graham arrived expecting to be losing Lee at any time, to find me overjoyed. He was totally confused. Then Lee showed him and we started laughing.

Graham and I were so thrilled, although the doctors warned us that if Lee was to recover he could be in a wheelchair. Graham went home that night, while I slept in the chair next to Lee. The next morning I woke to find Lee had wriggled his way down to the end of his bed.

He had his full voice back and he was saying very loudly, 'There is a Christmas party back in my ward. Have I missed it?'

Just then I saw three doctors looking stunned. One told me they were there to put Lee on a respirator. I thanked them and said I didn't think he needed that now. The intensive care doctor came in and was horrified that Lee was making so much noise. Lee was immediately thrown out of intensive care. He hadn't missed the Christmas party. He got his face painted like a green crocodile, and when he got back to his private room, Father Christmas came in to visit. A lovely memory.

Tests and a chest x-ray were conducted. His chest x-ray showed no sign of pneumonia. There are two ways of looking at this outcome—a huge, sudden injection of positivity, or a miracle. We made our choice about which we thought it was.

On Christmas Eve 1991 we were waiting for Lee's blood test results. If they were good he could go home, if not he would have to stay in hospital for Christmas. The results were good, and at 5 pm on Christmas Eve, our Lee walked out of hospital, albeit like a little drunk man, holding a blue helium balloon. We went straight to our local church Christmas service.

As we walked in there was a flood of happy tears for a little boy they thought they had lost.

Chronic Fatigue

At the age of 15, Lee was constantly tired. We put it down to teenage hormones at first, but it gradually became worse. We took him to the doctor only to discover he had Chronic Fatigue Syndrome, and that it was a relapse from the Guillain-Barré Syndrome.

The doctor rang me with the results and advised that Lee was too sick to go to school, and not to worry about his education. The doctor explained that it was vitally important for Lee to completely relax, and advised that we take all pressure off him. He went on to say that Lee was too sick to get into trouble, so just to let him do what he wanted, and not to wake him if he was sleeping, as he would need to sleep a lot.

We took the doctor's advice and the three of us floated into our new reality. Graham was working. Lee slept a lot, and when he was awake he played computer games. He would wander out from his room to eat and chat to us for a short while, and then go back to his room to play his games or to sleep. It might sound like teenage heaven, but when we get too much of a good thing we quickly get bored! Before too long, playing computer games wasn't holding Lee's attention, so he decided to find out about how to make them. He found some free tutorials on how to do 3D animation from a site called Blender, and became passionate about studying this art form.

Throughout this time, our friends and most of our relatives were very caring and supportive, but there were a few relatives who accused us of being irresponsible parents, and felt we were ruining any chance of Lee having a good education. We were so shocked and felt very hurt, but we shielded Lee from those verbal attacks. We were taking the doctor's advice, and even though we explained this to our relatives, it was not accepted. We realised later they were worried.

After studying the tutorials on 3D animation, and between sleeping for long periods of time, Lee started entering competitions in his online community. He soon began winning, and we got so excited with him. Winning meant that he got to choose the subject for the next competition. They would all vote for who they thought was the best, and this sharpened their skills. Of course, Lee didn't have any responsibilities, so he could put his full concentration into his animation when he wasn't sleeping.

After his 17th birthday his health started picking up. He would be like a hermit, shut away in his room, coming out to eat and then heading back into his room. One night he wandered out to the lounge room and announced that he had an email from a man named Ton who wanted to know if he could join a group of 3D animators in San Diego, America. Graham and I looked at each other and asked, 'Who's Ton?' Lee confessed that he didn't know, so we told him to find out who he was, what his surname was, and where he worked.

Lee returned with the relevant information and we checked him out. Ton Roosendaal was the creator of Blender, a free open-source 3D computer graphics software toolset used for creating animated films. It included the free tutorials that Lee had studied. Ton lived in Amsterdam in the Netherlands. Ton wanted Lee and other 3D animators to attend the 2003 Siggraph Conference in San Diego, and to meet each other at the Blender workshops. By this time Lee was in the last stage of recovering from chronic fatigue, and his doctor said he would be fine to travel, so we agreed that he could go. We also arranged for him to head to Denmark after the conference to meet my wonderful cousin Kirsten and her family.

Graham had retired in late 2002, so we could afford to send Lee, and felt it was more important for him to go overseas than us. All was arranged, and we were at the Adelaide Airport in September 2003 to see our seventeen-year-old boy off overseas—our boy who over the previous two years had been very sick, but safe in our home. Now we were smiling and wishing him a great time, but on the inside I just wanted to hold him, hug him, and keep him with me.

Meeting up with Ton and the others went well, but they were all shocked when Lee walked in and introduced himself. The standard of his work was so high that they had thought '17' had been a typo, in place of '27'. When Lee arrived home he told us of his wonderful trip to America and Denmark, and how lovely Kirsten had been, showing him around the tourist sites in Denmark, and he was thrilled to meet her granddaughters, Lotte and Ditte. Lee settled back into homelife and continued to study and create animations using Blender.

Not long after, Ton emailed Lee telling him should apply to work as an animator on a 3D film he was going to make in Amsterdam. He told Lee not to be disappointed if he didn't get it, because he was looking for the best animators in the world. Lee got busy sending Ton a heap of work. Finally, an email arrived from Ton. He said that Lee didn't want to know how close the competition was, but that he had been selected as one of six people chosen to work on the movie. The three of us were ecstatically happy.

Ton arranged for Lee to fly to Amsterdam for a week of meetings in July 2005, regarding the Project Orange workshop. At the end of that week, at 19 years of age, Lee signed the contract to work on Ton's movie and was flown home.

In September 2005, Ton flew Lee back to Amsterdam. Lee was chosen as lead artist on the film. In March 2006, 'Elephant's Dream', the world's first open-source animated movie, was released. Lee arrived home after seven months away. It was an amazing experience for him, and a wonderful start to his career.

After working in Adelaide and then Melbourne with 3D games companies, Lee teamed up with another Blender 3D animator living in Pennsylvania. With his American partner, Chris Plush, they now run their own business called, 'CG Masters—Blender Training and Tutorials.' They both work remotely from their homes. Lee continues to remain healthy and happy, and loves his work.

Lee was the winner of the South Australian Young Achiever in the Arts Award category in 2007.

'I remembered my parents being there for me as a child in hospital. Keeping cheery for me, always positive and never talking about any of their sad feelings in my presence. So here I was, passing on that wonderful quality. It didn't matter what was going on, we smiled at every opportunity.'

Jan Cocks-Salvemini

CHAPTER 17
Pole Sitting

I began pole sitting for the first time in the summer of 1996-1997 at Balfour's Mission SA Great Pole Sitting Event. This was the third pole sitting event run by Mission SA on the foreshore at Glenelg.

Pole sitting occurred at Henley Beach in the 1940 and 1950s. A vivid memory as a little girl was going to Henley Beach to watch in awe at people sitting on platforms on top of long wooden poles, stretching about five metres into the skies. The idea was to see who could last the longest. They only had a chair, a bucket for the necessary functions, and a rough curtain for privacy. Jill O'Toole, our next-door neighbour and family friend, had taken me to see the pole sitting. I was absolutely spellbound.

It was reinstated again in the summer of 1994-1995 by Mission SA, but now the event was held on the foreshore at Glenelg. The event ran from Boxing Day until Australia Day weekend, one month later.

Most participants would sit for one twenty-four hour period, starting early in the morning at around seven-thirty. The early morning was chosen as a good time to begin as the pole sitter would only need to take one day off work. To sit for twenty-four hours is an interesting process. The first step is registration, which required participants to raise at least $250.00 from sponsors.

I was so impressed with the event that I did the pole sitting for three years straight, until my lung started giving me trouble. I sat in the events that ran in 1996-1997, 1997-1998, and 1999-2000.

For the first year I took part in the pole sitting, I found myself, on the morning of the 7th of January 1996, sleeping bag and pillow in hand, standing at the base of the pole. Graham and Lee kissed me farewell for the next twenty-four hours, and up the pole I went, with the aid of a 'cherry picker.' I had raised the entry fee of $250.00, plus an additional $24.00 for good measure. Each pole sitter had a bucket on a rope to lower down for people walking by to put donations in. Our meals were donated and sent up via the bucket as well. My job was to encourage people to donate money. It was great fun, and in return I would throw them a wrapped up lolly. Each pole sitter would try to attract people to their bucket. Local sponsors donated all of the meals. And, yes, we had a portaloo with press buttons and a privacy curtain.

One year, our friends, Amanda and Greg Wood, who run a local business called 'A Class Metal Finishers', sponsored me for the pole sitting, which was wonderful. I was given a woman's racing driver's outfit to wear, which I loved—it felt fantastic. The outfit got people talking, and then I could get them to donate. I really didn't want to give the outfit back.

That first summer I raised a total of $488.80. Over the years that I enjoyed my 'penthouse' by the sea, I raised over $2,000.00, and I felt so good. In the last event I attended in the summer of 2000-2001, our son, Lee, also wanted to pole sit. I felt so proud of him. Even at three o'clock in the morning, when I had just dozed off, and was awoken by a voice saying, 'Mum, I'm awake, can we talk?' He coped well and raised about $400.00. That was the final year the event was held. And another dream had come true.

One year I decided to go up on New Year's Eve—it seemed like a great idea at the time. I would have a perfect view of the entertainment and the fireworks, but—and this was a big but—at midnight I was at the top of the pole, and Graham and Lee were at the bottom of the pole. Graham didn't want me to do that again, and neither did I!

'I still use the same principle of dreaming that my parents taught me from the age of three years old—to dream the biggest, wildest dreams and believe that they can become reality. When my dreams came true my parents would celebrate with me, and when my dreams didn't come true they would hug me and talk about the fact that I tried, then encourage me to find another dream. It was wonderful because it kept my mind full of happy thoughts. Five-year-old Lee was very sick but very happy.'

Jan Cocks-Salvemini

CHAPTER 18
Dad

My childhood was happy. I felt secure and loved by my wonderful parents, we lived in a safe neighbourhood in a middle-class suburb, just a kilometre from Adelaide Airport.

Dad drove a second-hand 1930's Morris, with a stepping plate that swept up over the back wheel, then down as a step, and up over the front wheel. As a child, I was allowed to wait at the front gate for Dad to come home. I would get excited seeing him travel down the road. He would stop at the gate, put his arm out of the window, and help me up on the step, holding onto me as we travelled slowly down the driveway.

In my eyes, my dad was strong and would always be strong. I maintained this illusion until I was about 11 years old, when we were away on holidays in Ceduna in country South Australia. Mother, Dad and I were with Auntie Bet, her son Paul, and Auntie Bet's dad, along with Trixie, our Australian terrier.

Dad was a person who would always be there for others. A man had driven his car over a lump of wood, and the wood couldn't be shifted, so Dad decided to lift the car back over the wood. Dad pulled all the muscles in his back and fell to the ground. Sensing something was terribly wrong, Trixie decided to sit on his stomach and got vicious when anyone went near Dad. I was back at the holiday house, so they ran to get me as I was the only one who was able to get Trixie off of him. It didn't worry me at all at that stage that my dad was lying on his back on the ground, as he seemed to be in good spirits. I was concentrating on encouraging Trixie to get off his stomach. While I was taking Trixie back to the house, the ambulance took Dad to hospital.

When we went to see Dad in the hospital he was in bed wearing a white hospital gown. I took one look at him and said I didn't feel well. He was furious with me, believing that I was attention seeking, but for the very first time in my life I fainted for real. The nurses rushed me to another room and I was put on oxygen. Seeing my dad looking vulnerable had been a huge shock to me.

After some bed rest, my dad gradually made a full recovery and our life returned to normal, with Dad back at work, Mother caring for me and her home duties, and me hating school.

Dad was an 80-a-day chain smoker, and by the time I was in my mid-twenties he needed an operation. I coped much better this time around. The doctor told my dad that because his lungs were so bad they couldn't operate on him for two days, until his lungs were clearer. The thought of the operation was clearly stressful, and he couldn't smoke to calm his nerves, on top of which he was in a great deal of pain. For those two days he was like a bear with a sore head.

Straight after the operation, Dad asked for a cigarette. He said it was the most foul tasting smoke he'd ever had. The doctors told Dad that his pancreas had been damaged during the operation, and that he would now be diabetic. After that, he told everyone he was not going to smoke for a while. He confided in me that if he'd said that he was stopping for good, it would have been too much pressure. He never smoked again.

In the early 1990's, Mother and Dad were going reasonably well. Mother's memory was deteriorating as a result of Alzheimer's disease. The more that Mother forgot, the more Dad had to do. Mother would walk over to the kitchen sink, stand there with a puzzled look, and then walk away. She knew that she was supposed to do something there, but she had forgotten what.

As Mother's health continued to decline, Dad divided his time between caring for her and playing lawn bowls. He would sometimes phone me and ask if I would like to go on a treasure hunt—Mother, with her sickness, had become very security conscious and would lock the back door and then hide the key. We found it in different places each time, such as in a tissue at the bottom of the sugar bowl or in her underwear drawer.

In 1993 I got concerned for Dad's health, so I called the Western Assessment Group to ask their advice. They suggested I talk to Dad, and propose that he take a three-week break from looking after Mother. Dad agreed, and Mother was placed in respite accomodation. Dad had the first week of his break at home, then spent a week on holiday in Alice Springs, before returning home for the final week. During the first week, Mother escaped and headed home, clutching a plastic bag with her knickers in it. A senior couple were worried and asked her if she was okay. She gave them her address and they drove her home. Dad was furious with the respite home, and on driving her back found that they had only just missed her and were about to raise the alarm. Dad gave them a good dressing down, and they didn't lose her again.

During the third week, I sat down with Dad and we talked over a coffee. He said he realised that he couldn't cope any more with trying to look after Mother, so we started looking for a retirement home that could accommodate both of them. I found one that was relatively new, and Mother and Dad's house was sold, after 41 years, with some of the money used for the entry fee to the retirement village. Mother was in an area with no access to the outside world, but she didn't realise it. Dad was in an adjacent house, and was free to come and go as he pleased. Selling the house gave Dad a chance to buy a new car, TV, and video player, and to go on holidays.

One day, when Dad and I were standing in the driveway, he said to me, 'So my home is sold. All you have to do now is throw the dirt on top of me.' He told me his dad had said that to him when his childhood home was sold. 'I swore to myself,' he said, 'that I would say the same when it was my turn to move on. That felt good.'

I was upset, but didn't show it—those words will never be said by me. The buck stopped there.

Mother broke her hip six months after moving into the

retirement village. I had assumed that there was a nursing home on the property, but this turned out not to be the case, and Mother was moved to a hospital a few kilometres away. Once she was released from hospital, she was admitted to a nursing home, so that she could receive proper care. Dad would visit Mother every day, until finally the 'girls' at his retirement village convinced him to cut back a bit, because Mother had forgotten who he was, even though he loved her and wanted to be there with her.

The people at the retirement village were deeply caring, and came to me one day to ask if I could talk my dad into changing doctors, as he had a mysterious lump on his back and his doctor was just giving him cream to put on it. I tried, but Dad was adamant that he would stick with his doctor. In his mind I was still his little girl, and he would give the advice to me, never the other way around.

In between visits to Mother and Dad, I looked after Lee's needs and enjoyed my home life with Graham. My Graham was working and Lee was in his first year at Cabra College on a piano scholarship. My lung infections were being quite annoying, which was slowing me down mentally and physically.

Dad phoned me one morning and asked me to visit and have a cuppa with him as soon as I could. When I arrived, he made the coffee and after a short chat he said, 'I'm going to tell you something, and I don't want you to cry, okay?' I froze. I was petrified at what was to come. He said, 'I have cancer.' I just sat there and took a deep breath. I think the fact that I was stunned helped me not to fall apart and cry.

I said, 'Okay, what can be done?' We talked over coffee and I left saying that I was going to visit Mother. By now, Mother was in the final stage of Alzheimer's. She weighed just 36 kilos, and her mental capacity was minimal. This was going to save her from the heartbreak ahead. I had been trying to mentally prepare for Mother's passing, and here I was now facing an uncertain future with my dad's health. The child in me had always assumed that they would live forever.

After leaving Dad, I began the two-kilometre drive to Mother's nursing home, slowly digesting the conversation I'd had with Dad. As I was driving along the shock started to wear off and the dreadful reality hit me like a train. I started crying and couldn't stop. I parked the car because I couldn't see for tears. I was distraught—Dad was my rock. My love for him was so deep. I felt as though I couldn't cope.

It was hard enough losing my very much-loved mother to Alzheimer's. She had lost her speech and didn't know who I was, but these changes had come on gradually and I'd had time to accept it, although I didn't like it at all. I was losing my mother but still had her physical presence. When I arrived at her nursing home, I had to pull myself together and put a smile on. This time, I was grateful that Mother didn't know what was going on.

Dad ended up with two different cancers, a melanoma, which was the lump his doctor had given him cream for, and bowel cancer. Each time he had an operation, I would think this would be the one that was going to make him better. He would smile for me when I came to visit, still trying to be strong for me.

On one occasion I went in to see him in hospital and he had a high temperature. The doctor told me he had blood poisoning, and to expect the worst. I sat with him. I wish I had understood the power of holding a loved one's hand. I went to the toilet and felt so very angry, I stood next to the hand basin, looked up to the celling and yelled, 'Don't you dare take my dad. Don't you dare. Do you hear me? He is my dad. You leave him here.'

I figure the message got through, because he slowly recovered from the blood poisoning, but he still had cancer. The Sunday before Dad died, I was sitting in the Adelaide Hospital cafeteria while he had his lunch. A lady came up and spoke to me, introducing herself as Mary. She was a hospital volunteer—a Lavender Lady and a Salvation Army volunteer. Mary gave me a cuddly toy rabbit with a little tag attached, which read 'God gives courage.' I had no idea how much courage Dad and I would need in the time ahead of us.

I left Mary and returned to Dad. He asked me what I had in the bag. I showed him the rabbit and read out what was on the tag. I suggested we call him Professor Ike—for 'I can cope with this', and asked him if he would like the rabbit to stay with him. I expected him to say 'no way', with his Australian macho attitude, but instead he said he would like the rabbit to stay.

As the week went on, Dad's health deteriorated. Mary came to visit Dad, and it was such a comfort for our family. Once again the Salvation Army was there for us. By mid-week he was heavily sedated. On Good Friday, the doctor told me that my father was slipping away fast and that I should call the relatives now, so I called everyone. I didn't want to leave Dad from then on. On Friday and Saturday night I slept by his side. Just before his last breaths he opened his eyes and stared into my eyes. I talked quietly to him and told him that he must set his spirit free from his broken body. He then took his last breath and passed away, just as the sun was coming up.

I sat there quietly, looking around the room. I said, 'Dad, what just happened? One minute you're here and the next you're gone. I didn't see anything.' I wanted to see angels or a ray of light or something, but there was nothing. I still didn't cry in front of him.

That afternoon we went to visit Mother—not to tell her, because it would not have registered anyway, but just to be with her. When we arrived at the door the nurses came running up to us and said that she was so different, and they could not understand why. She was alert and smiling. They didn't know that Dad had died earlier. I told them and they all gasped. We walked in, to find Mother sitting in a chair in the lounge room. Mother was focused and smiling, where usually she was distant and unresponsive.

Dad's funeral was planned for the Thursday following Easter. No-one wanted to give a eulogy, so I started to write a script. The funeral was so difficult. Afterwards, Graham and I took the flowers back to Mother's nursing home. We walked into her ward, where she was lying on her bed. She had the biggest grin and her eyes were smiling.

All that I could think of to say was, 'Hello Mother, it's wonderful, isn't it?' wondering why I wanted to say that. Mother nodded her head, even though I hadn't seen her do that for many years, and smiled broadly. Then I said to her that she looked as happy as she must have been on her wedding day, but just a bit older. She nodded her head quite definitely, and I knew that Dad hadn't been at the funeral, but at Mother's side.

Mother was never like that again.

CHAPTER 19
Mother

The first years of my life must have been horrific for Mother. Both my parents just had to cope, but Dad could go to work, while Mother was left at home alone with me, unable to go anywhere. My personality was stronger than Mother's gentle way, but we did get along very well and I always had her unconditional love—a fact I was well aware of—and I loved her a great deal, too.

Mother was the first to visit anyone she knew who got sick. In my mind's eye, I vividly remember looking through the venetian blinds in my room watching her in our front garden cutting flowers, then bringing them to the kitchen table. There, she would have the pretty paper cut out ready to make a posy of flowers to take to a sick friend or relative to cheer them up.

When I was getting to the age of going to discos I wanted to have nice dresses but we couldn't afford new dresses. Mother had started working at Maynard Catering. One of the ladies she worked with had a daughter who was described as being 'Ultra modern'. Her mother was a dressmaker and made her the most modern clothes to wear. The girl would wear the outfit once and then refuse to wear it again. Mother explained to me that these clothes were my size and would it worry me if I wore second-hand clothes. I was happy to look at them. They were magnificently made and to the latest fashions. So there I was, wearing the latest fashion clothes and feeling fantastic. Yes, I wore them again and again.

Mother was determined that I would feel good about who I was, regardless of my parability. Neither she nor my dad ever talked about my parability in a negative way to me or to anyone else. They gave me the confidence to feel equal at all times. To me, my parability was no different than some people having blonde hair and others having brown hair—it was just fact, a part of who I was.

The years passed by, and when 1990 arrived Mother's memory was beginning to go. She wouldn't remember things that I had told her, and would get cross with me for not telling her, but in everyday life she seemed quite okay. At first, we put it down to her being distracted, but gradually we realised there was something really wrong. Once Mother's doctor told us that she had Alzheimer's disease we had a name for her behaviour.

Alzheimer's is a very cruel disease, and Mother gradually changed from the loving, caring person we had known to a woman who had lost her memory, her personality, and her knowledge of her loved ones.

Dad and I took a ten-week course with the Alzheimer's Association, which was a great help to both of us. We learnt so much about how to care for Mother. We became very good at reacting to Mother's repeated conversation as if it was the first time, even when it was the tenth, because in her mind it definitely was the first time. We got into a rhythm of caring for her, but a lot rested on Dad's shoulders.

Over time, Mother became more and more childlike in her behaviour, until eventually we realised that we must get her in a nursing home. Once Dad died my life got harder. I coped for a while, until gradually depression started to creep in. I had no idea what was happening, and assumed I was just being lazy.

Towards the end, we hired a nurse to stay with her in the nursing home so that she wouldn't be on her own. Each day Mother got slowly weaker, until finally she was in a coma and I knew the end was very near. One afternoon, Charles came in to visit her. Graham suggested that I take a break, and that he would take me for a cuppa. We had just got our tea when the call came through that my dear mother had passed on. It was the 23rd of December 2000. We made our way back to her room. I went in and sat quietly with her. Mother's beautiful blue eyes were open, there was no sign of pain or confusion, just peace.

I knew that she and Dad were together again, and I felt at peace too.

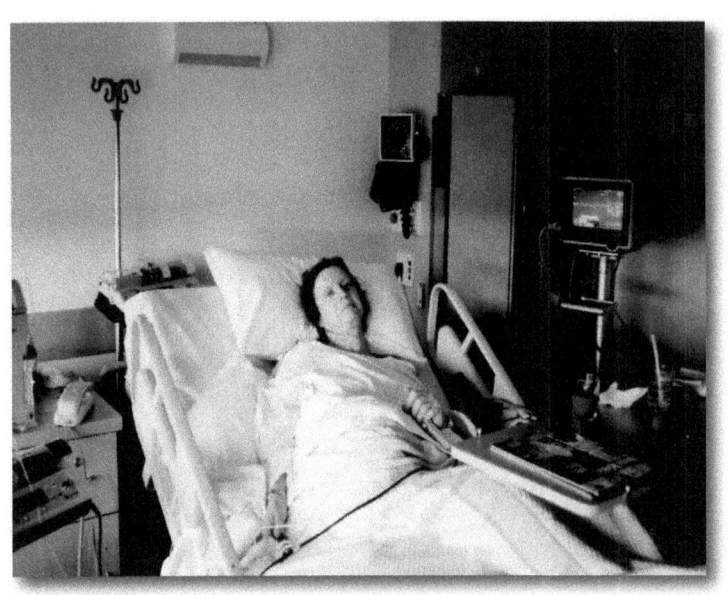

CHAPTER 20
The Partial Removal of My Lung

During the first half of 2002, I had a very sharp intense pain on the right side of my lung. Graham drove me to the emergency department, and the attending doctor suggested I make an appointment with my lung specialist.

I had got to the stage of having continual lung infections, and the antibiotics did not seem to be working. I was permanently lethargic and unwell. I told my family doctor that I felt I should see a different lung specialist to get a second opinion, as my present lung specialist was of the view that there was not really much more that could be done to help me.

At the first visit to my new lung specialist, I felt as though I was getting somewhere. He examined me and became quite concerned. Further tests showed that I had extensive lung damage to the middle right lobe of my lung. I had already had my top right lobe out when I was four years old. Now, it looked as though I would need to lose a second lobe. An appointment was made with a lung surgeon.

In my mind, I assumed that this young, good-looking smartly dressed surgeon, Dr. Craig Jurisevic, had come from an upper-class background and had been born with a silver spoon in his mouth. I felt hard done by—I was struggling with lung infections, my skin and hair were dreadful, and my energy level was very low. I felt like I was 90 years old, but I was only fifty-two. I sat there wishing I had an easy life with no dramas, like Dr. Jurisevic.

I later discovered that he was an amazingly brave man. Three years before my operation, he had decided to leave Australia and help in a war zone overseas. He had been in Kosovo with a gun in one hand, while working on a patient at the same time. He wrote a book about his experiences called *Blood On My Hands: A Surgeon*

At War. That was a true lesson for me, in never making assumptions about anyone.

Due to my lung condition and parability, I needed to be on the top level of private-health insurance. This meant no holidays or home improvements, but it was a necessity, not a choice. Dr. Jurisevic told me that my middle right lobe was extensively damaged and I needed to have it removed as soon as possible.

Two weeks later, I arrived at the Flinders Private Hospital to discover that not only did I have a beautiful private room, but there was a huge window. In the far distance was the sea, and I was able to see the sunsets. I asked the nurse if that was going to be my room after the operation and was told probably not, but that she would see what she could do. Directly after the operation I would be in intensive care.

My fear of this operation affected me more than any other operation. The last time I had part of my lung removed I was only four years old, and at that age I had no understanding of how vital the lungs are.

I awoke from the operation to find that I was in a glass room—the walls were all made from glass, and even the door was glass. Dr. Jurisevic came in to check me on me, and gently explained that over the next twenty-four hours it was important for me to breathe as deeply as possible, as much as possible, because the bottom right lobe now had a vast empty space above it, into which it could expand now that the middle lobe was gone. I had no idea that a lobe could expand, but I took his advice and every moment I could I did the deep breathing.

Dr. Jurisevic explained that taking my lobe out had been very difficult, because it had turned into a crumbly substance like honeycomb, so they had to break it off in sections. He said they had to break one of my ribs to get the lobe out. The collapsed lobe trapped infected phlegm, and the fumes from this were slowly poisoning my body, which is why I felt like a very old lady.

When my Graham came to visit we talked about whether our Lee should come in. He was 15 at the time, and I thought that it was important for him to come and see me, so that he could understand what was happening. I was so wrong. I hadn't talked the operation through with him enough. I hadn't been well enough or mature enough to prepare him for seeing me in that state. He did come in, and stood at the end of my bed with a shocked look on his face. He was deeply affected and refused to come in to see me again.

When I finally got home, I walked into our kitchen where Lee was leaning against the counter. He just said, 'So you're going to live then?'

It wasn't until about a year later that I realised the depth of fear he'd felt.

CHAPTER 21
Public Speaking

By 2001, I felt that many of my personal dreams had come true, and thought I would like to present my story to others to encourage them to achieve their own goals. To do this, I needed to acquire some expertise in public speaking.

A friend, Jenny, was a member of The Talking Owls Club, a training club assisting women to develop skills in communication and confidence. She suggested that I join. The group met twice a month for lunch, and members took turns to make a five-minute presentation to the other members. An adjudicator then critiqued the presentations.

I took up the offer and joined. It was challenging to prepare a presentation on an allocated subject, which one generally didn't really know much about beforehand. However, despite the challenge, it was rewarding. Not only that, it built up my confidence in presenting to groups of people, and the regular cycle of presenting enabled me to both grow and maintain my confidence.

My mother used to say that she would never join a women's only club, because there were fewer problems with mixed groups. Some women can be bitchy and spoil it for the other people in the group. This is what happened to me.

I had mentioned to the group that I wanted to be a professional speaker, and that I had made enquiries about joining another group. Not long after, for the Talking Owls Christmas meeting, I was asked to speak. I decided on the topic of Netherland Christmas Traditions. I found Wikipedia had a reference, and used this as the basis of my talk, explaining the way Kris Cringle's arrived in the Netherlands on a boat with Black Pete.

After I delivered my speech, a member of the group got up and presented a critique. It was scathing, and she finished up by saying that perhaps I needed to stay on with the Talking Owls, rather than trying to make it as a public speaker. There were about 30 people at the meeting, and I felt upset to have been spoken to that way in front of everyone, but I put on a brave face.

After the meeting ended, I was comfort eating at the afternoon tea, which is something I do when I'm nervous. I gradually began to feel better, with the combination of the afternoon tea and the kind words of some people who came up and complimented me on my speech. Then the person who had critiqued my speech approached me. She introduced me to a person who was visiting from the Netherlands, who proceeded to say in a clear voice, so that people around could hear, that my speech had not been accurate and I shouldn't have made it.

To top it off, the woman who had critiqued me said in an equally loud voice, 'Haven't you eaten quite enough now?' I was quite embarrassed, but I held myself together. I wasn't going to give them the satisfaction of seeing me dissolve into tears.

Undeterred, and still needing to acquire advanced skills in public speaking, I decided to attend some meetings of the South Australian chapter of the National Speakers Association of Australia. I timidly attended my first meeting in February 2003. The time spent with these speakers wasn't lost, and I learned a lot through listening to professional delivery.

I joined a local Toastmasters International group. The group gave me the confidence, knowledge and opportunity to speak with the important skills I had learnt. I had each speech evaluated and told the good parts of the speech and recommendations to help me in my next speech.

In 2013 I competed in a competition in Cairns for the International Speech Contest for Area 9 of the Northern Division and got through to the second level. To my surprise, I won the competition.

In 2015 I achieved the level of Advanced Communicator Bronze for exceptional achievements in the Toastmasters International Communication Program.

With my Graham's help I designed a PowerPoint presentation for when I did presentations. My presentations help people to understand parability and how to interact with confidence. I can talk from my perspective with over my 70 years of being para-abled.

I have presented to management of hotels, staff at hairdressers and other small businesses. So far I have only spoken at one conference. It was a South Australian Primary Health Care conference held at the Adelaide Convention centre.

CHAPTER 22
Karate

Following my lung operation in August 2002, I was advised by a medical practitioner to take up karate. My first reaction was to laugh hysterically, but she challenged me to have a go for a term, and so in early February 2003, I rolled up to a Monday evening class. Liz and her husband, Renshi Norrie, met me at the door. They greeted me with big smiles and welcomed me in, but I could see their concern and I fully understood it.

Renshi Norrie asked if I would like to join in or just watch for the first night. I said I was happy to follow along. Norrie asked me to take my caliper off, so I did. He asked what I could do without it, and when I explained that I couldn't really do anything, he asked me to put it back on and line up with the others. He wanted to introduce me to the rest of the group, and asked what should he call me. I said, 'Jan', but poor Norrie had meant should he refer to me as disabled or crippled or was there another term that I preferred.

'Oh!' I said, 'Anything, it is okay.'

Back then, being politically correct wasn't important to me—I hadn't decided on the words 'Para-abled' and 'Parability.'

I lined up with the other karate students. The youngest was 15, and the oldest was in their mid-twenties. Then there was me, at 53 years of age. The warm up consisted of star jumps and skipping, and I was hopeless at both. Norrie and I later decided that I should run at my own speed up and down the length of the hall for my warm up. After the third week I was accepted as a student. I signed the agreement and ordered my uniform. I felt so very proud to wear my new uniform. I also needed to get a pair of boxing gloves, which was the funniest shopping excursion I have ever had in my life.

Renshi Norrie and I talked about the fact that I needed to achieve a similar outcome to the other students, but in my individual way. So he would give instructions to the group, then come to me and work out how to adapt what I needed to learn to my needs. I didn't get out of doing anything—he had the same expectations of me, but with an understanding that there were times when we needed to take a different route to achieve a similar outcome.

My karate nights became routine, and working with Norrie went well. By the end of April he suggested that I prepare for my first grading—for the rank of 'blue belt.' The next regional assessment class was to be held at Mount Barker at the end of June, so I didn't have much time to prepare. I had a very hard time remembering the routine—the process just wouldn't stick in my head. The day of the grading quickly arrived, and I was overwhelmed by the crowd of people of all ages who were attending, from small children to adults. There were hundreds of people taking part in the grading. I had asked Norrie to tell the judges that I didn't want any favouritism. I struggled to remember the routine, but managed to get through it. I felt so proud to get my blue belt. I worked my way through to the green belt, and felt so proud of the hard work I put in, but then my right ankle collapsed while I was at home one day. It had nothing to do with the karate—I had osteoarthritis, and my bones were collapsing. My karate had to come to an end, but I was so grateful to Renshi Norrie for everything he taught me.

Years later, after attending a business dinner, two women approached me and offered to walk me to my car. I told them it would be better if I walked them to their car, as I was a green belt in karate.

They declined my offer.

'I lined up with the other karate students. The youngest was 15 and the oldest was in their mid-twenties. Then there was me, at 53 years of age.'

Jan Cocks-Salvemini

CHAPTER 23
Australasian Masters Games—Darts

In October 2007, the Australasian Masters Games were due to come to Adelaide. I wanted to be a part of the games, but had no experience at anything. Graham and I chatted about it, and decided I should have a go at playing darts.

I started practicing, but I was terrible, so I went to our local sports club and was given some tips. I kept practicing, until I could get the dart on the board—but only rarely by fluke where it was supposed to go.

I lost the singles competition of course, but I was matched up for the doubles with a gold-medal winner of past years. He was such a lovely man.

I managed to hit the board most times, and my partner played perfectly. We won the silver medal. I knew my partner would have won gold if it wasn't for me but he didn't care—he was as happy as I was. It was an amazing feeling to be presented with the silver medal, and I thanked my partner.

We sat and watched the rest of the presentations, and at the end the presenter said that each year they give a medal to someone who had shown good sportsmanship and participation, and my name was called. I couldn't believe what I was hearing, but was encouraged by the people around me to accept it. I am happy I had a go at darts. I have two lovely medals as a memory of the event.

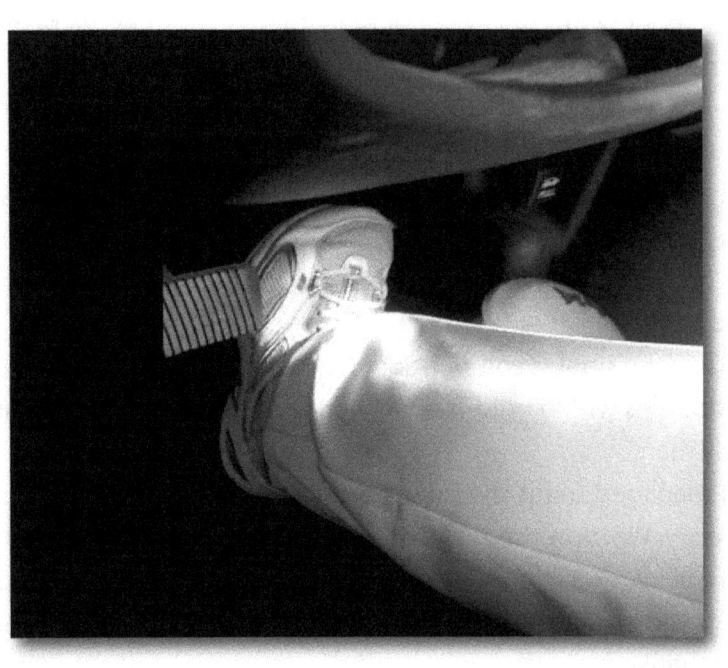

CHAPTER 24
Changing Driving Regulations

When I was first learning to drive, my instructor mentioned that I may have to get the brake and accelerator swapped over. I was astonished and I asked why on earth would I want to have that done. His answer completely surprised me. He told me it was because I was left-footed. I laughed because it sounded so ridiculous. I was quite defiant, and stated that the pedals would remain as they were. He said okay, let's see how you go. I went very well, and there were no issues with me being left-footed.

My driving test went well, and at 25 years old I was legally allowed to drive an automatic car. In all my years of driving I had one accident. I had mud on my shoe and my foot slipped off the pedal, causing me to roll into another car.

Many years later, a girl I knew had become para-abled after an epidural left her right leg partially para-abled. She wanted to get back to driving and asked me to help her. With a little practice, she was able to confidently drive an automatic.

We made an appointment for her to have her practical driving test. When we arrived at the Department of Motor Vehicles, the man behind the counter asked my friend why she was limping. When she explained that her right leg was partially para-abled he told her that she couldn't take the test, because the car with the brake and accelerator swapped over was out on the road. I explained that she could drive a normal car, but he insisted that she couldn't, and that it was the law.

By this time she was crying and I was extremely angry. I plonked my keys on the counter and said 'I have a partially para-abled right leg and I drive fine with my left foot. Take my keys or give her the driving test.' He returned my keys to me, and asked us to leave.

As soon as we were outside I asked her if I could ring Channel 7's *Today Tonight* program. She agreed, and they were interested in the story. The interview went straight to air, and the next day the Department of Motor Vehicles checked with their lawyers and realised I was right. After this, my friend was allowed to take her driving test, and passed without any problems.

Not every para-abled driver in South Australia has been as lucky. Some years later, I was introduced to a professional speaker named Peter Dempsey, by my friend Christine Sharkey. Due to COVID restrictions, we couldn't meet in person so we talked on the phone.

At the age of four, Peter had a stroke which affected his right side. When he learned to drive, he was instructed that he needed to have the accelerator placed on the other side of the brake. Although it isn't mandatory, The South Australian Department of Motor Vehicles insists that drivers with a para-abled right foot have the accelerator and the brake switched over. It is my belief that this is wrong on so many levels, as it forces para-abled drivers to be limited to using adapted cars. I am in exactly the same situation as Peter with my parabilities, and yet I can hire any automatic car I like in any state in Australia.

Peter uses an adapted car in South Australia, but when he travels interstate, his licence restrictions mean that he can't hire a car in other states.

We need to speak up whenever people in the para-abled community are underestimated by regulations or guidelines set by people who have no idea.

I have tried unsuccessfully to get this situation fixed, but no-one wants to do anything about it. The fact is that the authorities, including many doctors, are just doubly para-abling all, perhaps only for convenience.

I rang up the London Transport Department back in the 1990's and asked if they required people, with right leg permanent injuries, to get their car brake and accelerator swapped over. The London gentleman told me that they used to do that until they found that many people were getting involved in too many accidents as they had trouble changing their mind-set to the swap. So they modified the regulation to allow more flexibility in driver testing.

My understanding, here in Australia, is that the National Transport Commission's Assessing Fitness to Drive guidelines does not state that it is mandatory that the brake and accelerator be swapped over. It is only a recommendation, depending on the ability of the person being assessed by a driver assessor.

A person, with a right leg parability, should be allowed to show, if they wish, a driver assessor their ability to be able to drive competently with the brake and accelerator in the normal positions, before a swap recommendation is made by the driver assessor.

CHAPTER 25
Cairns

My thoughts of Queensland were originally of a magical wonderland, with warm comfortable weather all year round, where rich people would go to escape from the cold grey skies of winter.

On a cold wet day in August 2004, I was in a sad mood. The Adelaide winter felt endless and spring still seemed so far away. I sat in my favourite chair in the lounge room, sipping on a cup of tea and listening to the gas heater, as it softly churned out warm air.

I gazed out of the window at the wind forging its cold path through the branches of the trees, and thought, *I wish I could be in Queensland*. Winter has always been my enemy, as my health deteriorates in the cold weather. I wanted to escape the misery of constant lung infections.

Spring arrived, and I forgot about my silent wish as the sun warmed me enough to turn off the heater and escape to the outdoors. A few weeks later, the phone rang, and the caller told me that if they could ask me some questions I could win accommodation for two on the Gold Coast in Queensland. I won the free accommodation, as an incentive to buying into a timeshare. Graham and I found cheap flights and took the holiday that summer.

The accommodation was lovely and we had a fantastic time. Not long after we returned home, my lung specialist suggested that I should get out of Adelaide during the winter, and that somewhere on the coast of Queensland would be the most suitable destination.

My Graham suggested I write to the Lions Clubs in Townsville and Cairns. Both clubs responded, and both of the people who responded were called Dorothy. It was arranged that I would go to Queensland for three months, and spend most of my time with

Dorothy in Cairns, before going to Townsville for two weeks. As Dorothy from Townsville was married, I thought it would be harder for her and her husband to accommodate me for any length of time.

In June 2005, I sat in the plane watching the rain hitting the window. It was bitterly cold outside. Lee was over in Amsterdam with work, Graham was staying in Adelaide, and I was absolutely devastated that I had to leave him, our dogs, and our home for three months. To add to all that, I was absolutely petrified of flying. A friend, Libby Thompson, told me about a tablet that I could take to calm my nerves. My doctor wrote out the script, and I took one tablet before I left. When I reached Brisbane to catch the connecting flight to Cairns I decided it would be a good idea to take a second tablet. After a short while I felt quite foggy, and have little memory of what took place after that. I don't know how I got on the plane.

I vaguely remember Dorothy picking me up from the airport in her lovely sky-blue convertible. After that, I remember saying that I loved the dinner Dorothy had cooked for me, but the rest of the evening is a blur. I woke up the next morning in a strange room, and it gradually dawned on me that I must have overdosed on the medication. I found out later that Dorothy had called Graham to tell him I had arrived and that I wasn't in a good state. He suspected I must have taken an additional tablet.

A few days later, Dorothy asked if I would like to go to a birthday party with her. During the party, I wandered out onto the balcony to enjoy the warmth of the night. There was a couple sitting out on the balcony, called Maz and Bob. They were lovely, and took me under their wing, with afternoon teas at their home and sightseeing. I was amazed with Cairns, and loved everything I saw, from the city to the beach to the distant mountains.

In spite of how much I loved Cairns, I was desperately homesick the first winter that I was away. I cried myself to sleep at night, but the next morning I would behave as though everything was okay. I saw it as my responsibility to smile and act as if I had adjusted well.

Dorothy was lovely, taking me sightseeing, to the market stalls by the sea, and to the local jazz club. She also took me to the Lioness meetings, where I met some lovely people who have remained friends to this day. The people of Cairns have a warm and friendly nature.

After two months in Cairns I caught the train to Townsville, where I was met by the other Dorothy and her husband, Robert. They gave me a lovely warm welcome. The people of Townsville were so warm, welcoming, and inclusive. On my second visit to Townsville, I decided to stay longer. Again, I had the great welcome from Dorothy and Robert, and I was thrilled to spend more time with them.

Sadly, by this time Dorothy had cancer. I felt totally out of my depth, and had no idea how to cope with it all, which was so selfish of me. Some time after I returned to Adelaide I got a call from Robert to say that Dorothy had passed on. I haven't been back to Townsville since, although Robert and I still exchange Christmas cards.

The following year, rather than boarding in someone's home, I booked a room in a share house. Flying into Cairns on a beautiful sunny day was such a relief, having left Adelaide on a very cold wintery day. At that time I was overweight and not feeling well. I had a big black boot on my right foot and a walking stick. I arrived at the share house to find myself face-to-face with several people in their late teens and early twenties. Each of the girls was beautiful, and the young men were very handsome.

I was given the key to my room, and walked down the hall to my room, which was the last on the left. As I was unlocking the door a voice came from the dining room, asking, 'Are you staying here?'

'Yes,' I replied.

'I travelled 13,000 miles to get away from my mother and you turn up!' came the very grumpy reply.

I was speechless and hurried into my room, shutting the door behind me. I stood against the closed door, wondering if this was the beginning of a five-month nightmare.

My attention then focused on the room, which was lovely. I settled in and then rang my Graham to tell him about my first encounter with a housemate. He reassured me that the other housemates were probably better. I eventually got the courage to meet the other housemates, and was given a much warmer welcome.

As with any large group of people there were many different personalities. It felt a little like being on the TV show 'Big Brother.' All the young people had come from overseas or from other parts of Australia, and they would often only stay for a short time before moving on, at which point new housemates would move in.

The Cairns share house was such a wonderful place to stay that I went back year after year, and it became my second home. I got on well with many of my housemates, and the staff were fantastic. When I arrived each year I would be greeted with a cheerful, 'Welcome home!' from Catherine, Tammy and Phil. Seven years of staying at the share house meant that every time I went back I was a year older, while the young people were the same age as when I had first stayed, because each year would bring a completely new group of young travellers.

I made some wonderful friends through the Lioness club. One girlfriend, Robin Foster, had this adorable cat called Seraphina. She is a Tonkinese cat. When Robin went away I would housesit for her beautiful home and care for Seraphina. I loved staying there and was able to have the use of her car. In all my time in Cairns, Robin was always there to help if I needed it. Such as, giving me her spare woollen blanket in case I needed it, and I did need it sometimes.

Being in Toastmaster International clubs in both Adelaide and Cairns meant I could be involved all year round.

I decided after seven years that I wanted to get a studio apartment where I could have my own space. I was told that an apartment block had some studio apartments at a very reasonable price. The apartment block was lovely, with a bus stop close by. I chose an upstairs studio apartment. The grounds of the complex had a very tropical theme and every now and then I would spot one of my favourite butterflies, the big blue Ulysses.

The second year I chose a downstairs studio apartment. It was so much nicer than the previous one. It had been renovated and I loved it as there was a small stove. The owners put up security screens on the windows for my safety and quickly replaced the fridge when it failed.

The office management and staff of the complex were always ready to help me. Like storing my cases that stayed in Cairns and then delivering them to my apartment on my next arrival.

The last couple of years I have not been able to go to my 'second home' in Cairns due to the COVID situation.

While in Cairns, I wanted a meeting with Warren Entsch, Member of the Australian Parliament. I hoped that he could take the new words to Parliament. I explained my point about the need for the negative words, disabled and disability, needing to be replaced with para-abled and parabilty. Mr Entsch told me that he didn't see the need for a word at all for 'disabled'. WOW! I didn't see that coming.

I then suggested that the next time he goes to Canberra that he take a paper correction whitener and whiten out the word 'disabled' wherever it is written. He asked me what the 'para' stood for in the word para-abled. I said that 'para' was the Ancient Greek word for 'beside'. He laughed out loud. He told me that he just had a 'light bulb' moment. He said that his granddaughter has a parability and he believed that there doesn't need to be the word 'disability', because 'she is able to do so many things'.

He agreed that the new words were very positive words. I was delighted; I had his support. He understood. I am very grateful to Mr Entsch and his Executive Assistant, Tamara Srhoj, as they have been so supportive.

Warren wrote to both the Federal and Queensland state ministers for disability recommending that the new words be used. The words are now recorded in Hansard.

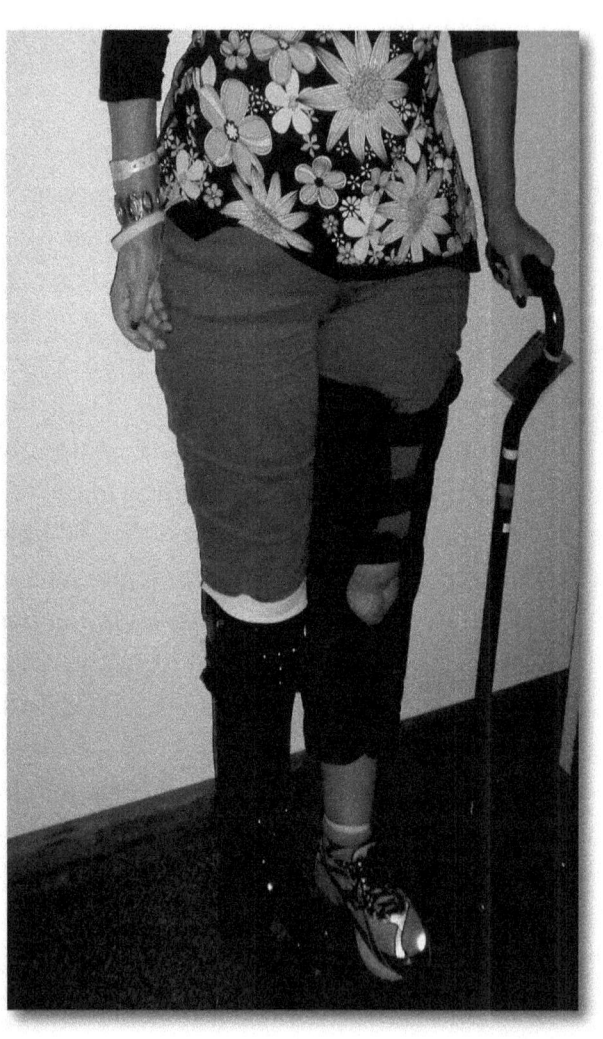

CHAPTER 26
Knee Replacement

As my left leg had to continually compensate for my para-abled right foot, I needed a knee replacement by the time I reached my sixties.

In early 2016 I made an appointment with a recommended orthopaedic surgeon. He was one of the few surgeons doing 3D knee replacements at that time. Measurements were taken of my knee and the hospital admission forms filled out before I flew to Cairns. All the knee information was sent to Europe where the replacement knee was made.

Three days after I arrived home from my five months in Cairns, I was admitted to hospital and the knee replacement done. I was in pain, and although the medication helped I could still feel the pain. That type of pain was all consuming and was monopolising my thoughts. The nurses that came in showed great empathy for my predicament and gently explained that I was having as much medication that is legal and that I would have to wait.

After two days I was transferred to a rehabilitation hospital. As my right hand didn't work, I was given a walker which I could lean my elbows and my forearms on and a handle was where my hands were. I held the left handle with my left hand. It worked well. I had been given a large room, which I loved, as the walker took space to manoeuvre.

The daytime nurses came in and showed compassion for my situation. The physio came in and asked why I was upset. I explained that I was having maximum pain killers. In a gentle caring voice he said he may be able to help and left. He returned with a little sashay of Vitamin E cream and rubbed it gently on the area around the bandage. In a couple of minutes it worked its magic and I felt peaceful. I was so grateful.

I would walk the corridors to exercise, and on one particular day I heard a familiar voice calling to me. It was my dear Auntie Bet—she had had a fall at home. We were thrilled to see each other, and I followed her to her room so that we could catch up properly.

Auntie Bet and I chatted nonstop, and it was good for both of us to be there together. At this time, her son Paul was in a hospice with terminal cancer. I had not been well enough to visit him, and it meant a lot to me that I could at least give Auntie Bet some support. She told me that she was having trouble sleeping because of the constant noise on her ward. I was able to arrange for her to be moved into a private room close to my own.

We talked about the old days when we had spent weekends together, and chatted about our families, and especially about our love for Paul. Auntie Bet and I spent every day together. One day, her grandchildren came and collected her so that she could visit Paul at the hospice. I was glad I could be there for her when she got back to the rehabilitation centre.

Not long after, I was resting in my room when I looked out of the window and saw two people getting out of a car. One was in a wheelchair, and I thought it looked like Paul, but dismissed that thought as not being possible. In spite of his illness, I had recognised my cousin, even at a distance, and was delighted when he was wheeled into my room. He slowly stood up and gave me a kiss on my cheek, saying, 'I love you, Jan.'

I told him I loved him too, then he left to have a visit with Auntie Bet. I saw Paul getting back in the car to return to the hospice. I waved, but he couldn't see me. That was the last time I saw my much-loved cousin.

Once Auntie Bet and I were allowed to go home, Graham drove me over to visit her every day. I visited her up until I went to Cairns, and then Graham would go to see her, and put her on the mobile phone so we could chat. While I was in Cairns my cousin Trena called to tell me Auntie Bet had passed away. I just stood motionless as the news sunk in. Our love and friendship, which spanned 60 years, had ended. I was so grateful to have had that special time together in the rehabilitation centre with my dear Auntie Bet.

I flew to Adelaide for the service and returned to Cairns a couple of hours later. When I got to my studio apartment I cried uncontrollably. My lung started playing up, and within a couple of days I couldn't breathe. I ended up in hospital with double pneumonia.

Dr. James Brown discovered that I had a superbug in my lungs. He gave me medication, which improved my future for the better.

Two weeks later I flew home, into the arms of my Graham.

CHAPTER 27
Para-abled and Parability

I see the words disabled and disability as negative. Many people don't think for a minute that becoming para-abled could ever happen to them. I call them the 'Not Me' group. They say they can't imagine how people with parabilities cope, because they believe they couldn't. The 'Not Me' group don't know what they don't know, and we can't expect them to.

As people with parabilities, it is our responsibility to gently educate the world community—not just for our sakes, but also for theirs. Aside from understanding the needs of para-abled people, it is important for the wider community to gain a greater understanding of parabilities so that if they or someone in their lives suddenly jumps from the 'Not Me' group into the para-abled group, the transition to accepting their new situation won't be so traumatic.

The word 'paralympic', which is used for the Paralympic Games, focuses on people's abilities, rather than their disabilities. So why not let everyone concentrate on our abilities all the time?

I feel strongly about the words 'para-abled' and 'parability' because they fit well with 'Paralympics', with the focused on possibilty, rather than limitation. The prefix 'para' comes from the Ancient Greek, and means 'alongside of' or 'beside.' So although our abilities may not be the same as people in the 'Not Me' group, these abilities are not less—as is suggested by the prefix 'dis', which means 'lack of'—we are just different. We are 'beside' the abilities of others, not beneath them.

I have asked hundreds of people in the 'Not Me' group whether they would prefer to be referred to as having a disability or parability, if their life circumstances changed. 95% have said that they would definitely prefer to be referred to as having a parability! The other 5% said they wouldn't care.

Of course, helping to educate the 'Not Me' group means that para-abled people need to feel good about who we are. The WHO states that in 2019 there were one billion people in our world with a parability. Every one of us is at a different stage of our feelings about ourselves and our parability.

Whether or not we have a parability, we are all individuals. Some people with parabilities can lip-read, and know more of what people are saying in a crowded room than people who are not para-abled. Some, who have impaired sight, can hear more because their hearing is sharper. Some people with parabilities are experts in maths and can outshine most other people in this field. I could go on and on. People with parabilities have so many qualities and abilities that are often completely underestimated by the majority of the population.

My goal is to go to the United Nations and the World Health Organisation to talk about my proposed words Para-abled and Parability.

About the Author

Life started in a normal manner for Jan as a healthy baby girl. But at ten months of age, she was bitten by a mosquito and became disabled. At this same time, she had bronchial pneumonia resulting in a permanent lung disease.

Jan prefers to be called 'para-abled' or having a 'parability', rather than 'disabled' and having a 'disability'.

Thanks Mosquito for the Great Ride is her first book. Jan lives in Adelaide, South Australia.

www.ingramcontent.com/pod-product-compliance
Lightning Source LLC
Chambersburg PA
CBHW071306110426
42743CB00042B/1187